GlassFish Security

Secure your GlassFish installation, Web applications,
EJB applications, application client module, and
Web Services using Java EE and GlassFish
security measures

Masoud Kalali

[PACKT] open source*
PUBLISHING   community experience distilled

BIRMINGHAM - MUMBAI

GlassFish Security

First published: May 2010

Production Reference: 1030510

Published by Packt Publishing Ltd.
32 Lincoln Road
Olton
Birmingham, B27 6PA, UK.

ISBN 978-1-847199-38-6

www.packtpub.com

Cover Image by Karl Swedberg (karl@englishrules.com)

Credits

Author
Masoud Kalali

Reviewers
Arun Gupta
Gaston C. Hillar
Kumar Jayanti
Ludovic Poitou
Antonio Gomes Rodrigues
Emmanuel Venisse
Deepak Vohra

Acquisition Editor
Rashmi Phadnis

Development Editor
Reshma Sundaresan

Technical Editor
Vinodhan Nair

Copy Editor
Sanchari Mukherjee

Editorial Team Leader
Gagandeep Singh

Project Team Leader
Lata Basantani

Project Coordinator
Joel Goveya

Proofreader
Lynda Sliwoski

Indexer
Monica Ajmera Mehta

Graphics
Geetanjali Sawant

Production Coordinator
Shantanu Zagade

Cover Work
Shantanu Zagade

About the Author

Masoud Kalali has a software engineering degree and has been working on software development projects since 1998. He has experience with a variety of technologies (.NET, J2EE, CORBA, and COM+) on diverse platforms (Solaris, Linux, and Windows). His experience is in software architecture, design, and server-side development.

Masoud has several articles published in Java.net and DZone, and has authored multiple refcards published by DZone, including Java EE security and GlassFish v3 refcards. He is one of founder members of the NetBeans Dream Team and a GlassFish community spotlighted developer.

Masoud's main areas of research and interest include Service Oriented Architecture and large-scale systems' development and deployment. In his leisure time he enjoys photography, mountaineering and camping.

Masoud blogs on Java EE, Software Architecture and Security at http://weblogs.java.net/blog/kalali/ and you can follow him at his Twitter account at http://twitter.com/MasoudKalali.

Masoud can be reached via Kalali@gmail.com in case you had some queries about the book or if you just felt like talking to him about software engineering.

About the Reviewers

Gastón C. Hillar has been working with computers since he was eight. He began programming with the legendary Texas TI-99/4A and Commodore 64 home computers in the early 80s.

He has a Bachelor's degree in Computer Science, graduated with honors, and an MBA (Master in Business Administration), graduated with an outstanding thesis.

He has worked as developer, architect, and project manager for many companies in Buenos Aires, Argentina. He was project manager in one of the most important mortgage loan banks in Latin America for several years. Now, he is an independent IT consultant working for several American, European, and Latin American companies, and a freelance author. He is always looking for new adventures around the world.

He also works with electronics (he is an electronics technician). He is always researching and writing about new technologies. He owns an IT and electronics laboratory with many servers, monitors, and measuring instruments.

He has written two books for Packt Publishing, *C# 2008 and 2005 Threaded Programming: Beginner's Guide* and *3D Game Development with Microsoft Silverlight 3: Beginner's Guide*.

He contributes to Dr. Dobb's Go Parallel programming portal at `http://www.ddj.com/go-parallel/` and is a guest blogger at Intel Software Network (`http://software.intel.com`).

In 2009, he was awarded as an Intel® Black Belt Software Developer.

Besides all this, he is the author of more than 40 books in Spanish about computer science, modern hardware, programming, systems development, software architecture, business applications, balanced scorecard applications, IT project management, the Internet, and electronics, published by Editorial HASA and Grupo Noriega Editores.

He usually writes articles for leading Spanish magazines Mundo Linux, Solo Programadores, and Resistor.

He lives with his wife, Vanesa, and his son, Kevin. When not tinkering with computers, he enjoys developing and playing with wireless virtual reality devices and electronics toys with his father, his son, and his nephew Nico.

You can reach him at: gastonhillar@hotmail.com.

You can follow him on Twitter at: http://twitter.com/gastonhillar.

Gastón's blog is at: http://csharpmulticore.blogspot.com.

Kumar Jayanti is a staff engineer at Sun Microsystems and works on the Web Technologies and Standards team. In his current role, Kumar is the implementation lead for GlassFish v3 Security, Metro Web Services Security, and also the specification and implementation lead for the SAAJ (JSR 67). Kumar holds an M.Tech degree in Computer Science from IIT Mumbai, India. His areas of interest include distributed computing, CORBA, XML, Web Services, and Security.

Ludovic Poitou is a directory services architect at Sun Microsystems and the community manager for the OpenDS project. For the past 15 years, he's been designing and developing numerous aspects of Sun's directory products, from management tools to protocols, security and multi-master replication.

Ludovic blogs about LDAP, directory services, OpenDS, and life at http://blogs.sun.com/Ludo.

Ludovic Poitou has been a technical reviewer for the following books:

- Solaris and LDAP Naming Services: Deploying LDAP in the Enterprise, by Tom Bialaski and Michael Haines, 2001, Sun Microsystems Press, a Prentice Hall Title.
- LDAP in the Solaris Operating Environment: Deploying Secure Directory Services, by Michael Haines and Tom Bialaski, 2004, Sun Microsystems Press, a Prentice Hall Title.

Antonio Gomes Rodrigues earned his Masters degree from the University of Paris VII in France. Since then, he has worked in various companies with Java EE technologies in the roles of developers, technical leader, and technical manager of offshore projects.

He currently works on performance problems in Java EE applications in a specialized company.

I would like to thank my friend Nadère for his motivation and support, my girlfriend Aurélie for her patience, and my family.

Emmanuel Venisse has been developing, architecturing, and integrating J2EE applications for twelve years for banks, government, holiday company projects, and so on. He's been working on several J2EE application servers such as JBoss, WebLogic, WebSphere, and more recently with GlassFish. For the last five years, he has worked as a freelancer. For the last seven years, he's been working, in his spare time, on Apache Maven, Continuum, and Archiva projects as a core developer and he's also the Continuum project leader. He has contributed to the majority of books written about Apache Maven.

Deepak Vohra is a consultant and a principal member of the software company NuBean.com. Deepak is a Sun Certified Java Programmer and Web Component Developer, and has worked in the fields of XML and Java programming and J2EE for over five years. Deepak is the co-author of the Apress book, Pro XML Development with Java Technology and was the technical reviewer for the O'Reilly book WebLogic: The Definitive Guide. Deepak was also the technical reviewer for the Course Technology PTR book Ruby Programming for the Absolute Beginner, and the technical editor for the Manning Publications book Prototype and Scriptaculous in Action. Deepak is also the author of the Packt Publishing books *JDBC 4.0 and Oracle JDeveloper for J2EE Development*, and *Processing XML documents with Oracle JDeveloper 11g*.

To My Parents

Table of Contents

Preface

We are living in a world full of dazzling wonders, and I for one always enjoy encountering them. Software development is one of the wonders that dazzles me because of its enormously vast domain, including many concerns and subjects of interest. Looking at this domain from any distance, we will see one big and sometimes blurry-edged spot named security.

Security, an orthogonal and inseparable part of software systems, is not for preventing others from accessing some information and system resources but for allowing them access in an appropriate way, by implementing necessary means to precisely check any attempt to access a resource and either allow it to go further or not and record all information related to examining this attempt for further review.

Java EE is the platform of choice for developing enormously large-scale applications, and provides plethora of features for implementing security plans for applications, starting from dealing with identity storages and identity solutions up to providing GUI-level support for security concerns and integration with other security providers.

Nowadays, integration is something that we hear in every software development meeting and session independent from what the session is about. Security integration, however, is a delicate matter compared to all other issues as it deals directly with the organization's assets. Java EE design allows it to delegate its security requirements to another entity in the enterprise, like a single sign-on solution, which on the other hand can integrate with other products and platforms in use in the organization.

The GlassFish Security book is an attempt to explain this domain considering Java EE, GlassFish, and OpenSSO capabilities and features.

What this book covers

Chapter 1, Java EE Security Model, discusses how we can secure different Java applications by using the declarative security model or by using the API exposed by Java EE containers to access the security enforcement layers programmatically. It also briefly introduces Web modules, EJB modules, and application client module's security in different levels, including authentication, authorization, and transport security.

Chapter 2, GlassFish Security Realms, discusses JAAS and GlassFish security realm, including File realm, JDBC realm, LDAP realm, and Certificate realm in detail as that will be required to develop a secure enterprise application. It also discusses GlassFish application server interaction with identity storages such as relational databases, Lightweight Directory Access Protocol (LDAP) servers, flat file storage, and so on.

Chapter 3, Designing and Developing Secure Java EE Applications, covers developing and deploying a secure Java EE application with all standard modules including Web, EJB, and application client modules. It also teaches us how we can secure EJBs using annotation and then use a web frontend to use the secured EJBs after a user provides correct identification information.

Chapter 4, Securing GlassFish Environment, helps you secure your operating system and environment from unprivileged access by applications deployed in GlassFish using the OS features and Java policy management. It also covers network communication security, GlassFish password security, and finally security auditing, which is a complementary function in software security.

Chapter 5, Securing GlassFish, covers GlassFish administration security tasks such as password security and listener security. This chapter will teach you to secure GlassFish by examining the administration security, password protection, and network listener security. It also discusses the benefits of virtual servers for isolating different applications deployed in a single machine with a single IP address.

Chapter 6, Introducing OpenDS: Open Source Directory Service, teaches you about directory service and the set of features OpenDS provides—installing, administrating, and monitoring OpenDS and using OpenDS in embedded mode. This chapter teaches you to set up a replication topology to ensure service and data availability in case of unpredicted disasters.

Chapter 7, OpenSSO, the Single sign-on Solution, covers projects security from an integration point of view. In this chapter you will install and configure OpenSSO and understand different methods of using OpenSSO. It also teaches you how to use OpenSSO RESTful Web Services for authentication, authorization, and acquiring SSO tokens.

Chapter 8, Securing Java EE Applications using OpenSSO, covers OpenSSO Policy Agents that let us as architects, system designers, and developers secure a Java EE application using OpenSSO without changing the application source code. It also discusses about Policy Agents, Policy Agent's installation, and administration, along with changing our sample application to place it under agent protection instead of using plain Java EE protection.

Chapter 9, Securing Web Services by OpenSSO, covers Web Services security and how we can use OpenSSO and OpenSSO agents to secure our Web Services deployed in GlassFish. It also teaches you to install OpenSSO Web Services Security Provider Agent and develop a simple, secure pair of WSP and WSC.

Conventions

In this book, you will find a number of styles of text that distinguish between different kinds of information. Here are some examples of these styles, and an explanation of their meaning.

Code words in text are shown as follows: "For the authentication method and a built-in realm named `file` as the security realm."

A block of code is set as follows:

```
<auth-constraint>
    <role-name>hr_management_role</role-name>
    <role-name>top_level_manager_role</role-name>
</auth-constraint>
```

When we wish to draw your attention to a particular part of a code block, the relevant lines or items are set in bold:

```
<user-data-constraint>
    <description/>highest supported transport security level
    </description>
    <transport-guarantee>CONFIDENTIAL</transport-guarantee>
</user-data-constraint>
```

Any command-line input or output is written as follows:

```
./start-ds
```

```
import-ldif --clearBackend --backendID userRoot --ldifFile
path/to/import.ldif
```

New terms and **important words** are shown in bold. Words that you see on the screen, in menus or dialog boxes for example, appear in the text like this: "clicking the **Next** button moves you to the next screen".

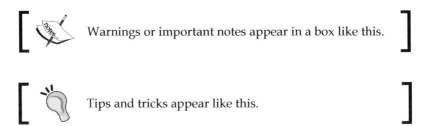

Warnings or important notes appear in a box like this.

Tips and tricks appear like this.

Reader feedback

Feedback from our readers is always welcome. Let us know what you think about this book—what you liked or may have disliked. Reader feedback is important for us to develop titles that you really get the most out of.

To send us general feedback, simply send an e-mail to feedback@packtpub.com, and mention the book title via the subject of your message.

If there is a book that you need and would like to see us publish, please send us a note in the **SUGGEST A TITLE** form on www.packtpub.com or e-mail suggest@packtpub.com.

If there is a topic that you have expertise in and you are interested in either writing or contributing to a book on, see our author guide on www.packtpub.com/authors.

Customer support

Now that you are the proud owner of a Packt book, we have a number of things to help you to get the most from your purchase.

Downloading the example code for the book

Visit https://www.packtpub.com//sites/default/files/downloads/9386_Code.zip to directly download the example code.

The downloadable files contain instructions on how to use them.

Errata

Although we have taken every care to ensure the accuracy of our content, mistakes do happen. If you find a mistake in one of our books—maybe a mistake in the text or the code—we would be grateful if you would report this to us. By doing so, you can save other readers from frustration and help us improve subsequent versions of this book. If you find any errata, please report them by visiting http://www.packtpub.com/support, selecting your book, clicking on the **let us know** link, and entering the details of your errata. Once your errata are verified, your submission will be accepted and the errata will be uploaded on our website, or added to any list of existing errata, under the Errata section of that title. Any existing errata can be viewed by selecting your title from http://www.packtpub.com/support.

Piracy

Piracy of copyright material on the Internet is an ongoing problem across all media. At Packt, we take the protection of our copyright and licenses very seriously. If you come across any illegal copies of our works, in any form, on the Internet, please provide us with the location address or website name immediately so that we can pursue a remedy.

Please contact us at copyright@packtpub.com with a link to the suspected pirated material.

We appreciate your help in protecting our authors, and our ability to bring you valuable content.

Questions

You can contact us at questions@packtpub.com if you are having a problem with any aspect of the book, and we will do our best to address it.

1
Java EE Security Model

Java EE is the mainstream platform for implementing applications in a broad range of use cases starting from high transaction backend for rich clients to a complex integration and mixture of web, transaction processing, and EIS integration layers.

Security is one of the main concerns of software developers whether in small and mid-scale range or in large-scale, distributed software. Starting from the smallest application to the largest one, all may need a similar set of security measures such as authentication, authorization, non-reputability, and transport security.

Java EE as a modular platform for developing enterprise-scale applications provides a great deal of functionalities and features to address security requirements in a declarative way instead of an intrusive code-changing way.

In this chapter we will discuss how we can secure different Java applications either by describing the security model using the **declarative** security or by manually enforcing the security needs using the API exposed by Java EE containers to access the security enforcement layers **programmatically**. In *Chapter 3* we will put into practice all that we will discuss in this and the next chapter to build a secure Java EE application.

A detailed list of what you will learn in this chapter is as follows:

- Java EE architecture
- Authentication and authorization
- Transport security
- Web module security
- EJB module security
- Programmatic and declarative security

We will discuss security annotations and programmatic security in addition to looking at security description elements, which we can include in the deployment descriptors.

Overview of Java EE architecture

Java EE platform is the dominant platform for developing enterprise-scale applications and in the past three years developers have started looking at Java EE for developing small and mid-scale applications.

We can define Java EE as a set of libraries and tools, developed on top of what Java SE provides as a language and platform. A Java EE application usually consists of three different modules, which include **Web module** and **EJB module** residing in the server, and the **Application Client Module** which is designated for the client applications. Each module is assembled from different components and deployed in a designated container or server. These containers are well integrated with each other and form the Java EE application server.

 We have another type of module called **connector module**; we will not include it in our discussion as it is not widely used compared to three other module types. The connector module allows developers connect different application servers together or connect application servers to EIS systems.

Each of these containers provides a unique set of functionalities in the overall application server architecture. We may use one or two types of containers to form our application without involving the other containers.

Understanding a typical Java EE application

We briefly discussed the Java EE architecture and we said it consists of three main modules which are deployed in different application server containers. The Web module running inside the Web container sits in front of an EJB module deployed in the **EJB (Enterprise Java Beans)** container. The EJB module drives the system's business logic and provides transaction processing capabilities. This middle layer, which is formed by EJBs, may interact with a database or any other **EIS (Enterprise Information System)** through a connector module.

The last module is an application client module, which is a Java-based client application that directly interacts with middle layer through a specific container named **Application Client Container (ACC)**. Following diagram shows a Java EE application which uses Web, EJB, and Application Client Container.

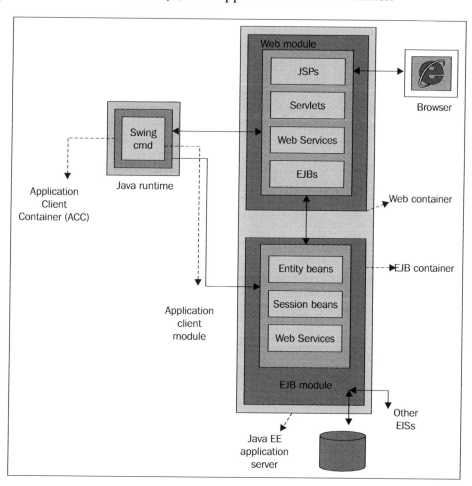

The previous figure assumes that no security measure is applied on user interaction with application or the interactions between different application modules. Each of these modules can be deployed independently or one or more of them can be included in a larger logical bundle named **Enterprise Application Archive (EAR)** and deployed together into the application server. Application server will decompose the archive and deploy each module into its designated container.

Each Java EE application, depending on which set of modules it uses, can have as few as one deployment descriptor or half a dozen. The deployment descriptors basically instruct the application server on how to deal with the application components. The following figure illustrates location and names of the deployment descriptors for a typical Java EE application designated for GlassFish application server.

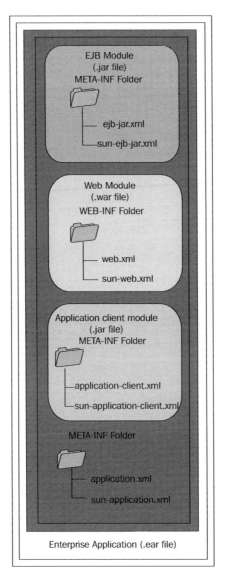

As you can see we have files with similar names, one without the sun- prefix and one with the prefix.

Files without the prefix are standard to Java EE and use the same schema across all Java EE application servers. These standard files deal with the configuration elements of a Java EE application and have nothing to do with the container the application is going to be deployed into. For example, definition of a Servlet, a Servlet filter, an EJB, and an EJB security constraint, among others can be configuration elements of the standard deployment descriptors.

The files prefixed with `sun-` specify the application server-specific configurations related to the application components. For example, mapping the Java EE security to application server-specific capabilities is one of functions of these files.

 Web browsers are the prominent clients for Java EE application and a fair deal of effort is devoted to secure and facilitate accessing Java EE applications through the browser without involving application client modules.

Accessing protected resource inside a Web module

A Web module represents resources inside the application server accessible using HTTP protocol. Each Web module is a deployable archive that contains JSP, Servlet, EJBs, and static contents like HTML page and graphical resources. A Web module is a ZIP file with **WAR** extension, a specific structure as shown in the previous figure, and one or more deployment descriptors.

The Web container responds to each HTTP request by executing `doPost` or other request processing methods of Servlet, processing a JSP or sending back a piece of static content like an HTML page. The following figure shows how users can access a protected resource in a Java EE application server.

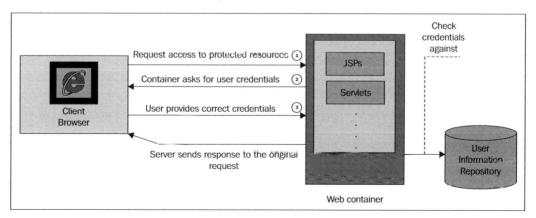

The previous figure illustrates steps the clients need to go through when they try to access some restricted resources. The Web container protects the Web module content by checking the requested URLs and decides whether it should send back the corresponding response or prevent the request going through the normal procedure until it ensures that the entity which requested the resource is permitted to access that specific resource.

Requests can be placed in one of the six different HTTP methods. Deciding on whether a specific method is acceptable for a resource or not is another factor which we can use to restrict access to a resource.

Web applications are complex and multi-purpose applications, which tons of different users may need to access. Each one of these users may need to have their own set of permissions and restrictions to specify which resources they can access and which resources they cannot.

To decide whether a request can get its corresponding response or not we should check who is requesting that specific resource and whether the requester is permitted to access the resource they are trying to reach.

An example can be a human resource manager, a role in the organization. We should validate his identity before we let him access the resources which are only available to a human resource department manager, such as an employee's contract record. At the same time we should prevent an accounting department employee, who in reality should only be able to issue the payrolls, from editing an employee's contract record.

To accomplish the identity validation and access authorization we should have a system to define users, assign one or more roles to each user, and later on define which roles and users are permitted to access different sets of our system functionalities. When it comes to users of our application, the users may already be defined in the organization where we want to deploy our application, thus we should be able to use already established identity storages when required.

We develop enterprise applications to ease the overall procedure of day-to-day tasks which an organization's employee needs to perform. We do not know whether the employee is going to access the application from an internal network or the communication between the employee and the application will go through an open network like the Internet.

We might be operating over an unknown open network where our requests and responses travel through many different nodes until they reach their destinations. So we need to think about our transport security as well as protecting our resources from unauthorized access. Transport security protects our content from unauthorized eyes that may be sitting between our clients trying to extract information from the transmitted packets.

To protect our information when we are operating in an unsecured network, we should apply some transport-level protection to ensure that our data travels in the unknown zone safely and no one can either monitor the content or tamper the requests or responses to manipulate our system in his or her favor.

Deployment descriptors

A Web module, which is an assembly of several different components, needs to have a deployment descriptor instructing the Web container the structure of the module, what its relation to external resources is, and what security measures the Web container must apply to protect the application resources. The deployment descriptor for a Web application is composed of two **XML** files and zero or more annotations directly placed in the components source codes. Two deployment descriptor files named web.xml and sun-web.xml are placed inside the WEB-INF directory of the Web application archive.

- The web.xml file contains all standard deployment instructions shared between all application servers. This file contains all instructions which an application server should apply internally.

- The sun-web.xml file contains GlassFish vendor-specific instructions, which can differ between different application servers. The instructions included in this file usually configures application server interaction with external resources in regard to the deployed application.

In the following sections we will see what features of the Java EE platform we can use to define access restriction on resources that need protection from unauthorized access.

Understanding Java EE security terms

Before we dig deep into Java EE application security we need to define some basic terms and the relation between these terms. They are:

- **User**: A user is an individual identity, which is defined in the identity storage. The individual can either be a program or a software operator. A user may be member of zero or more groups.

- **Group**: A group is a set of users classified with a set of common characteristics that usually leads to a set of common permissions and access levels. Individual users can be members of zero or more groups.

- **Security realm**: A security realm is the access channel for the application server to an identity storage system like a database or a flat file which contains user's authentication and grouping information. A sample of a security realm and authentication information storage can be the combination of a relation database as the users and groups information storage and GlassFish JDBC realm as the connector of Application server to this storage.

- **Role**: A role is an application-level concept that we have in almost every business application that we use. A role maps the access level defined in the Java EE application to users and groups defined in the security realm. Java EE platform provides the required functionalities to define roles and forms the access-level structure based on the defined roles.

- **Principal**: A principal is an identity that can be authenticated using an authentication protocol. The principal needs to have credentials to provide when it is going to the authentication process.

- **Credential**: A credential contains or references information used to authenticate a principal A password is a simple credential used for authentication.

The following figure shows an illustration of roles, users, groups and realms which we use to define the security view of our applications.

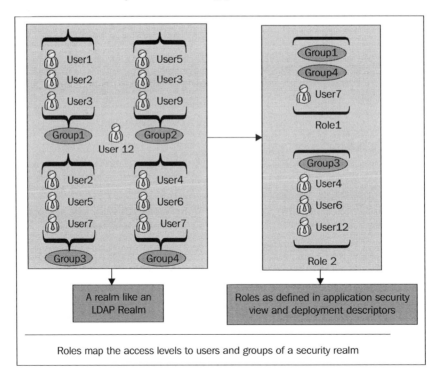

Roles map the access levels to users and groups of a security realm

Defining constraints on resources

Java EE platform allows us to define constraints on a URL or a set of URLs specified using wildcard characters. To define the constraints we determine which roles and users have the permission to access the URLs. An example of defining constraints on a set of JSP files is shown as follows:

```
<security-constraint>
    <web-resource-collection>
        <web-resource-name>HR Management</web-resource-name>
        <url-pattern>/jsp/hr/*</url-pattern>
        <http-method>PUT</http-method>
        <http-method>DELETE</http-method>
        <http-method>GET</http-method>
        <http-method>POST</http-method>
    </web-resource-collection>
    <auth-constraint>
        <role-name>hr_management_role</role-name>
        <role-name>top_level_manager_role</role-name>
    </auth-constraint>
</security-constraint>
<security-role>
    <role-name>hr_management_role</role-name>
</security-role>
<security-role>
    <role-name>top_level_manager_role</role-name>
</security-role>
```

This code snippet instructs the application server to check every incoming request to any URL matching /jsp/hr/* and only allows the request to go through when the user has one of the hr_management_role or top_level_manager_role roles.

We include the above listing in a deployment descriptor, deploy the application and try to hit a matching URL. The application server will forward us to the default **HTTP 403** error page which you can see in the following figure:

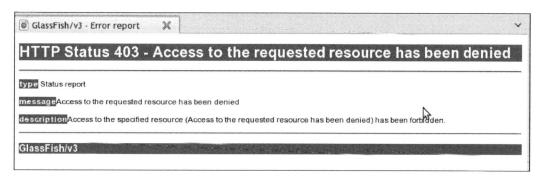

Why did the application server forward us to an access denied page? The reason is that the application server is not configured to authenticate the user and therefore it cannot determine what roles have been assigned to our user, so we need a way to instruct the application server to check our user identification information and decide whether the request should go through or not.

Authenticating and authorizing users

To make it simple, **authentication** is ensuring the users are who they claim they are by checking the credentials provided by them. **Authorization** is checking whether an authenticated user has the right to access the resource they requested to access. We perform authorization after we validate the user's identity.

The Java EE platform provides a broad range of options for enforcing the authentication procedure. Three different authentication methods are already provided in application servers and can be extended to cover the new requirements when they emerge.

In previous sections we discussed how access to some resources can be restricted to specific roles and users and we came to the conclusion that we should authenticate our users to check their permissions on accessing different system resources.

To address this requirement, authentication comes into play. Using authentication we can check whether a user is known to our system or not and if they are known, whether the requester is really who they claim to be or an imposter trying to get illegal access into our system.

The authentication process kick-starts when a user tries to access a restricted resource. If the user is not authenticated, the system will ask for his authentication information, including the username and password and commence with checking the username and password against the determined security realm. If the user fails to provide correct authentication information, the system will forward him to a HTTP 403 status page.

After the user is successfully authenticated, the system will continue the authorization process by checking whether the user has any of the roles permitted to access the requested resource. If user has one of the roles the request will go through. Otherwise, the user will be forwarded to a HTTP 401 status page.

The good news about Java EE authentication and authorization system is the **login once** feature, which ensures that when a user is authenticated he will not need to go through the authentication process again unless we discard the authentication token which the system assigned to the user after a successful authentication.

 We can configure our applications to use username-password pair, biometric tokens, **X.509 digital certificates**, **Kerberos** token, or any other form of authentication mechanism supported by the application server. Here we will discuss username and password as it is the most widely used authentication method.

Adding authentication to a Web application

To add authentication to a Web application we only need to include the required elements in the deployment descriptor. In the deployment descriptor we can determine which type of authentication we want the system to perform and which security realm we want the user to be authenticated against. The following code snippet shows the required elements that we can add to web.xml to enforce authentication where required.

```
<login-config>
    <auth-method>BASIC</auth-method>
    <realm-name>JDBC_REALM</realm-name>
</login-config>
```

The code snippet simply provides instructions for the application server to conduct a HTTP Basic Authentication when an unauthenticated user tries to access a restricted resource. The application server will check the provided credentials against a realm named JDBC_REALM. If we do not define which realm we want to use, the application server will use the default security realm. In GlassFish this realm is named file and its content are stored in a plain text file.

We will discuss application server realms in more detail in *Chapter 2*. For now consider the JDBC_REALM as a set of two tables that contains users, groups, and user to group association information.

The `auth-method` element specifies which authentication method we want to use. Different authentication methods provide different levels of security and protection. Four different authentication methods are provided in Java EE specification which vendors must implement. These four different authentication methods provided by application servers are listed in the following table.

Authentication method	Description	Pros and cons
HTTP BASIC Authentication (`BASIC`)	Server requests a username and password from the web client. The authentication dialog is standard.	• Easiest to implement. • Credentials transmitted in plain text if SSL or other network-level encryptions are not in place.
Form-Based Authentication (`FORM`)	We should provide a login form to ask username and password along with an authentication failed page in case authentication fails.	• Very flexible in look and feel. • Need extra work to develop required pages. • Password transmitted in plain text if SSL or other network-level encryptions are not in place.
HTTPS Client Authentication (`CLIENT-CERT`)	Both server and client or client alone will need to possess digital certificates to identify themselves.	• Very secure. • More expensive than other methods. • More complex in implementation and administration.
Digest Authentication (`DIGEST`)	Similar to HTTP BASIC Authentication with security enabled for transmitting credentials.	• Easy to implement but not widespread. • Credentials are encrypted prior to transmission.

If we do not specify an authentication method and therefore a security realm, GlassFish will automatically use HTTP BASIC Authentication (`BASIC`) for the authentication method and a built-in realm named `file` as the security realm. We will discuss file realm in more detail in *Chapter 2*.

We will discuss these authentication methods along with how we can configure the application server to support them in more detail in *Chapter 2*.

Authorizing using deployment descriptor

In the previous two sections we talked about roles and how we can configure the deployment descriptor to only let some of our web application resources be accessible to specific roles. But do these roles map to real world users and groups that security realms contain?

In the figure included in the *Understanding security terms of Java EE* section we saw a representation of the users and groups mapping to Java EE roles. To instruct the application server to perform these mappings we should use deployment descriptors to map a role to specific users or to groups (or both).

We define the mapping in the vendor-specific deployment descriptor (sun-web.xml) as it is where we should include the vendor-dependent deployment plan details. The following snippet assigns the hr_management_role role to HR_ADMIN user and all members of the HR_MANAGER group. The HR_MANAGER group and all of its possible members are stored in the security realm represented by the JDBC_REALM.

```
<security-role-mapping>
    <role-name>hr_management_role</role-name>
    <principal-name>HR_ADMIN</principal-name>
    <group-name>HR_MANAGER</group-name>
</security-role-mapping>
```

So far we have provided instructions for the application server to protect some of our resources and only allow specific roles to access those resources. But we still need to safeguard our application data on the open network from unauthorized eyes that may intercept our communication channels.

Managing session information

We discussed how when a user is authenticated they will stay authenticated unless we discard the authentication information or the validity period of the authentication information expires.

Here we can define a new term named **session** that can hold all kind of information either required by the programmer or by the application server during the time a visitor or a user is interacting with our system. Some examples for using session are holding the authentication information, the shopping cart content, the visited URLs, and so on. This information can be stored in different ways, including:

- **Cookies**: We can use cookies to store the session information on the client side. We usually encrypt sensitive information before setting it as a client-side cookie.

- **URL Rewriting** or **server side**: In this method we store the session information on the server side and assign each visitor a unique identifier to extract the session information when required. We usually append a field at the end of URLs which includes the session ID of that particular client.

- **Hidden form fields**: We can use hidden HTML fields like `<INPUT TYPE="HIDDEN" NAME="session" VALUE="...">` to transmit the session information.

The hidden form fields method's disadvantage is that all pages we use should be dynamically generated in order for us to include the session information as a hidden field along with other information. Unless we always know how many required fields are placed in the session, we create a placeholder field for them.

Java EE Servlet API provides a profound API for session management. We can access the session information using the `HttpSession` interface. An example of using `HttpSession` interface is as follows:

```
HttpSession session = request.getSession(true);
session. setAttribute("refPage",request.getHeader("Referrer"));
ShoppingCart sc = (ShoppingCart)session.getAttribute("sc");
sc.addItem(anItem);
```

We can put any serializable object into session and expect the application server to keep our session alive until we discard the session or the session times out and expires. But there are some pitfalls and best practices associated with using session to store our required properties. A short list of these precautions is as follows:

- Use `session-config` element of the `web.xml` to tune the session management capabilities of the application server

- Use `HttpSessionListener` to perform the necessary tasks after a session is created or invalidated

- Do not use long-term values like user IDs as a session identifier; instead use randomly generated short-lived tokens

- Do not store anything in the session unless it is encrypted with a proven encryption method.

- Invalidate all session variables after an absolute time like 10 hours or after a period of inactivity like 30 minutes

- Provide logout functionality to allow the users to logout when they want to, which is provided in Servlet 3 specification as a part of Java EE 6

- Do not store unnecessary information in the session and remove any variable which is no longer required from the session

The list can go on but the basics instruct us to use the server memory efficiently and make sure that our users' data will not get compromised if our session information is turned into the wrong hands.

 Different application servers may provide additional session management capabilities like specifying session maintaining method, cookies domain, cookies length, and so on. GlassFish application server stays with the standard to ensure that your application can be ported to any Java EE-compliant server if required.

Adding transport security

In many enterprise applications, transmitting information over open networks is inevitable. An open network like the Internet has its drawbacks alongside the many benefits that it brings to organizations. A drawback which can affect our applications is the unsecure nature of the data pathway between the client and the server. To address this drawback we should use some sort of encryption mechanism like secure **VPNs**, **IPSec**, manual encryptions, and so on.

Java EE application servers implement the required functionalities specified by the Java EE specification in providing SSL-based encryption for transferring sensitive data between the application server and its clients. The specification and the implementations make it as simple as adding required elements to the deployment descriptor for instructing the application server to use HTTPS for communication with clients. Here is a example snippet to add encryption support for a set of resources:

```
<security-constraint>
    <web-resource-collection>
        <web-resource-name>HR Management</web-resource-name>
            <url-pattern>/jsp/hr/*</url-pattern>
            <http-method>PUT</http-method>
            <http-method>DELETE</http-method>
            <http-method>GET</http-method>
            <http-method>POST</http-method>
    </web-resource-collection>
    <user-data-constraint>
        <description/>highest supported transport security level
        </description>
        <transport-guarantee>CONFIDENTIAL</transport-guarantee>
    </user-data-constraint>
</security-constraint>
```

Java EE specification followed by application servers provides different levels of transport guarantee on the communication between clients and the application server. The three levels follow:

- **Data Confidentiality** (CONFIDENTIAL): We use this level to guarantee that all communication between client and server goes through the SSL layer and connections won't be accepted over a non-secure channel.

- **Data integrity** (INTEGRAL): We can use this level when a full encryption is not required but we want our data to be transmitted to and from the client in a way that if anyone changed the data we could detect the change.

- **Any type of connection** (NONE): We can use this level to enforce the container to accept connections on HTTP and HTTPs.

Applying transport security measures brings additional overhead to perform the encryption and decryption. The amount of overhead greatly depends on the cipher suite we use in our HTTPS communication. If we use ciphers with longer key length our encryptions are harder to break compared to when using cipher suites with shorter keys. But we pay a price for better security and this price is more overhead on the server for encryption and decryption of data. We should always use cryptography with care not to introduce additional load on our systems. For example, where it is absolutely required to have data confidentiality, like when we are transmitting credit card numbers, we should use CONFIDENTIAL level, but when we are transmitting a set of numbers for calculation we can use INTEGRAL to ensure that our data is tamper-proof.

In production environment, we usually front the application server with a Web server or a dedicated hardware appliance to accelerate the SSL access among other tasks, such as hosting static content, load distribution, decorating HTP headers, and so on.

For security purpose, the frontend Web server or appliance (like a Cisco PIX 535, F5 Big IP, and so on) can be used to accelerate SSL certificate processing, unify the access port to both HTTP and HTTPS, act as a firewall, and so on.

Using programmatic security in web applications

Sometimes the declarative security in not enough to cope with a complex security requirement and we need to take control and program some security procedures instead of declaring them. There are seven methods of HTTPServletRequest class that we can use to extract security-related attributes of the request and decide manually about how to process the request. These methods are included in the following table.

Method	Description
String getRemoteUser()	If the user is authenticated returns the username, otherwise returns null.
boolean isUserInRole(String role)	Returns whether the user has the specified roles or not.
Principal getUserPrincipal()	Returns a java.security.Principal object containing the name of the current authenticated user.
String getAuthType()	Returns a String containing the authentication method used to protect this Servlet.

Method	Description
`void login(String username, String password)`	This method authenticates the provided username and password against the security realm which the application is configured to use. We can say this method does anything that the `BASIC` or `FORM` authentication does but it also gives the developer total control over how it is going to happen.
`Void logout()`	Establishes `null` as the value returned when `getUserPrincipal`, `getRemoteUser`, and `getAuthType` is called on the request.
`String getScheme()`	Returns the schema portion of the URL, for example HTTP or HTTPS.

We can use these methods when we are processing a request to decide what kind of response we should send back to our user. The programmatic login and logout is included in Java EE 6 and did not exist in Java EE 5 and previous versions.

We can use more descriptive names when we call the `isUserInRole` method to increase the readability of our source code. But we will need to include linking description for the role name we used in our source code to real names defined in the Web application descriptor, the `web.xml` file. The following sample snippet shows how we check the user role and decide where to redirect them:

```
protected void processRequest(HttpServletRequest request,
    HttpServletResponse response)
    throws ServletException, IOException {
        if (request.isUserInRole("human_resource_manager"))
                response.sendRedirect("/hr/index.jsp");
        else response.sendRedirect("/guests/index.jsp");
    }
```

We can use different aliases for a role name to make our code easier to read and maintain. For example, imagine we are using `human_resource_manager` in our source code to alias the `hr_management_role` role name. In case we use this sort of aliasing we should include `security-role-ref` elements in our deployment descriptor to describe the link between the aliases and names. For example, to describe the above aliasing we can use:

```
<security-role-ref>
    <role-name>human_resource_manager</role-name>
    <role-link>hr_management_role</role-link>
</security-role-ref>
```

If we do not include the `security-role-ref` element, the application server will assume that any role name we used in our source code is a role defined using `security-role` element and will look for its mapping in the `sun-web.xml` file.

We must include this referencing inside the Servlet element of the Servlet, where we used the alias in its implementation.

Using security annotations

Annotations included in Java EE starting from version 5 allows developers to use metadata to affect the way that a program is treated and interpreted by application servers, tools, and libraries. There are several annotations which we can use in configuring a Web application security.

`@DeclareRoles({"ROLE_1", "ROLE_2", "ROLE_N"})`: We can use this annotation on a Servlet class to define the roles that we are referring to them from that Servlet. To make it simple, this annotation is a replacement for `security-role` element of the `web.xml` file. We can declare one or more roles using this annotation.

`@RunAs(value="ROLE_NAME")`: Using this annotation we ask the container to only assign the given role to the current security identity for any outgoing invocation. For example, if placed on a Servlet, independent of what the current principal role is, the container will assign this role to the current security identity to access any resource. This annotation is the metadata twin of the `run-as` element, which we can use in deployment descriptor.

> We use the run-as element or its counterpart annotation to assign an specific role to all outgoing calls of a Servlet or an EJB. We use this element to ensure that an internal role which is required to access some secured internal EJBs is never assigned to a client and rather stays fully in control of the developers. Note that the role of the current principal does not change the current identity as seen by the `getCallerPrincipal()` method of the `EJBContext`, or `getUserPrincipal()` of the `HTTPServletRequest` will return the actual roles.

`@ServletSecurity`: Using this annotation we can define the security and access control of a Servlet right inside the source code instead of using the deployment descriptor `security-constraint` element. The `@ServletSecurity` can optionally get a `@HttpMethodConstraint` and `@HttpConstraint` as its parameters. The `@HttpMethodConstraint` is an array specifying the HTTP method-specific constraint while `@HttpConstraint` specifies the protection for all HTTP methods which are not specified in the `@HttpMethodConstraint`.

For example we can use the following annotation:

```
@ServletSecurity(@HttpConstraint(rolesAllowed = {"employee",
"manager"}))
```

This allows only users with a `manager` or `employee` role to access this Servlet. This one single line of code is equal to the following deployment descriptor elements.

```
<security-constraint>
    <web-resource-collection>
        <url-pattern>/ourServlet</url-pattern>
    </web-resource-collection>
    <auth-constraint>
        <security-role-name>manager</security-role-name>
        <security-role-name>employee</security-role-name>
    </auth-constraint>
</security-constraint>
```

In the next section we will discuss EJB annotations, learn more about these annotations, different types of target (class and method), and what kind of components (EJB or Servlet) can be annotated using security annotations.

With this we've finished with the basics of Web module security; we will discuss the Web module security in further detail in *Chapter 3* when we will develop a secure application using Java EE. Now it is time to take a look at EJB module security.

Understanding the EJB modules

We saw that a Web module is mostly responsible for interactive with users, including receiving the requests as HTTP methods, processing the requests, calling business logic when required to generate the response, and finally sending the generated response back to clients.

The EJB modules are simple ZIP files with **JAR** extension, with a predefined structure, formed by several Enterprise JavaBeans implementations, which are called enterprise beans. Three types of EJBs defined by the specification and supported by different application servers are **Session Beans**, **Entity Beans**, and **Message-Driven Beans (MDB)**.

Message-Driven Beans are provided to process the **JMS** messages in the context of enterprise application to support complex transaction schemas. There is no security constraint which we may need to define for an MDB.

Java EE specification followed by application servers provides a complete security model for Entity Beans and Session Beans as they are in direct contact with the clients either through the Application Client Container, through a web application, or from another container developed by third-party companies to integrate a new container in a Java EE application server.

We can define constraints on Entity Beans and Session Beans in two ways—by adding required elements to deployment descriptor or adding necessary annotations to the EJB's source code.

These annotations or deployment descriptor elements instruct the application server about which roles are allowed to access the EJB as a whole or one or more methods of the business interface, home interface, component interface, and/or web service endpoints.

If you are thinking about the authentication, I should say that authentication process usually happens in the first layer of user's interaction with application. In our case this is the Web module or the application client module. Thus we are not involved with authentication in the EJB layer and instead we rely on the authentication information we receive from the Web layer and we only go through the authorization process in the EJB layer. Following figure illustrates how EJB container relies on Web container or Application Client Container for authentication process.

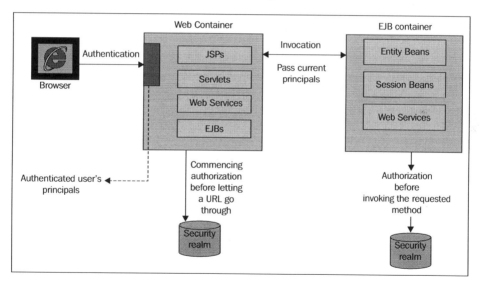

Whenever the Web container needs to invoke some methods from an EJB module in the EJB container it sends the authenticated user's principal to the EJB container, which goes through authorization to see whether the current user has the permission to invoke the method or not.

Similar to Web modules where we could use annotation and deployment descriptor elements to instruct the container to apply constraints on our resources, we can use annotation and deployment descriptor to define constraints on EJBs. Through this section we will use Entity Beans to demonstrate how we can define constraints either by using annotation or through the deployment descriptor. The listing below shows the `Employee` Entity Bean.

```
@Entity
public class Employee implements Serializable {
    public String getName() {
        return "name";
    }
    public void promote(String toPosition) {
        //promote the employee
    }
    public List<EvaluationRecords> getEvaluationRecords() {
        List<EvaluationRecords> evalRecord;
        //return a list containing all
        // EvaluationRecords of
        //this employee
        return evalRecord;
    }
    public List<EvaluationRecords> getEvaluationRecords(Date from,
            Date to) {
        List<EvaluationRecords> evalRecord;
        //return a list containing all
        //productivity evaluation of
        //this employee
        return evalRecord;
    }
    @Id
    private Integer id;
    public Employee() {
    }
}
```

The `Employee` Entity Bean has several methods and we should only allow certain roles to invoke them. The `getName` method can be accessed by any caller that has the `employee_role` role. The `promote` and `getEvaluationRecords` method can be called by any employee with the `hr_management_role` role assigned to them. Finally, we should allow all top-level managers to invoke different overloads of the `getEvaluationRecords` method. For instructing the application server to protect our entity bean with the security view we have just defined, we should provide the corresponding declaration in the `ejb-jar.xml` file. The following listing shows how we should add the security view we defined to our `ejb-jar.xml` file.

```xml
<security-role>
    <description>human_resource_manager
    </description>
    <role-name>hr_management_role</role-name>
</security-role>
<security-role>
    <description> top level managers
    </description>
    <role-name>top_level_manager_role</role-name>
</security-role>
<method-permission>
    <role-name>hr_management_role</role-name>
    <method>
        <ejb-name>Employee</ejb-name>
        <method-name>getName</method-name>
    </method>
</method-permission>

<method-permission>
    <role-name>hr_management_role</role-name>
    <method>
        <ejb-name>Employee</ejb-name>
        <method-name>*</method-name>
    </method>
</method-permission>

<method-permission>
    <role-name>top_level_manager_role</role-name>
    <method>
        <ejb-name>employee</ejb-name>
        <method-name>getEvaluationRecords</method-name>
        <method-params>
            <method-param>from</method-param>
            <method-param>to</method-param>
        </method-params>
    </method>
</method-permission>
```

This snippet shows some basic instructions for application servers to restrict access to different methods of Employee bean for certain roles.

Using `security-role` we can define roles which we want to use in the EJB module. By using the `method-permission` element we can define which roles can access one or all methods in our entity bean. The `role-name` is the name of the rule which we want to define its permissions in the current `security-role` element. The value can either be a role name or it can be `unchecked` to permit all roles to invoke methods we determine by using the `method-name` element. In the `method-name` element we can use a method name or we can use * to grant permission for invoking all of our EJB methods to the roles we set in `method-name` element.

In our entity bean we have two overloads of the `getEvaluationRecords` method and sometimes we just need to let different roles invoke different overloads. In such a condition we distinguish different overloads by providing the list of parameters for the method for which we want to define permission.

Like in web applications, we sometimes need to assign a specific role to all outgoing calls of an EJB. To do this, we can use the `run-as` element of the standard deployment descriptor as shown in the following snippet:

```
<enterprise-beans>
<entity>
    <ejb-name>employee</ejb-name>
    <ejb-class>book.glassfish.security.chapter01.Employee
      </ejb-class>
    <security-identity>
        <run-as>
            <role-name>payroll_dept</role-name>
        </run-as>
    </security-identity>
</entity>
</enterprise-beans>
```

This sample code instructs the application server to assign the `payroll_dept` to all outgoing calls from `Employee` bean using the `payroll_dept` role. Using the `run-as` element does not change the current authenticated user or their role, but it's just in case the method invocation uses the given role.

Securing EJB modules using annotations

Annotations play an important role in Java EE 5 and later releases, especially in the EJB layer. We can almost forget about the standard deployment descriptor, `ejb-jar.xml`, and define every runtime aspect of EJBs using annotations. Although using annotations lifts the necessity of the `ejb-jar.xml` presence, we still need to have vendor-specific descriptor `sun-ejb-jar.xml` in place to define dependency of our EJB module to external resources like security realms.

The following table below shows important security-related annotations in Java EE 6 that we can use to secure different components of enterprise applications.

Annotation	Class Level	Method Level	EJB	Servlet	Description
@PermitAll	X	X	X		Permitting everyone to access the annotated method. In case of class-level annotation, all methods of annotated EJB are accessible to all roles unless the method is annotated with a @RolesAllowed annotation.
@DenyAll		X	X		If placed on a method, no one can access that method. In case of class-level annotation, all methods of annotated EJB are inaccessible to all roles unless a method is annotated with a @RolesAllowed annotation.
@RolesAllowed	X	X	X		In case of method-level annotation, it permits the included roles to invoke the method. In case of class-level annotation, all methods of the annotated EJB are accessible to included roles unless the method is annotated with a different set of roles using @RolesAllowed annotation.
@DeclareRoles	X		X	X	Defines roles used by the application. It is similar to using the security-role element of the deployment descriptor.
@RunAs	X		X	X	Specifies the run-as role for the given components. We discussed how this annotation works in the *Using security annotations* section.

Some of the security annotations cannot target a method like @DeclareRoles while some others can target both methods and classes like @PermitAll. Annotation applied on a method will override the class-level annotations. For example, if we apply @RolesAllowed("employee") on an EJB class, and we apply @RolesAllowed("manager") on one specific method of that EJB, only *admin* role will be able to invoke the marked method while all other methods will be available to the employee role.

You should remember two of these annotations from the Web module section and now you are going to learn four other security-related annotations. Let's rewrite the Employee entity bean using annotations. A revision of the Employee entity bean enriched by annotation is in the following listing:

```
@Entity
@DeclareRoles({"employee_role","hr_management_role"top_level_manager_
role})
@RolesAllowed(" hr_management_role")
public class Employee implements Serializable {
    @RolesAllowed("employee_role")
    public String getName() {
        return "name";
    }
    public void promote(String toPosition) {
        //promote the employee
    }

@RolesAllowed("top_level_manager_role ")
    public List<EvaluationRecords> getEvaluationRecords() {
        List<EvaluationRecords> evalRecord = null;
        //return a list containing all
        // EvaluationRecords of
        //this employee
        return evalRecord;
    }
@RolesAllowed("top_level_manager_role ")
    public List<EvaluationRecords> getEvaluationRecords(Date from,
      Date to) {
        List<EvaluationRecords> evalRecord = null;
        //return a list containing all
        // EvaluationRecords of
        //this employee
        return evalRecord;
    }

    @Id
    private Integer id;
    public Employee() {
    }
}
```

We simply used `@DeclareRoles({"employee_role","hr_management_role","top_level_manager_role})` to define all roles that we are going to use in our EJB and then we used `@RolesAllowed("top_level_manager_role")` to permit the `top_level_manager_role` role to invoke all methods in the `Employee` EJB. Finally, we defined which roles can invoke individual methods by marking them with different `@RolesAllowed` annotations.

To instruct the application server to execute the EJB methods using a specified role instead of the caller role, we can place `@RunAs(value="payroll_dept")` on the EJB class level.

Mapping roles to principals and groups

In the Web applications we saw that we should define the mapping between roles, principals, and groups in the `sun-web.xml`, which is the vendor-specific deployment descriptor for web applications. In the same way, we need to define the role mapping in the EJB applications to ensure that application server can determine whether a user has a required role assigned to it or not. The following snippet of the `sun-ejb-jar.xml` shows how we can map the `hr_management_role` role to an individual user and a group of the realm.

```
<security-role-mapping>
    <role-name>hr_management_role</role-name>
    <principal-name>HR_ADMIN</principal-name>
    <group-name>HR_Manager</group-name>
</security-role-mapping>
```

This role mapping declaration, `hr_management_role` is assigned to `HR_Manager` group as well as for an individual user, identified by `HR_ADMIN` username.

Accessing the security context programmatically

Similar to web applications for which we had some level of programmatic access to the context security information, we have some methods which allow us to access the security context and extract the required information when the declarative security and annotations are not enough.

The `javax.ejb.EJBContext` interface provides two methods for accessing the security information. First, `getCallerPrincipal` method which lets us access the caller principal and second, the already introduced `isCallerInRole` method to check a specific role against the roles assigned to the caller. It is highly recommended that we only use the annotations and deployment descriptor and turn to programmatic security only when we have no other way to address our requirement. Imagine that our `Employee` bean has a new method named `raisePaygrade(int amount, String raisedBy)`, this method needs the username of the manager who will raise the pay grade of the employee. When we are calling this method of `Employee` bean we can extract the caller principal and use it when we are invoking this method.

```
@Stateless
public class EmployeeServiceBean
  {
    @Resource
    SessionContext ctx;
    public void raiseEmployeePaygrade(int amount, long empID){
      Employee employee = null;
      //find the employee
      String raisedBy =ctx.getCallerPrincipal().getName();
      employee.raisePayGrade(850000, raisedBy);
      //persist the employee
    }
}
```

We simply extract the principal of the caller and store who raised the pay grade for our employee. Our sample method only accepts two parameters; while it may be way more complex than this, the concept and the procedure is the same.

We should follow the same rules when we are using the `isCallerInRole` method, meaning that we need to either use the role name as defined in the deployment descriptor, or we should define the link between the role name we used in the source code and real name of the role which is defined in the `security-role` element.

Using EJB interceptors for auditing and security purposes

We can use `AroundInvoke` interceptor to intercept EJB business method calls. Intercepting the call lets us access the method name, its parameters, and EJB context (and therefore `isCallerInRole` and `getCallerPrincipal` methods). We can perform tasks such as security check, logging and auditing, or even changing the values of method parameters using interceptors.

```
public class SampleInterceptor {
    @Resource
    private EJBContext context;
    @AroundInvoke
    protected Object audit(InvocationContext ctx) throws Exception {

        Principal p = context.getCallerPrincipal();
        if (userIsValid(p)) {
        //do some logging...
        }else{
        //logging and raising exception..
    }
        return ctx.proceed();
    }
}
```

To use this interceptor we only need to place an annotation on the designated EJB. For example to intercept any method call on `EmployeeServiceBean` we can do the following:

```
@Interceptors(SampleInterceptor.class)
@Stateless
public class EmployeeServiceBean {
// Source code omitted.
}
```

The `@Interceptors` can target classes, methods, or both. To exclude a method from a class-level interceptor we can use `@ExcludeClassInterceptors` annotation for that method.

We can use interceptor element of `ejb-jar.xml` deployment descriptor to specify interceptors if preferred.

Enforcing authentication in EJB modules

So far we have assumed that the EJB module itself does not require conducting an authentication and relies on authentication information it receives from the caller container. But we may need to instruct the EJB container to commence with authentication process when necessary by including required configuration elements to `sun-ejb-jar.xml` file.

We usually require enforcing authentication in the EJB layer when we know that client applications, which may access our EJBs, are deployed into other containers like ACC or another application server's different containers.

The EJB container uses Inter-ORB security standards to declare constraints over EJBs which have some level of constraints applied on them. A simple configuration to ensure that any call to a constraint method of the `Employee` entity bean will go through authentication is similar to the following listing.

```
<sun-ejb-jar>
    <enterprise-beans>
        <unique-id>1</unique-id>
        <ejb>
            <ejb-name>employee</ejb-name>
            <jndi-name>employee</jndi-name>
            <ior-security-config>
                <transport-config>
                    <integrity>NONE</integrity>
                    <confidentiality>NONE</confidentiality>
                    <establish-trust-in-target>
                    NONE
                    </establish-trust-in-target>
                    <establish-trust-in-client>
                    NONE
                    </establish-trust-in-client>
                </transport-config>
                <as-context>
                    <auth-method>USERNAME_PASSWORD</auth-method>
                    <realm>default</realm>
                    <required>true</required>
                </as-context>
            </ior-security-config>
        </ejb>
    </enterprise-beans>
</sun-ejb-jar>
```

The snippet simply means that we want to have authentication of HTTP Basic type in place when a user tries to access a constrained part of our EJB. Using IOR we can declare transport security in addition to authentication, but I leave it to you to study the `sun-ejb-jar.xml` to see what else we can do using IOR declarations. In *Chapter 3* we will discuss `sun-ejb-jar.xml` in more detail.

Understanding the application client module

Application client modules are regular Java programs that directly interact with the EJB modules. These modules depend on another type of container named Application Client Container for the services that are required for operation. Each application client module is assembled in a JAR file that contains a deployment descriptor named `application-client.xml`.

The `application-client.xml` descriptor file determines how the application accesses enterprise beans and web resources. When the resources which the application client requires to access are secure the client will be authenticated accordingly.

Assume that we have a Swing application interacting with an EJB module with several constrained EJBs that we need to use during our application runtime. As we want to access a secure resource, we should go through the authentication and authorization phases. In order to go through these two phases we should provide our authentication information to the container so it can validate our identity and check whether we have a role permitted to invoke the EJB method we want to invoke.

When we want to access a constraint EJB resource from an application client module, the ACC will perform the authentication and send the authenticated subject along with the context when it accesses the EJB. Then the EJB module performs the authorization to check whether we have the required access permission (we have the required role) to further proceed with the invocation.

There is no standard authentication API for plain (not application clients) Java SE applications to access the EJB module. So, if we have a plain Java SE application and we need to access a secured EJB, we should either use the vendor-specific solutions or we should change the Java SE application into a application client module.

Forget about how we can develop the client application which runs on the ACC; we can talk about deployment descriptors which we should make it possible for our client application to send the authentication information to the server, so an authorized user can access what it is authorized to access. These configurations are provided through different deployment descriptor files. The first file is the standard Java EE deployment descriptor for the application client named `application-client.xml` and a companion vendor-specific deployment descriptor named `sun-application-client.xml`. We use these two files to configure a callback handler which asks the user to provide specific credentials like username and password or a digital certificate, or it can use the credential which the user used to log into his operation environment.

Two files are bundled with our application client module and deal with internals of our application client such as which resources our application wants to use and how it responds to an authentication request coming from the server.

We need another descriptor file to define where our server is located, how secure our communication channel should be, and which security realm our user should be checked against. This deployment descriptor which provides us with a fair deal of security-related configuration is named `sun-acc.xml` but we can change the name to something more meaningful.

This file is not bundled with the application client module but rather we pass this file as an argument of the Application Client Container launcher when we want to launch our client application. If we do not pass this file address as an argument, the ACC launcher will try to use a default one. We discuss more about this file in *Chapter 3*.

By default the Application Client Container uses a simple Swing dialog to collect the username and password when we try to access a restricted EJB from our client application. But we can override the configuration and instruct the Application Client Container to use our own callback handler to collect the authentication information. We may show a very polished Swing frame to collect the username and password or collect any other necessary credentials. The following snippet is a part of the `application-client.xml` file that instructs the Application Client Container to use our callback handler instead of showing the default dialog box.

```
<callback-handler>
    book.glassfish.security.chapter1.SwingCallbackHandler
</callback-handler>
```

We simply let the ACC know what the callback handler is and the ACC takes care of initiating and calling its methods when necessary. In addition to a lazy authentication that kick-starts the authentication when we try to access a resource, we can specify a default username and a password for each one of the resources that our client application can access in the `sun-application-client.xml` file. For example:

```
<resource-ref>
    <res-ref-name>TaskQueueFactory</res-ref-name>
    <jndi-name>jms/TaskQueueFactory</jndi-name>
    <default-resource-principal>
        <name>user</name>
        <password>password</password>
    </default-resource-principal>
</resource-ref>
```

The GlassFish application server or any other application server has a default realm which Web Container, EJB container, or ACC will authenticate the users against when an authentication is defined, but for all of them we can override this default realm name with the realm name we require using different types of deployment descriptors.

We can use the `sun-acc.xml` file for declaring several types of security measures, starting from the authentication down to transport-level security. You may study which options are available in this file to increase you understanding of available ACC security measures.

Declaring security roles in Application level

So far we discussed several types of deployment descriptors for Web, EJB, and application client modules. But we know that we usually deploy an archive including all three types of modules known as an enterprise application module. This module is again a ZIP file with EAR extension.

The enterprise application module has its own deployment descriptors named `application.xml` and `sun-application.xml` for the vendor-specific deployment descriptor, which in addition to the application structure we can include declarations common between different modules inside them.

In our case, one of the common declarations are security role declarations which are defined using the `security-role` element inside the `application.xml`, which is the standard deployment descriptor.

The other common declarations are role-to-group and individual mapping using `security-role-mapping` element. We put this declaration, which is a vendor-specific declaration, inside the application vendor-specific deployment descriptor, the `sun-application.xml` file.

We can use `sun-application.xml` to specify the default authentication realm for the entire application. The default realm specified in the `sun-application.xml` will be used if an included module does not specify which authentication realm it wants to use. Following snippet shows how we can specify the authentication realm in `sun-application.xml`.

```
<sun-application>
    <realm>JDBC_REALM</realm>
</sun-application>
```

Summary

Java EE security is a very broad topic which can address small and day-to-day security requirements to large, complex, and unique issues which only can rise for large-scale complex applications.

In this chapter we briefly introduced Web modules, EJB modules, and application client module's security in different levels including authentication, authorization, and transport security. We discussed users, groups, and role mapping down to a good level of detail, along with small topics like HTTP session and performance issues of using cryptography.

In next chapter, we will discuss JAAS and GlassFish security realm in more detail to complete the basic information we need to develop a secure enterprise application in *Chapter 3*.

2

GlassFish Security Realms

Java EE application servers require interaction with many external systems to address the requirements of the organization they are hosting applications for. Two of these external systems are **Identity management systems (IDM)** and **identity storages.** Identity management systems are end-to-end products covering all functionalities related to provisioning, authentication, and authorization. IDM products can interact with tons of external sources and support major security-related standards to facilitate security integration and interaction of separate enterprise applications. Identity storage is any type of storage containing user identification information, including identity and credentials. We will discuss the **OpenSSO** IDM system in chapters 7 to 9. In this chapter, we discuss GlassFish application server interaction with identity storages like relational databases, **Lightweight Directory Access Protocol (LDAP)** servers, flat files storage, and so on. This chapter follows *Chapter 1* to complete the Java EE applications' security configuration and prepare us for completing a sample application in the next chapter. This chapter covers the following topics:

- Security realms
- GlassFish security realms
- File realm
- JDBC realm
- LDAP realm
- Certificate realm
- Developing custom realm

There are sample codes to see how each of the above topics can be used to secure the sample application.

Security realms

Security realms, like many other standards, functionalities, and capabilities, are provided to address the requirement of enterprise application developments when it comes to reusing security assets.

Authenticating using security realms

Security realms provide a standard way for application servers to authenticate the identity provided by a user, or an entity like another software or hardware against a set of already defined identity stored in identity storages. Some of the common identity storages are as follows:

- Flat files for development time or for small applications
- Relational databases for applications of all sizes
- LDAP servers for mid or enterprise-scale applications
- Microsoft Active Directory, which is an LDAP implementation
- Operating system realms like Solaris realm for integrating the applications security with operating system security and using the same login for it
- Biometric databases like thumbprint identifications for applications with sensitive applications
- Smart card identification for sensitive roles applications and roles like administration sections

Several security realms are available in GlassFish to support authentication against different identity storage types. We create security realms using available realm types to authenticate users against an identity storage known to that realm type. For example, a **JDBC** realm knows how to interact with a database to authenticate user credentials.

Sometimes we need to authenticate our users against a custom identity storage that is not supported by GlassFish; for these occasions we can develop new realms by extending some GlassFish-specific classes that let an application server authenticate a user against our custom identity storage. GlassFish uses **Java Authentication and Authorization Service (JAAS)** under the hood of its security realms implementations.

Reusing security assets

The reason that security realms are included in Java EE specification and the application server is the need in the enterprise to reuse some already established IT assets like identity storage in new software systems, to reduce the overall costs and prevent duplication in the enterprise.

The realm in Java EE under `login-config` element just says "the realm name that should be used for this application". The Java EE specification does not really expand more on what a realm is. Each application server implements the concept of realm separately and includes as many security realms in the application server as they see required.

The specification ties the security realm to authentication method, which are mandatory parts of the specification with a statement like:

> *HTTP Basic Authentication is the authentication mechanism supported by the HTTP protocol. This mechanism is based on a username and password. A web server requests a web client to authenticate the user. As part of the request, the web server passes the realm in which the user is to be authenticated. The web client obtains the username and the password from the user and transmits them to the web server. The web server then authenticates the user in the specified realm (referred to as HTTP realm in this document).*

The presence of security realms ensures that all of the software systems driving a business are using the same set of identities stored centrally. By using security realms and central identity storage we guarantee that identity management does not need to be scattered between several application and application server administrators.

GlassFish security realms

GlassFish provides a fair set of security realms out of the box by supporting all major identity storages like file-based storages, databases, LDAP servers, digital certificates, and so on. In addition to providing a wide set of supported realms, GlassFish left the door open for developing new security realms and plugging the realm to the set of application server's security realms.

Administrating security realms

GlassFish provides us with multiple administration channels, including **command-line interface (CLI)**, Web Administration Console (Web Console), and **Java Management Extensions (JMX)**. Through this book we will use CLI and Web Console to change the configuration of objects we need to administrate.

 CLI is available through `asadmin` utility, which is located at `glassfish_home/bin` directory. The Web Console is available at `http://{host}:{port}` in which "host" is where the application server administration console is listening and "port" is administration listener port number. Default values for host and port are `localhost` and `4848`. Default username and password for using CLI and Web Console are `admin` and `adminadmin`.

Before digging deep into different security realms in GlassFish application server, let's see how we can create a security realm using Web Console and CLI.

To create a new realm based on any of the available realm types we can use Web Console and navigate to **Tree | Configuration | Security | Realms**. The **Realms** page will open, then click on the **New** button to start our journey for creating a realm. We will discuss all of the following realms in the subsequent sections of the book.

- File realm
- JDBC realm
- LDAP realm
- Certificate realm

GlassFish CLI provides a set of commands to administrate security realms. These commands are briefly listed in the following table.

Command	Description
`create-auth-realm`	Creating a new realm based on one of the available realm types.
`delete-auth-realm`	Deleting a realm from list of the available realms.
`list-auth-realms`	Listing all security realms defined in the system.

We will discuss some of these commands later in this chapter.

Creating a file realm

A file realm is the most basic security realm available in GlassFish. This realm is useful for test and development cycles and not for a production environment where we have tons of users and groups. Any security realm defined using this type uses a flat file to store the users, passwords, and users' group assignments.

To create a file realm we can navigate to **Tree | Configuration | Security | Realms** and after the **Realms** page opens, click on the **New** button. Now we can select which realm type we want to use for our new realm. Each realm has some properties for which we should provide values to configure the realm. Some of these properties are mandatory while some others arc optional. The following table lists all properties we can specify for file realm. Optional properties are marked with "*" sign.

Attribute	Description
Name	This is the realm name which we will use in our web or enterprise applications.
Class Name	Specifies which type of realm we want to create.
JAAS Context	This is the JAAS Context for our realm which defines the login module. Each realm type has at least one JAAS Context.
Key File	Specifies location of the file where we want to store our users information. The file does not need to exist because GlassFish will create the file. It is important that GlassFish has write access in the specified location.
Assign Groups*	A list of comma-separated groups we want to assign to any authenticated user.

Let's see the values we want to provide for our security realm. The following figure shows values for all of the mandatory and optional properties:

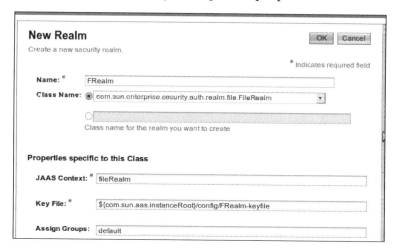

Two properties need some more description, which are as follows:

- The **JAAS Context** property should specify a name that points to a specific configuration element in `domain_dir/config/login.conf`. The element specifies which JAAS login module we can use for this realm. We will discuss JAAS in more details in last section of this chapter.

- The **Key File** uses a relative path for it. The relative path indicates that our key file is located at domain's configuration directory.

Now we can press the **OK** button to finish creating the new realm.

 In the figure you can see that I specified key file path relatively to the domain directory using the `${com.sun.aas.instanceRoot}`. The path can be anything like `C:/FRealm-keyfile` or `/home/user/FRealm-keyfile`.

File realm is native to GlassFish application server and usually we use it for development purposes, therefore GlassFish developers tried to ease the application development by providing us with a user provisioning interface for this realm.

To use the provisioning interface:

1. Navigate to **Tree | Configuration | Security | Realms | FRealm** and click on **Manage Users** button. It will open an interface to add new users.

2. Click on **New** and use the following information for each attribute.
   - User ID: jack
   - Group List: manager, hr_manager
   - Password: jack

Now press the **OK** button to store the information in the file we specified in previous section.

Let's examine how this information will be stored in the key file, whose location we specified when we were creating the new realm. The following listing shows content of `FRealm-keyfile` which contains user information for `FRealm`.

```
jack;{SSHA}r1Inju5avfgMCQ3DRl+vuWsfJevTuD+80xFcxQ==;
    managers,hr_managers
```

Looking at the file content we can understand that user attributes are separated using semicolons. While usernames in the first column and group names in the third one are stored in plain text, only a hashed representation of passwords are stored in the second column.

File realm stores passwords in hashed mode to prevent any unauthorized access to the list of passwords if the realm file is compromised.

Let's develop a simple web application to test our new realm. We will use this application throughout the chapter to study how different realms work.

 Complete source code and build scripts for this application is available at `https://www.packtpub.com//sites/default/files/downloads/9386_Code.zip`.

Application build and deployment system is based on Maven (`http://maven.apache.org`). You may need an active Internet connection in order for the build script to get its required libraries.

Our sample application has three JSP files located in three different directories. We define constraint over URLs opening these directories using URL patterns and allow specific roles to access these URL patterns. The following figure illustrates the web application file and folders layout:

The application is assembled using some JSP files and folders along with the `web.xml` file and the `sun-web.xml` file to declare the security constraints and role to group mappings. The following listings shows the `web.xml` file content.

The following part of the `web.xml` file shows how we can use the `security-constraint` element of the `web.xml` to limit access to any resource inside the `managers` folder to `top_level_manager_role`.

```xml
<security-constraint>
    <display-name>Managers Constraint</display-name>
    <web-resource-collection>
        <web-resource-name>Managers Content</web-resource-name>
        <description/>
        <url-pattern>/managers/*</url-pattern>
        <http method>GET</http-method>
    </web-resource-collection>
```

```
        <auth-constraint>
            <description/>
            <role-name>top_level_manager_role</role-name>
        </auth-constraint>
    </security-constraint>
```

The following portion demonstrates how we can permit multiple roles to access a set of resources. In this part of `web.xml` we are permitting `hr_management_role` and `top_level_manager_role` to access any resources inside the `hrmanagers` directory.

```
    <security-constraint>
    <display-name>HR Managers Constraint</display-name>
        <web-resource-collection>
            <web-resource-name>HR Management Section</web-resource-name>
            <description/>
            <url-pattern>/hrmanagers/*</url-pattern>
            <http-method>GET</http-method>
        </web-resource-collection>
        <auth-constraint>
            <description/>
            <role-name>hr_management_role </role-name>
            <role-name>top_level_manager_role</role-name>
        </auth-constraint>
    </security-constraint>
```

The following portion defines how we can specify the authentication mechanism, which is BASIC in this case, and the security realm which we want the application server to authenticate our users against. In this case we are using FRealm which we created previously.

```
    <login-config>
        <auth-method>BASIC</auth-method>
        <realm-name>FRealm</realm-name>
    </login-config>
```

Finally, we should define the roles that we used in the application and in the descriptor file.

```
    <security-role>
        <description/><role-name>hr_management_role </role-name>
    </security-role>
    <security-role>
        <description/>
        <role-name>top_level_manager_role</role-name>
    </security-role>
```

We discussed the necessity of a vendor-specific deployment descriptor for defining roles to group mappings for authorization purposes. This code shows how we can use the GlassFish-specific deployment descriptor `sun-web.xml` file to define the roles to principal and group mappings.

```
<sun-web-app error-url="/errors/error.jsp">
    <context-root>/SecurityRealms</context-root>
    <security-role-mapping>
        <role-name>top_level_manager_role</role-name>
        <group-name>manager</group-name>
        <group-name>hr_manager</group-name>
    </security-role-mapping>
    <security-role-mapping>
        <role-name>hr_management_role</role-name>
        <group-name>hr_manager</group-name>
    </security-role-mapping>
</sun-web-app>
```

We simply assigned different groups to roles we declared in the `web.xml` file. Reviewing the first chapter is recommended if you cannot understand these elements. After deploying the application any attempt to access a restricted resource fires Basic HTTP authentication, which shows a dialog similar to the following figure:

We just need to enter the username and password to pass the authentication barrier and continue working with the application.

Creating the JDBC realm

The JDBC realm is one of the most common realms in the production environment after the LDAP realm. Basically, the JDBC realm allows us to use a set of tables containing usernames, passwords, and user's group membership as an authentication source.

Assuming a simple database schema for defining users, passwords, and user's group membership, we should have two tables—one for users and another one for groups with a foreign key to assign multiple groups to a user. The following figure shows a simple schema for a database useable for the JDBC realm:

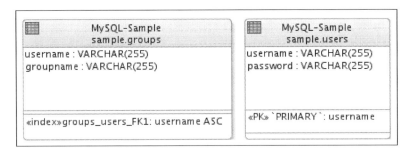

A sample SQL to create the required tables and populate them with some sample data is shown in the following code. I am using **MySQL** to create the database and related tables, which we need to configure a JDBC realm. You may use any other databases that you are more comfortable with.

```
Create database jdbc_realm_db;
Use jdbc_realm_db;
CREATE TABLE users
(username VARCHAR(255) NOT NULL
, password VARCHAR(255) NULL
, CONSTRAINT PRIMARY KEY(username));
CREATE TABLE groups
(username VARCHAR(255) NULL
, groupname VARCHAR(255) NULL );
CREATE INDEX groups_users_FK1 ON groups(username ASC);
insert into users values('jack','jack');
insert into groups values('jack',manager);
insert into groups values('jack','hr_manager');
```

We should now create the database and execute the script to load sample data before we continue to the next steps. The SQL script performs the following tasks:

- Creating the `users` and `groups` tables
- Inserting a user into the users table. The username and password are `jack/jack`
- Assigning `MANAGER` and `HR_MANAGER` groups to the previously inserted user

For MySQL, the procedure of creating the database and executing the script is as follows:

- Make sure that MySQL server is up and running. You can check the Services section in Windows or you can use the following command on a **Debian**-based Linux:

  ```
  sudo  /etc/init.d/mysql status
  ```

- If MySQL is not running, right-click on the service name and select **Start** in **Services** section of Windows or the following command in Linux:

  ```
  sudo  /etc/init.d/mysql start
  ```

 You can find the script file named `jdbc_realm.sql` in the `chapter02/scripts` directory of the source code bundle that is available at `https://www.packtpub.com//sites/default/files/downloads/9386_Code.zip`.

After starting the database, use the following to execute the script file:

```
mysql -uUSER_ -pPASSWORD_
mysql>source /path/to/jdbc_realm.sql
```

In the above command, you should replace the `USER_` and the `PASSWORD_` with your database administration user and password.

Now that we have the database created we can continue with creating the JDBC realm. Navigate to **Tree | Configuration | Security | Realms** and click on **New** button. Enter a **Name** like **DBRealm** and for **Class Name** select `com.sun.enterprise.security.auth.realm.jdbc.JDBCRealm`. Selecting the class name shows all optional and required properties for which we can specify values directly without involving the **Additional Properties** table.

Name: *	DBRealm
Class Name:	⦿ com.sun.enterprise.security.auth.realm.jdbc.JDBCRealm ▾
	○
	Class name for the realm you want to create

Properties specific to this Class

JAAS context: *	jdbcRealm
JNDI: *	jdbc/security
User Table: *	users
User Name Column: *	username
Password Column: *	password
Group Table: *	groups
Group Name Column: *	groupname
Assign Group:	default
Database User:	
	Allows you to specify the database user name in the realm instead of the JDBC connection pool
Database Password:	
	Allows you to specify the database password in the realm instead of the JDBC connection pool
Digest Algorithm:	
	Digest algorithm (default is MD5)
Encoding:	
	Encoding (allowed values are Hex and Base64)
Charset:	
	Character set for the digest algorithm

Additional Properties (0)

[Add Property] [Delete Properties]

Name	Value	Description
No items found.		

The following table shows a list of these properties along with their descriptions for the previous screenshot.

Attribute	Description
JAAS context	JAAS context for this realm, it's `jdbcRealm` or `jdbcDigestRealm`.
JNDI	JNDI address for JDBC data source connecting application server to users identity database.
User Table	Table containing users.
User Name Column	Username column in the table.
Password Column	Password column in the table.
Group Table	Group table name.
Group Name Column	Group name column.
Assign Group	A comma-separated list of group names which all authenticated users are assigned to.
Database User, Database Password	We can specify database username and password here instead of the connection pool.
Digest Algorithm	Usually we store a hashed copy of password to prevent password recovery. This property specifies the hash algorithm used to hash the password before storing it. We should use `jdbcDigestRealm` for **JAAS context** if we choose to go with a digest algorithm instead of none which specifies no digesting is required.
Encoding	We can either use Hex or Base64 if we want to use a digest algorithm. If digest algorithm is specified, the default is **Hex** unless we specify otherwise. Selecting the algorithm is just matter of choice and overall system requirement.
Charset	The character set for the digest algorithm.

The `JdbcDigestRealm` is not to be used unless the authentication method is `DIGEST`. In other words we should not configure the JAAS context of `jdbcDigestRealm` when we are using the `BASIC` authentication method. You can find more information at `http://blogs.sun.com/swchan/entry/jdbcrealm_in_glassfish`.

Looking at the set of mandatory properties, we know we need to create a JDBC connection pool and data source to allow the JDBC realm to retrieve information from database tables. Before we dig into creating the connection pool we should add the required JDBC driver to the GlassFish classpath. Copy the database driver library to the `domain_dir/lib` directory. I am using MySQL, so my driver library is `mysql-connector-java-5.0.4-bin.jar`. Now we can continue with creating the connection pool and the data source. To create a connection pool named `security_pool` we can use the following CLI command:

```
asadmin create-jdbc-connection-pool --datasourceclassname
com.mysql.jdbc.jdbc2.optional.MysqlConnectionPoolDataSource --restype
javax.sql.DataSource --property
User=root:Password=root:URL="jdbc:mysql://127.0.0.1/sample"
security_pool
```

If you are not into using CLI, you can use administration console to create the connection pool. Just navigate to **Resources | JDBC | Connection Pools** and press the **New** button and follow the onscreen tips to create the connection pool.

 To see our newly-created connection pool and further examine it we can use the web-based administration console and navigate to **Resources | JDBC | Connection Pools | security_pool**. We can use the **Ping** button to check whether the connection pool is operational or not.

The following command creates a data source named `jdbc/security` on top of our connection pool.

```
asadmin create-jdbc-resource --connectionpoolid security_pool    jdbc/
security
```

We can use the administration console to create the JDBC resource. To do so navigate to **Resources | JDBC | JDBC Resources** and press the **New** button.

Here we are ready to commence with the final step and create the JDBC realm for which we are prepared with prerequisites.

Now that we have all prerequisites we can go back to the JDBC realm creating page and specify required values for different properties. The previous screenshot shows values we specify for each property of JDBC realm. Properties which are not shown in the figure are required, having value in our case.

To test our application with the JDBC realm, we can simply change the authentication realm we created in `web.xml` when we test our application with the file realm. We should change the realm name from `FRealm` to `DBRealm` and redeploy the application. It is the beauty of using realm and container security. Just change the realm name in the production environment and we are done with setting up the authentication and authorization for our application.

We usually store passwords in a one-way hashed format in the database and when required we should hash the user-provided password using the same algorithm and compare it with the stored value in the database. Java supports several hashing algorithms, including MD2, MD5, SHA-1, SHA-256, SHA-384, and SHA-512. We should ensure that the algorithm we use for the **Digest Algorithm** property is the same as the algorithm used to hash the passwords prior to storing them in the database.

Selecting a digest algorithm is highly dependent on the required security assurance. For example, the MD5 algorithm produces a 128-bit digest while the SHA-1 produces a 160-bit digest. The pros associated with MD5 is its speed while the pros associated with the SHA-1 is the smaller possibility to reverse the generated digest because of its longer length.

 MD5 algorithm is considered broken as it is possible to create two documents which result in the same digest. So, it is basically better to use SHA-1, as it is widely used and almost supported by any platform.

Using the LDAP realm to secure web applications

Lightweight Directory Access Protocol (LDAP) was developed to allow the IT world easily access the directory servers in an effective and reliable way. Organizations store their users' identity information in a tree structure which represents the structure of the enterprise itself. We can store identification information like username, passwords, groups, organizations, organization unit, home address, and so on into the directory server and when required, retrieve it using LDAP API.

A well-known LDAP is **Microsoft Active Directory**, which contains information about any network object in addition to users, groups, and user group assignments. In this section we discuss how the LDAP realm works and how we can configure it to use **OpenDS** as an authentication source.

When we specify a LDAP realm in our web or enterprise application, the application server sends the username and password it received from users to the specified LDAP realm. Then the LDAP realm conducts a search in the directory server and after finding the given username it tries to bind to the LDAP server using the given password. After a successful bind operation, the authentication is done and the LDAP realm returns back to the application server with a list of group names for which our user has membership.

To fully understand the LDAP and LDAP realm we will install an LDAP server and use it as an identity storage which our LDAP realm will connect to.

Downloading and installing OpenDS 2.2

We will discuss OpenDS installation in detail in *Chapter 6*, but here we are going to look at the installation briefly to get the ball rolling for our test application. If you have any difficulties with OpenDS installation, you can take a look at *Chapter 6* under the *Installing and administrating OpenDS* section.

Download OpenDS version 2.2 from `https://www.opends.org/promoted-builds/2.2.0/OpenDS-2.2.0.zip` and install it according the following instructions.

1. Unzip the archive in an appropriate directory; we call this directory `opends_home`.
2. Execute the `setup` script. It is either a BAT or a Shell script.
3. Continue with the wizard like any application setup. Make sure you remember the password you specified for **Root User DN** in Server Settings step. I used `123456` as a password to ensure I won't forget it.
4. Accept default values for remaining steps and finish the installation process.

Now we have a LDAP server installed and we need to import some users and groups to test our LDAP realm in the next step. The following code shows content of `import.ldif` file available inside the sample source code provided for this book.

The `import.ldif` format is **LDAP Data Interchange Format (LDIF)** which is a standard plain text format used for LDAP information exchange. Content of an LDIF file describes changes which should be applied on the LDAP data tree.

We need to import the content of this file into our LDAP server to ensure that we can use our sample application to test our LDAP realm without any extra modification. The following snippet shows what an LDIF file content looks like. We discuss more about LDIF format in *Chapter 6* under the *Storing hierarchical information: Directory services* and *Importing and exporting data* sections.

```
dn: dc=example,dc=com
objectClass: domain
objectClass: top
dc:: Z2xhc3NmaXNoIA==
entryUUID: c016ceef-5811-3b23-886b-3fd366b062b5

dn: cn=jack,dc=example,dc=com
objectClass: person
objectClass: inetOrgPerson
objectClass: organizationalPerson
objectClass: top
givenName: Jack
uid: jack
cn: jack
sn: Thomas
userPassword: {SSHA}mzQ6QYMrR946gRALVj4swqxHNGhx7lVbSEzmhg==
entryUUID: ee765366-e23a-4ddf-9ca2-5cbb9c530d48
createTimestamp: 20100113232013Z
creatorsName: cn=Directory Manager,cn=Root DNs,cn=config
pwdChangedTime: 20100113232013.678Z

dn: cn=manager,dc=example,dc=com
objectClass: groupOfUniqueNames
objectClass: top
cn: manager
uniqueMember: cn=jack,dc=example,dc=com
entryUUID: c274266b-d352-4fbc-9286-8987a5f529a3
createTimestamp: 20100113232032Z
creatorsName: cn=Directory Manager,cn=Root DNs,cn=config

dn: cn=hr_manager,dc=example,dc=com
objectClass: groupOfUniqueNames
objectClass: top
cn: hr_manager
uniqueMember: cn=jack,dc=example,dc=com
entryUUID: f4b0f882-17b1-45ac-a7a2-02bc3c8f8f95
createTimestamp: 20100113232049Z
creatorsName: cn=Directory Manager,cn=Root DNs,cn=config
```

The content is human-readable except for the passwords which are stored as hashed values instead of plain text. To import the file into the installed LDAP server, navigate to `opends_home/bin` and execute following commands sequentially.

```
./start-ds
```

```
import-ldif --clearBackend --backendID userRoot --ldifFile
path/to/import.ldif
```

We simply start the server and import the content into LDAP server storage. Now we are ready to create the LDAP realm in the LDAP creation page.

 We can use plain text to specify the password in the LDIF file, but when we export the content of LDAP, the server will export the password in hashed value to protect the passwords. The above snippet is an exported file and therefore passwords are shown in hashed instead of plain text.

Creating the LDAP realm

To create the LDAP realm navigate to **Tree | Configuration | Security | Realms** and click on the **New** button to create a new realm. The following table shows a list of LDAP realm properties along with their description.

Property	Description
JAAS context	JAAS context for this realm, it's `ldapRealm`.
Directory	LDAP Server connection URL, for example: `ldap://127.0.0.1:1389`.
Base DN	Location in the tree where search for the provided identity should begin. We usually narrow the search to the smallest possible part of the LDAP hierarchy.
Assign Group	A comma-separated list of group names, where all authenticated users are assigned to these groups.

We can use additional properties which we should insert in **Additional Properties** table to further fine-tune and customize the LDAP realm. These properties are listed in the following table.

Property	Description
search-filter	Search filter used to find the user. The default value is uid=%s (%s expands to the subject name). We can use a custom search filter if the userid attribute is different than the default one.
group-base-dn	Base DN for the location of group data. If group data is stored under a separate Base DN we can use this property to further fine-tune the performance.
group-search-filter	Search filter to find group memberships for the user. Defaults to uniquemember=%d (%d expands to the user element DN). We can use a custom search filter if the uniquemember attribute is different than default one.
group-target	The LDAP attribute name that contains group name entries. The default is CN. We can use a custom name for the attribute containing group name entries when required.
search-bind-dn	We can specify a DN so LDAP realm uses it to perform the search-filter lookups. It is only required for directories that do not allow anonymous search.
search-bind-password	The LDAP password for the DN specified in search-bind-dn.

After we understand all properties of the GlassFish LDAP realm we can create a new LDAP realm. Navigate to the realm creating page and create a new realm using the values shown in the following figure:

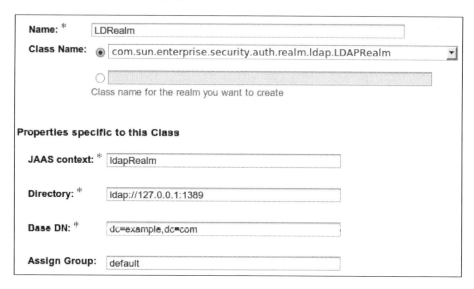

This realm uses the OpenDS server we installed and configured in the previous section. To test the LDAP realm we can use our sample application. The only required modification is changing the value of the `realm-name` element in `web.xml` from `FRealm` to `LDRealm`.

Configuring the GlassFish LDAP realm for Microsoft Active Directory

Microsoft Active Directory is a common LDAP server in the enterprise. The following screenshot shows how we can configure LDAP realm to use Microsoft Active Directory.

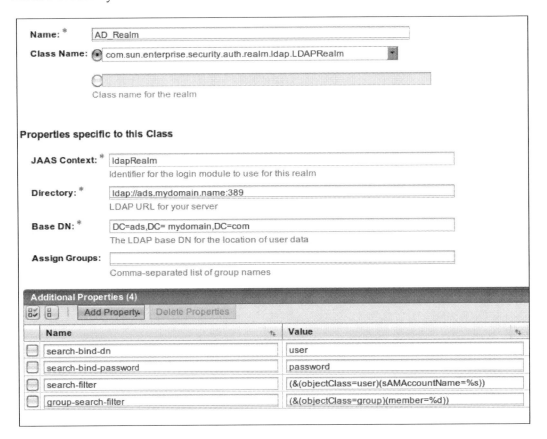

We should change the **Directory** and **Base DN** fields to address different Active Directory instances while other properties do not need to be modified to tailor the realm for different instances.

We also need to specify a runtime parameter for application server **JVM** for cases where we have multiple Active Directory servers in the enterprise completing the hierarchy together. In such cases one Active Directory can refer to another Active Directory for a searched object. Our policy should be following the referrals unless we are just interested for the results coming from our specified server.

```
-Djava.naming.referral=follow
```

We can add this parameter to GlassFish JVM by navigating to **Tree** | **Configuration** | **JVM Settings** and switching to the **JVM Options** tab.

Creating the certificate realm

We discussed three different types of security realms which were based on username and password for authentication. We configured our web application and GlassFish to use those realms to authenticate and check the authorization of users. In this section we are going to discuss a custom realm which works on a different type of credential for authenticating the users.

We use the certificate realm with the CLIENT-CERT authentication type. In this type, clients need to prove their identity using a digital certificate. You may have noticed that in many cases when you visit an e-commerce website the URL changes to **https** and a notification icon is shown in browser URL indicating that the server is identified using a digital certificate and assures you that you are communicating with the genuine site and not a phishing website. In such cases the server identifies itself using a digital certificate. In CLIENT-CERT authentication type not only must the server identify itself to the clients but also clients must provide a valid certificate in order for the communication to continue.

Before digging deep into the certificate realm we should have some basic understanding about what a digital certificate is and how it can be used to authenticate an entity.

Assume a digital certificate is like a passport which one can use to travel around. A passport contains several identification attributes such as name, age, picture, birth date, and signature. A passport is trusted to be valid because a passport-issuing office sealed it either electronically or using classic seals. Passports have expiration dates and they are considered invalid after the expiration date.

Digital certificates follow the same rules but instead of representing the owner in a physical way, they represent their owners digitally and let them be recognized and authenticated in the digital world. Passports are issued by passport offices that we trust. In the same way certificates are issued by certificate authorities like VeriSign, which we trust. When a certificate authority issues a certificate it digitally signs the certificate to validate the certificate.

Digital certificates can be used to identify individuals, web servers, governments, and so on. Digital certificates are hard to forge and more reliable than hand-written signatures.

The certificates are signed by certificate authorities and we should have a way to validate whether the signature belongs to a trusted certificate authority before we commence on validating the certificate itself. To understand how we can validate the certificate authority's signature we should review some related concepts like public key cryptography and certificates stores.

Public key cryptography

When we talk about **cryptography** and **encryption** the first thing that comes to our mind is a secret phrase which is used to encrypt data and decrypt it. This type of cryptography is called **symmetric cryptography** in which the encryption and decryption keys are the same.

In contrast with symmetric cryptography we have **asymmetric cryptography** in which the encryption and decryption keys are not the same. In asymmetric cryptography we have a set of two keys named **public key** and **private key**. We can use the public key to encrypt information and the private key to decrypt it. It is practically impossible to decrypt some information without having the private key corresponding to the public key used to encrypt the information.

We let everyone we want to communicate with have our public key so they can encrypt the data packet prior to sending it to us. When we receive the data we can decrypt it using our private key which is paired with our public key. Benefits of this method are as follows:

- The risk for the secret key to be discovered by a third party is minimal because we do not have a common secret key
- Encrypted data can only be decrypted with the private key of the same public key used to encrypt the information
- Communicating parties' identity can be verified
- Using public key methods, communicating parties cannot deny that they participated in the communication

 Explanation of how public key algorithms work is beyond the scope of this chapter as there is some complex mathematical computation in play to make asymmetric cryptography a reality.

So far we understood that there are a set of two keys which can be used to encrypt and decrypt information; now it is time to see how these keys are used by certificates authorities to issue and sign a digital certificate.

Digital signature

When we transmit a document encrypted using the receiver's public key we can sign that document to assure the receiver that the document is genuine and no one else tampered with it during transmission.

To sign the document we create a hash representing the document named **Message Digest**. Then we encrypt it using our private key and send the encrypted digest along with the document to receiver. Receiver decrypts the document using his private key, computes a hash for document, decrypts our digest, and compares his hash with our computed hash. If both values are the same the document is genuine and has not been tampered with during transmission.

The digital signature can be used to sign any type of digital content to let any qualified party verify the document origin.

Key stores and trust stores

Now we come to an important part of the story. How can we trust a signature or an entity which issued a digital certificate? The answer to this question relies on the fact that any software which uses a public key for security purposes has at least one database containing a public key for any entity it wants to verify their signatures. When we add a certificate to this storage we are telling the software that we trust any digital certificate signed by the owner of the imported certificate.

Another type of certificate store which public key-based software may have is a key store in which they store their own private key(s) and certificates they want to identify themselves using.

So we have this trust store that can store any CA's certificate to instruct our application to trust digital certificates signed by them. But are we able to store all certificate authorities' certificates in our trust store? The answer is no, we do not need to store any single certificate authorities' certificate. We can instead store the root certificate authorities' certificate and use certificate authorities chain to verify a new CA's certificate.

If a certificate is signed by a CA whose certificate is signed by a root CA we can verify the certificate as a valid certificate. This process is called **certificate chain**. The chain can have as many nodes as required.

A **root certificate** is a certificate signed by the issuer itself, such as VeriSign root certificate that is signed by VeriSign. We trust root certificates because they represent the companies we can trust. We trust any other party with a digital certificate signed by VeriSign or similar companies because we trust they will not cross the law by issuing invalid certificates.

Large corporations that use digital certificates as an identification token for their employees and software systems set up their own certificate authority and include their certificate in their servers and clients trust store files.

Now we have acquired enough basic knowledge about digital certificates to dig into GlassFish certificate and the certificate realm.

Managing certificates

We discussed the necessity of a trust store for applications that just need to verify other parties' messages and certificates, and of a key store for applications that need to present a certificate to the other party, in addition to validating the other parties' certificate and messages.

By default GlassFish v3 uses **Java keystore (jks)** format for trust and key stores. By default these files are placed inside the domain_dir/config directory. The file names are keystore.jks that contains GlassFish private key and certificate and cacerts.jks that contains all mainstream CA's certifications.

We can use other types of certificate stores such as PKCS11, PKCS12, and so on with GlassFish v3. For more information on using other types of certificate stores take a look at the following article:

http://weblogs.java.net/blog/kumarjayanti/
archive/2009/08/26/configuring-non-jks-keystore-
glassfish-v3.

Listing the content of keystore.jks and cacert.jks

Java Development Kit provides an efficient tool for working with keystore files. The utility name is keytool and is located inside the java_home/bin directory. To list keys stored in the keystore.jks file we can use following command; we need to be in the domain_dir/config directory to use the command.

```
keytool -list -v -keystore keystore.jks -storepass changeit
```

The output value for the command should be similar to the following screenshot, with some extra information about extensions and number of keys and so on.

```
Keystore type: JKS
Keystore provider: SUN

Your keystore contains 1 entry

Alias name: slas
Creation date: Oct 19, 2009
Entry type: PrivateKeyEntry
Certificate chain length: 1
Certificate[1]:
Owner: CN=HAL10000, OU=GlassFish, O=Sun Microsystems, L=Santa Clara, ST=California, C=US
Issuer: CN=HAL10000, OU=GlassFish, O=Sun Microsystems, L=Santa Clara, ST=California, C=US
Serial number: 4adb9dbb
Valid from: Mon Oct 19 02:29:07 IRST 2009 until: Thu Oct 17 02:29:07 IRST 2019
Certificate fingerprints:
         MD5:  90:5F:1E:F7:6A:4E:E2:76:1F:E1:0A:73:24:C1:61:E6
         SHA1: 52:0D:79:0B:05:FF:BC:73:B8:5C:54:6D:76:3B:0F:28:7B:97:57:02
         Signature algorithm name: SHA1withRSA
         Version: 3
```

The output tells us that there is one private key stored in the keystore under `slas` alias. The certificate chain length is `1` therefore this entry is self-signed and no certificate authority signed it.

This keystore works fine as long as we do not use SSL or mutual authentication in a production environment where visitors and users need to verify the server validity using the server's provided certificate. For a better understanding of the certificate verification concept, start GlassFish and visit `https://127.0.0.1:8181/` in your web browser. The browser will warn you about an invalid certificate and when you check the details you can see that the certificate is issued for "Your computer name" and not for `127.0.0.1`. To skip this warning, try visiting `https://compute_name:8181/`. This time you will get a warning which complains about a self-signed certificate, or a certificate signed by an unknown certificate authority. We can approve the certificate manually and continue using SSL for our development purposes but in a production environment users want assurance and certificates that their browser can validate automatically.

Now let's view the content of the `cacerts.jks` file to see how certificate authority's certificates are stored in the `cacerts.jks` file. We can execute the following command to view this list:

```
keytool -list -v -keystore cacerts.jks -storepass changeit
```

You should see a long list of certificates rolling in the terminal window. The entries are similar to the following figure and represent different certificate authorities.

```
*******************************************
*******************************************


Alias name: verisignclass2ca
Creation date: Oct 27, 2003
Entry type: trustedCertEntry

Owner: OU=Class 2 Public Primary Certification Authority, O="VeriSign, Inc.", C=US
Issuer: OU=Class 2 Public Primary Certification Authority, O="VeriSign, Inc.", C=US
Serial number: 2d1bfc4a178da391ebe7fff58b45be0b
Valid from: Mon Jan 29 03:30:00 IRST 1996 until: Wed Aug 02 04:29:59 IRDT 2028
Certificate fingerprints:
        MD5:  B3:9C:25:B1:C3:2E:32:53:80:15:30:9D:4D:02:77:3E
        SHA1: 67:82:AA:E0:ED:EE:E2:1A:58:39:D3:C0:CD:14:68:0A:4F:60:14:2A
        Signature algorithm name: MD2withRSA
        Version: 1


*******************************************
*******************************************
```

This snippet shows the VeriSign certificate. It is self-signed and is treated as a root CA certificate.

Now that we understand the contents of these files we should see how we can obtain and install a valid certificate signed by a certificate authority. In the next section we will obtain and install a test certificate from **Thawte Inc**.

Obtaining and installing a valid certificate

A server should have a valid certificate representing the server authenticity to the clients. To obtain and install the valid certificate for GlassFish we can use the following steps:

Generate a self-signed certificate using `keytool` and store it in a separate keystore:

```
keytool -genkey -alias glassfishcert -keyalg RSA -keysize 2048 -dname
"CN=HAL10000.md.com,OU=Learning,O=A Publishin,L=London,S=London,C=GB" -
keypass changeit-keystore glassfishKS.jks -storepass changeit
```

This command will generate a keystore along with a key stored under `glassfishcert` alias inside the keystore. The most important factors are:

- CN should be the exact name that browser will use to access our server. It also needs to be a fully-qualified name like a domain name. The most simple name can be `www.domain_name.com`.

- We are using the same password that GlassFish keystore uses, for sake of simplicity. Otherwise we should change GlassFish master password before we point GlassFish to use our new certificate store.

Now list the content of the keystore and see what we have inside it using the following command:

```
keytool -list -v -keystore glassfishKS.jks -storepass changeit
```

The next step is generating the **Certificate Signing Request (CSR)**. We will submit this CSR to our certificate authority to put their signature on it. A certificate signed by a known CA is trusted by major web browsers. We can use the following command to generate the CSR file:

```
keytool -certreq -v -alias glassfishcert -file glassfish-cert-csr.pem -
keypass changeit-storepass changeit-keystore glassfishKS.jks
```

The above command will generate a file named `glassfish-cert-csr.pem` which is text file containing encrypted information. Navigate to `https://www.thawte.com/cgi/server/try.exe` and select **SSL Web Server Certificate (All servers)** and paste the content of `glassfish-cert-csr.pem` into the input area provided on the Web page. The following figure shows the certificate signing request:

Now click **Next** which takes you to the page with the generated certificate. Copy the encrypted content and save it to a file named `glassfish-signed-cert.pem`.
To see content of the signed certificate we can use the following command:

```
keytool -printcert -v -file glassfish-signed-cert.pem
```

We have one more step to complete importing the certificate before we instruct GlassFish to use the new keystore containing the obtained certificate.

1. First we need to download the thawte test CA certificate from
    `https://www.thawte.com/roots/`.

2. The download archive contains several directories, open the `Thawte Test Root` directory and extract `Thawte Test CA Root.pem`.

3. We are going to import this file into our trust store to let GlassFish trust any client with the certificate signed by the Thawte test certificate. To do so use the following command:

    ```
    keytool -import -v -noprompt -trustcacerts -alias thawtetestcert -file "Thawte Test CA Root.pem" -keypass changeit-keystore cacerts.jks -storepass changeit
    ```

4. We need to import the CA certificate into our keystore in order to create a trust chain to let our certificate issued by the CA get imported into the keystore. To do so use the following command:

    ```
    keytool -import -v -noprompt -trustcacerts -alias thawtetestcert -file "Thawte Test CA Root.pem" -keypass changeit -keystore glassfishKS.jks -storepass changeit
    ```

5. Now that we have CA's certificate in the trust store, along with the private key we generated in the earlier steps, we should import the server certificate into the keystore to complete the certificate chain from our server certificate up to the CA certificate. The following command does the magic:

    ```
    keytool -import -v  -alias glassfishcert -file glassfish-signed-cert.pem -keypass changeit-keystore glassfishKS.jks -storepass changeit
    ```

6. After completing the previous command we can change GlassFish settings so it uses the new certificate. For configuring GlassFish to use our new keystore we can use Web Console and navigate to **Tree | Configuration | JVM Settings** and select **JVM Options.** We should look for an entry like `-Djavax.net.ssl.keyStore=${com.sun.aas.instanceRoot}/config/glassfishKS.jks` and change the path to our own keystore file.

Now we are done with server certificate installation. However we will need to configure listeners to use our new key alias instead of old s1as alias. To change each listener's alias for HTTP listeners we need to navigate to **Tree | Configuration | Network Config | Protocols** and change the **Certificate NickName** to our selected name, glassfishcert. The simplest way to change the nickname is by replacing s1as with the new alias name in the domain.xml file located inside the domain.dir/ config/ directory. Before starting the replace make sure that the domain is stopped.

Remember that if you changed the GlassFish master password you will need to manually change the key pass, as the related command cannot change our key password because its alias is different than s1as. To change the password we can use the following command:

```
keytool -keypasswd -alias glassfishcert -keystore
glassfishKS.jks -storepass <new master password>
```

To learn more about GlassFish support for digital certificates and different types of certificate stores refer, to GlassFish documentation.

- Using keytool: http://docs.sun.com/app/docs/doc/821-0185/ablqz?a=view
- Using **NSS**: http://docs.sun.com/app/docs/doc/821-0185/ablrf?a=view

To see how we can install GoDaddy certificate in GlassFish, take a look at my weblog at:

http://weblogs.java.net/blog/kalali/
archive/2010/02/27/how-install-godaddy-certificate-your-glassfish-v3

Now that all GlassFish-related configuration is finished we can go back and create a certificate realm and use it in our web application. To create the certificate realm navigate to **Tree | Configuration | Security | Realms** and create a new realm named gcertificate. Make sure to assign a default role like authorized to **Assign Group** attribute to ensure that any user who provides a valid certification is assigned to this group. For the digital certificate realm we do not have any out of the box authorization mechanism. Although we can tweak the sun-web.xml to get some level of authorization, that is not enough for a large-scale application.

We need to change the `login-config` element of the `web.xml` as follows to make it use `client-cert` authentication.

```
<login-config>
    <auth-method>CLIENT-CERT</auth-method>
    <realm-name>gcertificate</realm-name>
</login-config>
```

Now we have two choices for the authorization roles we defined in the `web.xml` file and we used them in previous section. First, we remove all authorization declaration and only define one role which we will map to the `authorized` group we defined when we created `gcertificate` realm. We can rely on the fact that anyone authenticated using the `CLIENT-CERT` method is authorized to access all resources.

The second way is to keep our old roles and define the corresponding groups by assigning individual principals to each group in the `sun-web.xml` file. Mapping groups to a set of individuals works if we know all of our clients' **distinguished names (DN)**. The DN includes `Common Name`, `Organization Unit`, and `Organization` attributes. For example, we can have a `web.xml` file with the following declaration to let specific accepted digital certificates fall under `manager` and `hr_manager` groups.

```
<security-role-mapping>
    <role-name> top_level_manager_role </role-name>
    <principal-name>CN=Jack Thomas, OU=Management,
      C=Coopers</principal-name>
    <principal-name>CN=Sin Lava, OU=Management, C=Coopers
      </principal-name>
</security-role-mapping>
<security-role-mapping>
    <role-name> hr_management_role </role-name>
    <principal-name>CN=Jack Thomas, OU=Management,
      C=Coopers</principal-name>
</security-role-mapping>
```

Starting with GlassFish 3.1, the GlassFish team is making enhancements to GlassFish authentication realms, whereby developers can write custom certificate realms to address issues like integration of username and password authentication, along with digital certificate authentication.

Creating the Solaris realm

GlassFish integration with Solaris is far beyond its integration with other operating systems when it comes to large-scale management and administration. In the same way, GlassFish has some out of the box features that provide us with required functionalities to configure GlassFish to authenticate users against Solaris users.

The Solaris realm is provided for us to allow our web applications to authenticate the users through this realm against the operating system users.

We can create a Solaris realm in the same way that we created other realms. The only difference is the value of **JAAS context** property, which in this case is `solarisRealm`. We can use Solaris Realm with Basic HTTP and Form-based authentications.

Developing custom realms

Developing custom realms comes handy when we need to authenticate our users against a custom security realm or a standard authentication mechanism not supported in GlassFish, like **OpenID**. Developing a new realm requires some basic JAAS experience, so we start this section with an introduction to JAAS.

Developing the custom realm

Under the hood, GlassFish security realms are developed on top of JAAS but we do not need to have experience with JAAS to develop a custom security realm due to the fact that GlassFish security realm development is further simplified by its additional layer of abstraction. There are three steps which we should follow for developing a custom realm:

1. Implementing a Java Authentication and Authorization Service (JAAS) `LoginModule`.
2. Implementing a realm class.
3. Installing and configuring the realm and `LoginModule` into the server.

Now let's get down to business and see what we should do about each step.

Implementing a JAAS LoginModule

To extend the number of GlassFish security realms we do not directly extend the JAAS `LoginModule`. Instead we should extend `com.sun.appserv.security.AppservPasswordLoginModule`. This class extends the JAAS `LoginModule` and adds GlassFish specific methods and properties.

The following code shows our `SimpleLoginModule`, which extends `AppservPasswordLoginModule` class.

```
public class CustomLoginModule extends AppservPasswordLoginModule {

    @Override
    protected void authenticateUser() throws LoginException {

        if (!authenticate(_username, _password)) {
            //Login fails
            throw new LoginException((new
                    StringBuilder()).append("Login Failed for:
                    ").append(_username).toString());
        }
        String[] groups = getGroupNames(_username);
        commitUserAuthentication(groups);
    }

    private boolean authenticate(String username, String password) {
    /*
     Check the credentials against the authentication source,
        return true if authenticated, return false otherwise
    */
        return true;
    }

    private String[] getGroupNames(String username){

    // Return the list of groups this user belongs to.
    }
}
```

The above code reveals a lot of information about GlassFish security realms, including that we only need to override one single method named `authenticateUser` and in this method we have access to the username and password provided by the user whom we want to authenticate. Two inherited `String` variables named `_username` and `_password` represent the information provided by us and we should authenticate the user based on them.

The `authenticateUser` method should perform the authentication and it should either throw a `LoginException` indicating that login has failed or should commit the list of groups the user belongs by invoking the `commitUserAuthentication` method and passing a `String` array containing a list of groups to it. Returning from this method without a `LoginException` means that authentication was successful.

The next step in developing a new security realm is implementing the realm class, which is as simple as implementing the `LoginModule` class.

Implementing a realm class

To implement the realm class we should extend the `com.sun.appserv.security.AppservRealm` class. Our implementation must provide a set of basic information about the realm. Although we can include more functionalities in this class we are not required to. The following code shows `CustomRealm` class extending `AppservRealm`.

```
public class CustomRealm extends AppservRealm {

    @Override
    public void init(Properties properties)
        throws BadRealmException, NoSuchRealmException {
        //initialize the realm
    }
     @Override
    public String getAuthType() {
        return "Custom Realm";
    }

}
```

The class simply requires implementing two methods. The `init` method is called during GlassFish startup to initialize the realm. If `init` does not throw any exception GlassFish assumes this realm is ready for later use, otherwise GlassFish disables the realm to prevent further security problems. We can access all properties that are provided during the realm creation using the `properties` parameter of the `init` method. The next required method is `getAuthType`, which should return a descriptive name about this security realm.

Installing and configuring

The first step in installing a custom realm is providing GlassFish with the realm implementation classes and all dependent libraries. We can copy all JAR files to the domain_dir/lib directory to let the application server add them to its classpath. Next is configuring application server to know which LoginModule it should use when we specify a custom security realm. To do so, open domain_dir/config/login.conf file and add the jaas-context and login module description to it. For our custom realm it is like:

```
gfCustomRealm{
        org.glassfish.book.CustomLoginModule required;
};
```

In previous sections we were specifying authentication context for our new realms. That authentication context is mapped to description provided in login.conf file to choose which LoginModule implementation should be used.

The next step is creating an authentication realm based on our new realm. We will not be able to use administration console for this step and thus we should either use CLI commands or should manually edit the domain.xml file. The following CLI command can create the new authentication realm based on our custom realm.

```
asadmin create-auth-realm --classname .org.glassfish.book.CustomRealm
--property  "jaas-context=gfCustomRealm:auth-type=simplecustomrealm"
gfcustom_realm
```

Now that we have created the realm we can configure our web application's authentication to use this realm for a basic authentication method.

> For more information about GlassFish v3 custom realm development you can take a look at the following articles:
> - http://blogs.sun.com/nithya/entry/modularized_osgi_custom_realms_in
> - http://blogs.sun.com/nithya/entry/groups_in_custom_realms

Adding a custom authentication method to GlassFish

In *Chapter 1* we discussed HTTP BASIC Authentication and Form-Based Authentication among other authentication methods supported by the GlassFish application server. We learned that they are quite capable of addressing authentication requirements of all normal enterprise applications. GlassFish supports **JSR 196** (Java Authentication Service Provider Interface for Containers), which let us plug any **Server Authentication Module (SAM)** implemented according to JSR 196 into the GlassFish Servlet container.

The JSR 196 specification makes it possible for the Servlet container to use the plugged SAM without requiring to change the application security declaration included in the web.xml file or added as annotations into the source code.

Basically JSR 196 allows us to plug a new message processing module into the Servlet container and let this module take care of the preprocessing of HTML messages. The SPI defined by the JSR 196 provides the third-party developers with some pluggable interaction points with Servlet container request processing. The integration with Servlet message processing is made possible by introducing some contracts, by using which module developers can intercept a requests, analyze them, and decide whether the request has a valid authentication token to go through or if it is not authenticated and cannot be further proceed.

The contract interface that SAM modules need to implement is named ServerAuthModule and it is located inside the javax.security.auth.message. module package. The interface has five methods that we should implement. These methods, along with their basic Javadoc, are listed in the following table.

Method	Description
validateRequest	Authenticate a received service request.
secureResponse	Secure a service response before sending it to the client.
cleanSubject	Remove method-specific principals and credentials from the subject.
getSupportedMessageTypes	Get one or more Class objects representing the message types supported by the module.
initialize	Initialize this module with request and response message policies to enforce, a CallbackHandler, and any module-specific configuration properties.

For more information about the JSR 196 support and how to develop and install a SAM, take a look at the article available at `http://blogs.sun.com/enterprisetechtips/entry/adding_authentication_mechanisms_to_the`.

To study a more complete sample of using JSR 196 to implement support of well-known authentication standards, take a look at the Spnego project, which uses JSR 196 to implement **SPNEGO** and **Kerberos** plugin for Glassfish. The Spnego project is located at `https://spnego.dev.java.net/`.

 SPNEGO is a standard for negotiating and selecting a shared **Generic Security Services Application Program Interface** (**GSSAPI**) mechanism and establishing a security context based on the selected mechanism. Kerberos allows peers communicating over an unsecure network to prove their identity to one another in a secure manner. The GSSAPI provides a generic API for performing client-server.

Summary

We covered in detail all of the GlassFish security realms including file realm, JDBC realm, LDAP realm, and certificate realms to see how easily we can integrate GlassFish with external sources to reuse identity storages already established in the enterprise. We covered all basics of how we can create and install new certificates for the GlassFish application server.

We reviewed how we can install and use OpenDS as identity storage and how we can import directory server entries into OpenDS backend and use them for authentication and authorization purposes.

So far we learned about the Java EE security model and its related annotations and configuration elements, in addition to mastering GlassFish security realms. In the next chapter, we will put all of the knowledge we gathered into practice to develop and deploy a secure Java EE application with web, EJB, and application client module.

3

Designing and Developing Secure Java EE Applications

In previous chapters we discussed how we can utilize Java EE capabilities to secure our Java EE applications. In this chapter, we are going to put what we learned into practice and develop a secure Java EE application with all standard modules including Web, EJB, and application client modules.

Security is an orthogonal concern for an application and we should assess it right from the start by reviewing the analysis we receive from business and functional analysts. Assessing the security requirements results in understanding the functionalities we need to include in our architecture to deliver a secure application covering the necessary requirements.

Security necessities can include a wide area of requirements, which may vary from a simple authentication to several sub-systems. A list of these sub-systems includes identity and access management system and transport security, which can include encrypting data as well.

In this chapter we will develop a secure Java EE application based on Java EE and GlassFish capabilities. In course of the chapter we will cover following topics:

- Analyzing Java EE application security requirements
- Including security requirements in Java EE application design
- Developing secure Business layer using EJBs
- Developing secure Presentation layer using JSP and Servlets
- Configuring deployment descriptors of Java EE applications
- Specifying security realm for enterprise applications
- Developing secure application client module
- Configuring Application Client Container

Understanding the sample application

The sample application that we are going to develop, converts different length measurement units into each other. Our application converts meter to centimeter, millimeter, and inch. The application also stores usage statistics for later use cases.

Guest users who prefer not to log in can only use meter to centimeter conversion, while any company employee can use meter to centimeter and meter to millimeter conversion, and finally any of company's managers can access meter to inch in addition to two other conversion functionalities. We should show a custom login page to comply with site-wide look and feel.

No encryption is required for communication between clients and our application but we need to make sure that no one can intercept and steal the username and passwords provided by members. All members' identification information is stored in the company's wide directory server.

The following diagram shows the high-level functionality of the sample application:

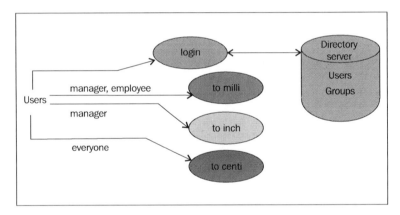

We have login action and three conversion actions. Users can access some of them after logging in and some of them can be accessed without logging in.

Analyzing sample application business logic

Before looking at security requirements and factors affecting the software security let's see what we need to provide in our business layer. Our business logic consists of conversion operations and persistence of the conversion operations usage statistics. We can use a stateless Session Bean with three methods, one for each type of conversion. And for statistics persistence we can use EJB 3 entity beans.

After studying the application description we can extract the following security-related requirements which we need to address to comply with the application description:

- Authentication is required
- Authentication should happen over a secure channel
- Authorization is required
- We need to use LDAP security realm

So far we translated the business analysis to technical requirements and now we are going to check each requirement in further detail to extract the implementation details. For implementing the sample application we can use a simple **bottom-up** procedure.

The following diagram shows the application blocks down to JSP files, Servlet, and EJBs.

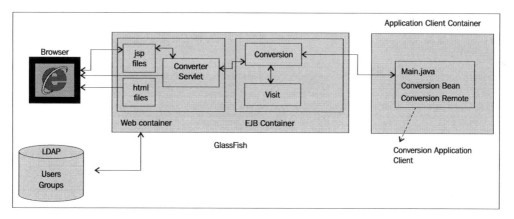

As you can see we have Web module, EJB module, and an application client module. The Web module and the application client module presents a frontend for the EJB layer that performs both business logic, which is the conversion operations, and storing the conversion operation invocation statistics using Entity Beans. GlassFish uses the LDAP realm to authenticate the users against the specified directory server.

Implementing the Business and Persistence layers

The Persistence layer consists of an Entity Bean named Visit; we use this entity bean to store information about each visit. We will use a session bean with three business methods to convert a given length in meter to centimeter, millimeter, and inch.

Implementing the Persistence layer

We are using EJB 3 to develop the Persistence layer so we will only need to implement the entity bean and define the persistence unit. The following listing shows the `Visit` class.

 Complete code for this class is available in the book's source code: https://www.packtpub.com//sites/default/files/ downloads/9386_Code.zip.

```
@Entity
public class Visit implements Serializable {

    private static final long serialVersionUID = 1L;
    @Id
    @GeneratedValue(strategy = GenerationType.AUTO)
    private Long id;
    @Temporal(javax.persistence.TemporalType.DATE)
    private Date visitDate;
    private String username;
    private String operationName;
    private int conversionValue;
        public Visit() {
    }

    public Visit(Date visitDate, String username, String Operation,
      int conversionValue) {
        this.visitDate = visitDate;
        this.username = username;
        this.operationName = Operation;
        this.conversionValue = conversionValue;
    }
}
```

Now that our entity bean is ready we can start looking at our session bean that drives the application business logic and also stores information about each invocation using the `Visit` entity bean. The following listing shows Conversion session bean local interface.

```
@Local
public interface ConversionLocal {
    float toInch(int meter);
    int toCentimeter(int meter);
    int toMillimeter(int meter);
}
```

All of these methods are implemented in Conversion bean implementation which is as follows:

```
@Stateless
public class ConversionBean implements ConversionLocal {
    @PersistenceContext(unitName = "chapter3")
    private EntityManager em;
    @Resource
    private SessionContext ctx;

    @RolesAllowed({"manager_role"})
    public float toInch(int meter) {
        persist(meter, "toInch");
        return Math.round(meter * 39.37);
    }

    @PermitAll
    public int toCentimeter(int meter) {
        persist(meter, "toCentimeter");
        return meter * 100;
    }

    @RolesAllowed("employee_role")
    public int toMillimeter(int meter) {
        persist(meter, "toInch");
        return meter * 1000;
    }

    private void persist(int value, String operationName) {
        String userName = ctx.getCallerPrincipal().getName();
        Visit v = new Visit(new Date(), userName, operationName,
            value);
        em.persist(v);
    }
}
```

Starting from the first line we are using @Stateless to mark this class as a stateless Session Bean. Later on we are using @PersistenceContext to inject an entity manager into the instance. We will use this entity manager to store Visit entities. Then we are using @Resource to inject the current SessionContext into the session bean. Later on we will use it to extract the current principal and username of the invoker. The first security-related annotation is @RolesAllowed({"manager"}), which instructs the application server to only permit an authenticated user with manager role to invoke this method. After this we have @PermitAll which instructs the application server to allow anyone, either authenticated or not, to invoke this method. And finally we are using @RolesAllowed("employee") to instruct the application server that any authenticated user with employee role can invoke this method.

The persist method stores the invocation information. This information includes the current invoker username, which we extract from SessionContext using the getCallerPrincipal().getName() method.

Finally we have a persistence unit that uses sample data source and sample database which is bundled with GlassFish. The listing shown below contains a snippet of persistence.xml file, which configures a persistence unit for chapter3.

```xml
<?xml version="1.0" encoding="UTF-8"?>
<persistence version="1.0"
  xmlns="http://java.sun.com/xml/ns/persistence"
  xmlns:xsi="http://www.w3.org/2001/XMLSchema-instance"
  xsi:schemaLocation="http://java.sun.com/xml/ns/persistence
  http://java.sun.com/xml/ns/persistence/persistence_1_0.xsd">
    <persistence-unit name="chapter3" transaction-type="JTA">
        <provider>oracle.toplink.essentials.PersistenceProvider
          </provider>
        <jta-data-source>jdbc/sample</jta-data-source>
        <class>book.glassfish.security.chapter3.Visit</class>
        <exclude-unlisted-classes>true</exclude-unlisted-classes>
        <properties>
            <property name="toplink.ddl-generation"
              value="drop-and-create-tables"/>
        </properties>
    </persistence-unit>
</persistence>
```

Now that we have our Persistence and Business layers ready we can start looking at the Web layer and how the Web layer can complement the inner layer in securing the system.

Developing the Presentation layer

The Presentation layer is the closest layer to end users when we are developing applications that are meant to be used by humans instead of other applications. In our application, the Presentation layer is a Java EE web application consisting of the elements listed in the following table. In the table you can see that different JSP files are categorized into different directories to make the security description easier.

Element Name	Element Description
Index.jsp	Application entry point. It has some links to functional JSP pages like toMilli.jsp and so on.
auth/login.html	This file presents a custom login page to a user when they try to access a restricted resource. This file is placed inside auth directory of the Web application.
auth/logout.jsp	Logs users out of the system after their work is finished.
auth/loginError.html	Unsuccessful login attempt redirect users to this page. This file is placed inside the auth directory of the Web application.
jsp/toInch.jsp	Converts given length to inch, it is only available for managers.
jsp/toMilli.jsp	Converts given length to millimeter, this page is available to any employee.
jsp/toCenti.jsp	Converts given length to centimeter, this functionality is available for everyone.
Converter Servlet	Receives the request and invokes the session bean to perform the conversion and returns back the value to the user.
auth/accessRestricted.html	An error page for error 401 which happens when authorization fails.
Deployment Descriptors	The deployment descriptors which we describe the security constraints over resources we want to protect.

Now that our application building blocks are identified we can start implementing them to complete the application. Before anything else let's implement JSP files that provides the conversion GUI. The directory layout and content of the Web module is shown in the following figure:

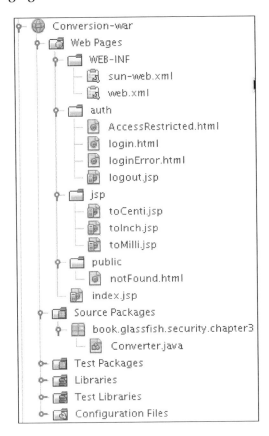

Implementing the Conversion GUI

In our application we have an `index.jsp` file that acts as a gateway to the entire system and is shown in the following listing:

```
<html>
    <head><title>Select A conversion</title></head>
    <body><h1>Select A conversion</h1>
        <a href="auth/login.html">Login</a>
        <br/>
        <a href="jsp/toCenti.jsp">Convert Meter to Centimeter</a>
        <br/>
        <a href="jsp/toInch.jsp">Convert Meter to Inch</a>
        <br/>
```

```
        <a href="jsp/toMilli.jsp">Convert to Millimeter</a><br/>
        <a href="auth/logout.jsp">Logout</a>
    </body>
</html>
```

Implementing the Converter servlet

The Converter servlet receives the conversion value and method from JSP files and calls the corresponding method of a session bean to perform the actual conversion. The following listing shows the Converter servlet content:

```
@WebServlet(name="Converter", urlPatterns={"/Converter"})
public class Converter extends HttpServlet {
    @EJB
    private ConversionLocal conversionBean;

    protected void processRequest(HttpServletRequest request,
      HttpServletResponse response)
            throws ServletException, IOException {
    }
    @Override
    protected void doPost(HttpServletRequest request,
      HttpServletResponse response)
          throws ServletException, IOException {
            System.out.println("POST");
            response.setContentType("text/html;charset=UTF-8");
            PrintWriter out = response.getWriter();
            try{
              int valueToconvert =
                Integer.parseInt(request.getParameter("meterValue"));
              String method = request.getParameter("method");
              out.print("<hr/> <center><h2>Conversion Result is: ");
              if (method.equalsIgnoreCase("toMilli")) {

                out.print(conversionBean.toMillimeter(valueToconvert));
                } else if (method.equalsIgnoreCase("toCenti")) {

                out.print(conversionBean.toCentimeter(valueToconvert));
              } else if (method.equalsIgnoreCase("toInch")) {
                  out.print(conversionBean.toInch(valueToconvert));
              }
              out.print("</h2></center>");

          }catch (AccessLocalException ale) {
              response.sendError(401);
          }finally {
              out.close();
          }
      }
}
```

Starting from the beginning we are using annotation to configure the servlet mapping and servlet name instead of using the deployment descriptor for it. Then we use dependency injection to inject an instance of Conversion session bean into the servlet and decide which one of its methods we should invoke based on the conversion type that the caller JSP sends as a parameter. Finally, we catch javax.ejb.AccessLocalException and send an **HTTP 401 error** back to inform the client that it does not have the required privileges to perform the requested action. The following figure shows what the result of invocation could look like:

Each servlet needs some description elements in the deployment descriptor or included as deployment descriptor elements.

Implementing the conversion JSP files is the last step in implementing the functional pieces. In the following listing you can see content of the toMilli.jsp file.

```html
<html>
    <head><title>Convert To Millimeter</title></head>
    <body><h1>Convert To Millimeter</h1>
        <form method=POST action="../Converter">Enter Value to
         Convert: <input name=meterValue>
            <input type="hidden" name="method" value="toMilli">
                <input type="submit" value="Submit" />
        </form>
    </body>
</html>
```

The toCenti.jsp and toInch.jsp files look the same except for the descriptive content and the value of the hidden parameter which will be toCenti and toInch respectively for toCenti.jsp and toInch.jsp.

Now we are finished with the functional parts of the Web layer; we just need to implement the required GUI for security measures.

Implementing the authentication frontend

For the authentication, we should use a custom login page to have a unified look and feel in the entire web frontend of our application. We can use a custom login page with the FORM authentication method. To implement the FORM authentication method we need to implement a login page and an error page to redirect the users to that page in case authentication fails. Implementing authentication requires us to go through the following steps:

- Implementing `login.html` and `loginError.html`
- Including security description in the `web.xml` and `sun-web.xml` or `sun-application.xml`

Implementing a login page

In FORM authentication we implement our own login form to collect username and password and we then pass them to the container for authentication. We should let the container know which field is username and which field is password by using standard names for these fields. The username field is `j_username` and the password field is `j_password`. To pass these fields to container for authentication we should use `j_security_check` as the form action. When we are posting to `j_security_check` the servlet container takes action and authenticates the included `j_username` and `j_password` against the configured realm. The listing below shows `login.html` content.

```
<form method="POST" action="j_security_check">
    Username: <input type="text" name="j_username"><br />
    Password: <input type="password" name="j_password"><br />
    <br />
    <input type="submit" value="Login">
    <input type="reset" value="Reset">
</form>
```

The following figure shows the login page which is shown when an unauthenticated user tries to access a restricted resource:

Implementing a logout page

A user may need to log out of our system after they're finished using it. So we need to implement a logout page. The following listing shows the `logout.jsp` file:

```
<%
session.invalidate();
%>
<body>
    <center>
    <h1>Logout</h1>
    You have successfully logged out.
    </center>
</body>
```

Implementing a login error page

And now we should implement `LoginError.html`, an authentication error page to inform user about its authentication failure.

```
<html>
    <body>
        <h2>A Login Error Occurred</h2>
        Please click <a href="login.html">here</a> for another try.
    </body>
</html>
```

Implementing an access restricted page

When an authenticated user with no required privileges tries to invoke a session bean method, the EJB container throws a `javax.ejb.AccessLocalException`. To show a meaningful error page to our users we should either map this exception to an error page or we should catch the exception, log the event for audition purposes, and then use the `sendError()` method of the `HttpServletResponse` object to send out an error code. We will map the HTTP error code to our custom web pages with meaningful descriptions using the `web.xml` deployment descriptor. You will see which configuration elements we will use to do the mapping. The following snippet shows `AccessRestricted.html` file:

```
<body>
    <center>  <p>You need to login to access the requested
        resource. To login go to <a href="auth/login.html">Login
        Page</a></p></center>
</body>
```

Configuring deployment descriptors

So far we have implemented required files for the FORM-based authentication and we only need to include required descriptions in the `web.xml` file. Looking back at the application requirement definitions, we see that anyone can use meter to centimeter conversion functionality and any other functionality that requires the user to login. We use three different HTML pages for different types of conversion. We do not need any constraint on `toCentimeter.html` therefore we do not need to include any definition for it. Per application description, any employee can access the `toMilli.jsp` page. Defining security constraint for this page is shown in the following listing:

```
<security-constraint>
    <display-name>You should be an employee</display-name>
    <web-resource-collection>
        <web-resource-name>all</web-resource-name>
        <description/>
        <url-pattern>/jsp/toMillimeter.html</url-pattern>
        <http-method>GET</http-method>
        <http-method>POST</http-method>
        <http-method>DELETE</http-method>
    </web-resource-collection>
    <auth-constraint>
        <description/>
        <role-name>employee_role</role-name>
    </auth-constraint>
</security-constraint>
```

We should put enough constraints on the `toInch.jsp` page so that only managers can access the page. The listing included below shows the security constraint definition for this page.

```
<security-constraint>
    <display-name>You should be a manager</display-name>
    <web-resource-collection>
        <web-resource-name>Inch</web-resource-name>
        <description/>
        <url-pattern>/jsp/toInch.html</url-pattern>
        <http-method>GET</http-method>
        <http-method>POST</http-method>
    </web-resource-collection>
    <auth-constraint>
        <description/>
        <role-name>manager_role</role-name>
    </auth-constraint>
</security-constraint>
```

Finally we need to define any role we used in the deployment descriptor. The following snippet shows how we define these roles in the web.xml page.

```
<security-role>
    <description/>
    <role-name>manager_role</role-name>
</security-role>
<security-role>
    <description/>
    <role-name>employee_role</role-name>
</security-role>
```

Looking back at the application requirements, we need to define data constraint and ensure that username and passwords provided by our users are safe during transmission. The following listing shows how we can define the data constraint on the login.html page.

```
<security-constraint>
    <display-name>Login page Protection</display-name>
    <web-resource-collection>
        <web-resource-name>Authentication</web-resource-name>
        <description/>
        <url-pattern>/auth/login.html</url-pattern>
        <http-method>GET</http-method>
        <http-method>POST</http-method>
    </web-resource-collection>
    <user-data-constraint>
        <description/>
        <transport-guarantee>CONFIDENTIAL</transport-guarantee>
    </user-data-constraint>
</security-constraint>
```

One more step and our web.xml file will be complete. In this step we define an error page for HTML 401 error code. This error code means that application server is unable to perform the requested action due to negative authorization result. The following snippet shows the required elements to define this error page.

```
<error-page>
    <error-code>401</error-code>
    <location>AccessRestricted.html</location>
</error-page>
```

Now that we are finished with declaring the security we can create the conversion pages and after creating these pages we can start with Business layer and its security requirements.

Specifying the security realm

Up to this point we have defined all the constraints that our application requires but we still need to follow one more step to complete the application's security configuration. The last step is specifying the security realm and authentication. We should specify the FORM authentication and per-application description; authentication must happen against the company-wide LDAP server.

Here we are going to use the LDAP security realm LDAPRealm which we created in *Chapter 2*. We need to import a new LDIF file into our LDAP server, which contains groups and users definition required for this chapter. To import the file we can use the following command, assuming that you downloaded the source code bundle from https://www.packtpub.com//sites/default/files/downloads/9386_Code.zip and you have it extracted.

```
import-ldif --ldifFile path/to/chapter03/users.ldif

 --backendID userRoot --clearBackend --hostname 127.0.0.1 --port 4444 --
bindDN cn=gf\ cn=admin --bindPassword admin --trustAll --noPropertiesFile
```

The following table show users and groups that are defined inside the users.ldif file.

Username and password	Group membership
james/james	manager, employee
meera/meera	employee

We used OpenDS for the realm data storage and it had two users, one in the employee group and the other one in the manager group. To configure the authentication realm we need to include the following snippet in the web.xml file.

```
<login-config>
    <auth-method>FORM</auth-method>
    <realm-name>LDAPRealm</realm-name>
    <form-login-config>
        <form-login-page>/auth/login.html</form-login-page>
        <form-error-page>/auth/loginError.html</form-error-page>
    </form-login-config>
</login-config>
```

If we look at our Web and EJB modules as separate modules we must specify the role mappings for each module separately using the GlassFish deployment descriptors, which are `sun-web.xml` and `sun-ejb.xml`. But we are going to bundle our modules as an **Enterprise Application Archive (EAR)** file so we can use the GlassFish deployment descriptor for enterprise applications to define the role mapping in one place and let all modules use that definitions. The following listing shows roles and groups mapping in the `sun-application.xml` file.

```
<sun-application>
    <security-role-mapping>
        <role-name>manager_role</role-name>
        <group-name>manager</group-name>
    </security-role-mapping>
    <security-role-mapping>
        <role-name>employee_role</role-name>
        <group-name>employee</group-name>
    </security-role-mapping>
    <realm>LDAPRealm</realm>
</sun-application>
```

The `security-role-mapping` element we used in `sun-application.xml` has the same schema as the `security-role-mapping` element of the `sun-web.xml` and `sun-ejb-jar.xml` files.

You should have noticed that we have a `realm` element in addition to role mapping elements. We can use the `realm` element of the `sun-application.xml` to specify the default authentication realm for the entire application instead of specifying it for each module separately.

Deploying the application client module in the Application Client Container

The application client module can be a first layer Java SE application which directly communicates with the EJB container and uses services like transaction and security management of EJB container through the **Application Client Container**.

When it comes to software structure an application client is not different from a simple Java SE application. It has a `main` method, which is the software entry point and we can access different Java EE services simply with annotation or using deployment descriptors.

The following listing shows the `main` method for our application client, which invokes the `Conversion` Session Bean and prints the result.

```
public class Main {

    @EJB
    private static ConversionRemote conversionBean;
    public static void main(String[] args) {
        System.out.println(conversionBean.toInch(10));
    }
}
```

You may ask how this application can use injection and access an EJB instance. The secret is, as we saw in *Chapter 1*, hiding in another type of container called the Application Client Container. We deploy an application client module in the ACC and later execute it in the machine either as Java Web Start application or simply using GlassFish-provided scripts. When we run this application the following procedure takes place:

1. Application client (launched using Web Start or directly) results in the ACC trying to inject the secured EJB.

2. The EJB method requires authentication, so GlassFish calls the default `CallbackHandler` to get user login.

3. The default `CallbackHandler`, which is a simple username and password collecting dialog, appears on the client's screen.

4. The collected username and password are sent back to application server for authentication and authorization.

5. After a successful authentication, the method invocation goes through.

This procedure happens even if we do not add any single line of configuration to our EJB module deployment descriptor or Application Client deployment descriptor. The following figure shows more detail about the interaction between different modules when a secure EJB is called from an application client.

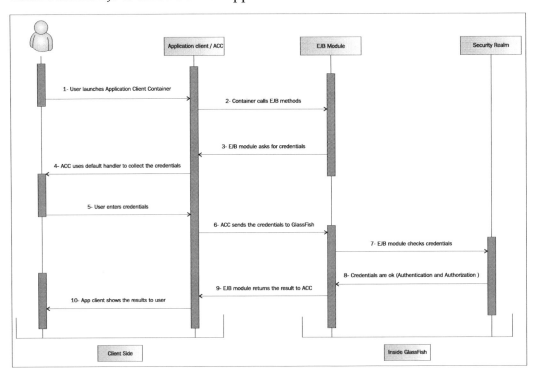

The default configuration for application client authentication is summarized in the following table:

Security Measure	Description
Security Realm	If no realm specified in sun-application.xml EJB container will use GlassFish default security realm. Default realm is file realm if not configured otherwise.
Authentication CallbackHandler	Default CallbackHandler is a simple swing dialog, which collects username and password.
Transport security	No encryption is applied on data transportation.

All of these measures are configurable either through the Application Client deployment descriptor or the EJB deployment descriptor or the ACC deployment descriptor. The following table shows which attributes are configurable through each one of these deployment descriptors.

Attribute	Deployment descriptor
Authentication mechanism	`sun-ejb-jar.xml`
Security Realm	`sun-acc.xml` and `sun-ejb-jar.xml`
SSL and transport security	`sun-acc.xml` and `sun-ejb-jar.xml`
`CallbackHandler` to collect username and password	`application-client.xml`

Two of the deployment descriptors included in the above table are specific to each vendor and may differ between different application servers. The only standard descriptor is `application-client.xml`, which is a part of the application client standard. This descriptor is placed inside the `META-INF` directory of the client application and contains information like which resources our application is using, how the application is accessing these resources, and finally definitions of the callback handler we want to use to collect user credentials.

The following figure shows default the `CallbackHandler`, which is fired to collect username and password before the container lets the application invoke a method with security constraint.

We can change the default `CallbackHandler` in `application-client.xml` by specifying a new `Callbackhandler`. The new callback should implement the `javax.security.auth.callback.CallbackHandler`. The following snippet shows the `callback-handler` element in `application-client.xml`.

```
<callback-handler>
  book.glassfish.security.chapter3.SwingCallbackHandler
</callback-handler>
```

We can use a programmatic way to provide the ACC with username and password instead of using the callback mechanism to have more control over the authentication procedures. To conduct programmatic login we can use `com.sun.appserv.security.ProgrammaticLogin` class to login before we access any EJB method which has security constraints, defining security measures for communication over IIOP.

We can use the GlassFish-specific deployment descriptor for EJB modules to define several types of configuration elements. We can use one set of these elements to define security measures for communication between the EJB container and the clients over **IIOP** (**Internet Inter-Orb Protocol**).

The super element for the IOR security is `ior-security-config`, which includes the following sub elements:

- The `transport-config` for specifying transport security
- The `sas-context` for specifying the caller propagation options
- The `as-context` for specifying the authentication method, the security realm we want to use for authentication.

Following snippet shows what we should include in the EJB deployment descriptor to get SSL transport security along with username and password-based authentication using the `LDAPRealm` we defined in *Chapter 2*.

```
<ior-security-config>
    <transport-config>
        <integrity>required</integrity>
        <confidentiality>required</confidentiality>
        <establish-trust-in-target>Required
          </establish-trust-in-target>
        <establish-trust-in-client>none</establish-trust-in-client>
    </transport-config>
    <as-context>
        <auth-method>username_password</auth-method>
        <realm>LDAPRealm</realm>
        <required>true</required>
    </as-context>
    <sas-context>
        <caller-propagation>supported</caller-propagation>
    </sas-context>
</ior-security-config>
```

Starting from the top, this snippet instructs the EJB container's IIOP listener to use SSL for data transmission to ensure the integrity and confidentiality of data which is transferred between client and server. Other possible values for `integrity` and `confidentiality` elements are `Supported` and `None`, which means server supports SSL if requested by clients or it does not provide them even if the client asks for data integrity and confidentiality.

We can have SSL mutual authentication by changing the value of `establish-trust-in-target` and `establish-trust-in-client` to required. This way the client will authenticate itself to the server using its digital certificate and in the same way the server will authenticate itself to the client using the digital certificate we specified for IIOP listeners.

When using mutual authentication, we should ensure that the trust store of the client trusts the certificate of the server and the trust store of the server trusts the certificate of the client. To achieve this we should:

1. Add the digital certificate of the client's certificate issuer to the server trust store.
2. Include the digital certificate of the server's certificate issuer to the client's trust store.

Later in the code snippet we have the `as-context` element that we can use to specify which authentication method and security realm we want to use for authenticating clients that need to invoke a secure method of an EJB. The only supported authentication method is `USERNAME_PASSWORD`.

The last element is `sas-context`. We can use it to specify whether EJB container accepts propagated caller identities or not. Possible values are `Supported`, `Required`, and `None`.

Configuring Application Client Container security

The Application Client Container hosts a Java SE layer application that interacts with the EJB container of the application server using IIOP. Each instance of the container can only host one instance of the client application and can be configured for that client application instance.

When we want to run a client application deployed in GlassFish we can either use Java Web Start or the script file provided in the GlassFish `bin` directory. Command format for using the script file is as follow:

`./appclient -client /opt/dev/Conversion-app-client.jar -xml /opt/dev/sun-acc.xml`

It means that we want to launch the `Conversion-app-client.jar` using a configuration file named `sun-acc.xml`.

The `sun-acc.xml` structure follows the schema defined in the `http://www.sun.com/software/appserver/dtds/sun-application-client-container_1_2.dtd` and allows us to configure every aspect of the ACC. The following shows the content of `sun-acc.xml`, which has both authentication and transport security configured.

```
<client-container>
    <target-server name="localhost" address="127.0.0.1" port="3700">
        <security>
            <ssl cert-nickname="s1as"
              ssl2-enabled="false"
              ssl2-ciphers="-rc4,-rc4export,-rc2,-rc2export,-des,
              -desede3"
              ssl3-enabled="true"
              ssl3-tls-ciphers="+rsa_rc4_128_md5,
              -rsa_rc4_40_md5,+rsa3_des_sha,+rsa_des_sha,
              -rsa_rc2_40 _md5,-rsa_null_md5,-rsa_des_56_sha,
              -rsa_rc4_56_sha"
              tls-enabled="true"
              tls-rollback-enabled="true"/>
            <cert-db path="ignored" password="ignored"/>
            <!-- not used -->
        </security>
        <auth-realm name="LDAPRealm"
    classname="com.sun.enterprise.security.auth.realm.ldap.LDAPRealm">
            <property name="directory"
              value="ldap://127.0.0.1:1389"/>
            <property name="base-dn" value=" dc=example,dc=com "/>
            <property name="search-bind-password" value="123456"/>
            <property name="jaas-context" value="ldapRealm"/>
        </auth-realm>
    </target-server>
    <client-credential user-name="james" password="james"/>
</client-container>
```

Starting from the top, we are instructing the container to use a certificate identified by `client` nickname. Later on we will see how we can specify which keystore and trust store we want our client container to use when we launch our application.

All other properties of the `ssl` element specify which SSL version and cipher suites are available to the ACC to choose from. During the negotiation between server and client to establish an SSL session, the strongest cipher suite supported by both server and client is selected.

In addition to configuring the transport security we can configure the authentication mechanism for ACC in order to let ACC collect the identification information and send them back to server when required. Following the security element we have the `auth-realm` element which specifies the authentication realm that ACC must use to conduct the authentication.

You should know all of these properties as we discussed them in great detail in *Chapter 2*. The only thing that you should remember is the fact that this configuration has nothing to do with the LDAP realm we configured in the server. This configuration affects only the client container instance running in the client machine and using this particular `sun-acc.xml` file.

The Application Client Container process exists in the clients machine and anything we configure using the `sun-acc.xml` affects the client machines and has nothing to do with the server or other clients, which run another instance of the application client.

Next we have the `client-credential` element which we can use to specify the default client credential that ACC sends to server instead of collecting the username and password. This element ensures that a single principal is used for all invocation without end users knowing about it.

Using SSL always bring out the issue of keystore and trust store which the application requires using during the SSL handshake and SSL session. There is no vendor-specific way to pass the trust and key store information to Java runtime and rather we can use the JVM environment variables to set these values.

When JVM starts and needs to use SSL, it looks for some environment variables to initiate the SSL session. These variables are included in the following table.

Variable	Description
`javax.net.ssl.keyStore`	Path to keystore containing the client certificate.
`javax.net.ssl.trustStore`	Path to trust store containing certificate issuer's certificates.
`javax.net.ssl.keyStorePassword`	The keystore password.
`javax.net.ssl.trustStorePassword`	The trust store password.

In Linux, we can use the following command to export these variables before launching the application client using the `appclient` script.

```
export VMARGS="-Djavax.net.ssl.keyStore=key-store-path -Djavax.net.ssl.
trustStore= trust-store-path -Djavax.net.ssl.keyStorePassword=key-store-
password -Djavax.net.ssl.trustStorePassword=trust-store-password"
```

For Microsoft Windows we can use the `set` command to set VMARGS value as follows:

```
set VMARGS="-Djavax.net.ssl.keyStore=key-store-path -Djavax.net.ssl.
trustStore=trust-store-path -Djavax.net.ssl.keyStorePassword=key-store-
password -Djavax.net.ssl.trustStorePassword=trust-store-password"
```

To create a working pair of certification stores we can follow the same steps we followed to create keystore and trust store for GlassFish application server. Using the same certificate issuer will guarantee that GlassFish will accept the certificate provided by the client and the client will accept the certificate provided by GlassFish.

Now that we have set the required runtime arguments for JVM we can run the client application and be assured about data confidentiality and integrity. The sample application for this chapter is included in the source code archive of the book.

Summary

In this chapter we studied Java EE security in action and developed a secure Java EE application with all of standard modules including EJB, Web, and application clients.

We studied how we can secure EJBs using annotation and then use a web frontend to use the secure EJBs after the user provides correct identification information. We developed a client application to access the secure EJB and later on we studied how we can use SSL and mutual authentication between the application client module and EJB container.

In the next two chapters we will look at GlassFish security independent of the Java EE security and what measures we should consider to have a safe GlassFish installation.

4
Securing GlassFish Environment

Any interaction between us and the environment in which we live can affect both sides of the interaction in a reversible or irreversible way. Software systems are just like us and are in constant interaction with the environment that host them and provides them with basic requirements, such as I/O resource and resource management.

Just like we are protected from environmental conditions like extreme heat in summers and extreme cold in winters or similar to the way we put precaution in place for earthquake and floods, we should implement precautions to protect the software system from disasters happening to the OS that could affect them.

In the same way that we are trying to protect the environment from pollution and unnecessary consumption we should protect the operating system of a software system from unnecessary access and consumption by the software itself.

In this chapter we are going to discuss how we can secure our operating system and environment from unprivileged access by an application deployed in GlassFish. For example, an application may delete a file or open a records file, which it is not permitted to do.

We will also look at protecting the GlassFish application server and its deployed applications from unprivileged access by operating system users and other software which are running in the same operating system.

We will look at following topics in this chapter:

- Operating system-level resource control
- Preparing the operating system for GlassFish installation
- Restricting GlassFish user's access to resources like network interfaces and file system
- Installing and securing GlassFish
- Using policy manager to restrict GlassFish access to OS resources at JVM level
- Enabling and using auditing to audit the security-related activities
- Developing custom auditing module

Securing a host operating system

Installing and using any server-side system introduces some concerns about the security of the server-side application itself and the effects that the installed server can have on the hosting operating systems. When we decide to install GlassFish on a server, we should be prepared to address several security aspects of the installation.

Defining security at the OS level

The operating system either in a virtualized or a non-virtualized model is where we are installing the application server, which can be running alone or in conjunction with some other software.

The operating system provides application server with the resources it requires to serve the clients requests in a proper way. The resource can include filesystem, network access, CPU cycles, memory, and so on. The operating system that hosts the application server may host multiple other systems like batch processors, legacy integrators, databases, and so on. We may need to prevent the application server from accessing all data available in the host operating system or we may need to ensure that the application server can only access particular network interfaces and not all of them. The following figure further illustrates the concept of shared resources. All operating systems can contain applications or users using only a specific set of resources, which we will demonstrate throughout this chapter.

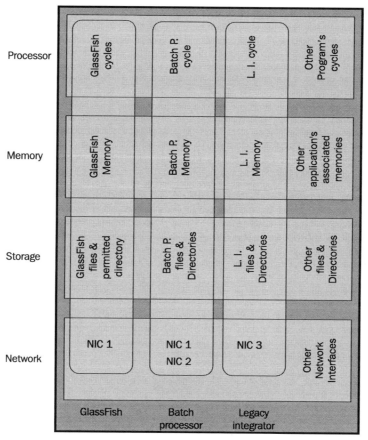

Operating System

NIC: Network Interface Card

 OpenSolaris is an open source distribution of the Oracle Solaris operating system with advanced features like resource control and management, and integrated virtualization which can be used to contain process or users to a specific amount of CPU cycles. specified amount of memory, or network traffic.

There are two different ways to accomplish securing the operating system from unwanted access by GlassFish as follows:

- Using the operating system level access control
- Using Java SE policy enforcement

In real-life scenarios, we use both of these techniques together to double the measure and keep our sweet sleeping time for ourselves, instead of digging into logs to see what has happened that lead to leakage of some EXCEL files containing financial information or customer records which were waiting to be imported into the database at midnight.

First let's look at how operating systems help us restrict the GlassFish application server from accessing anything that is not required for it. The following table shows operating system features and how we can use them to secure the operating system from GlassFish.

Feature	Functionality
Defining new user	We can define a new user and limit the user access levels to other resources and then run GlassFish under this user.
File system access control	We only allow a GlassFish user to have access to a set of required files and not the entire filesystem.
File system quota implementation	It is a good idea to specify disk space quota for a GlassFish user. But it is not a hard requirement.
Network interfaces access control	We should specify which network interfaces GlassFish users have access to, prevent unwanted access to other interfaces.

Now that we know which functionality is the answer for which one of our requirements we can start looking at how we can use these functionalities. All commands and steps provided in this section assume that the host operating system is **Ubuntu** or any **Debian**-based distribution of Linux operating system.

 The kernel version can be anything starting from 2.x. We can detect the kernel version using a simple command like:
`uname -r`

Here is our task list for installing GlassFish in a secure way:

1. Create a directory like /opt/app-server; it is where we will install GlassFish.
2. Create a user like glassfish and give full permission over /opt/app-server.
3. Login as glassfish user to commence with the installation.
4. Install GlassFish in/opt/app-server and revoke all access permissions to this directory from groups who we do not want to allow to access the resource.

5. Prevent `glassfish` user from accessing network interfaces it does not require to access.

6. Define a quota for `glassfish` user to double the safety.

Now, let's get our hands dirty with some shell commands to realize each item of the tasks list.

Creating the installation directory

To create the installation directory we can simply invoke a command like the following in the shell. I am using Ubuntu so I use `sudo` to get root privileges. You may need to log in as `root` in some other distributions instead of using `sudo`.

```
sudo mkdir /opt/app-server
```

If you are using a non-Debian-based distribution then you can use `su` command to fake the `root` permission and continue with rest of this chapter's commands without prefixing any command with `sudo`. The following command will give your terminal `root` permission:

```
su root
```

When it asks for the password, enter your `root` password to continue working in the terminal as `root` user. Make sure you use `logout` command when you want to use the terminal with your current user.

Now we can go to the next step and create the `glassfish` user and commence with the installation.

Creating the GlassFish user

To create the user we can use `useradd` command as follows:

```
sudo useradd glassfish -p glasspass --system --shell /bin/bash
```

We have just created a user named `glassfish` with `glasspass` as its password. The user is a system user and uses `bash` as its default shell.

Now it's time to get full privileges over `/opt/app-server` to this newly-created user. We can do it using the `chmod` and `chown` commands as follow:

```
sudo chown -R glassfish /opt/app-server
sudo chmod -R 700 /opt/app-server
```

Logging in as a GlassFish user

Now it's time to install GlassFish, so login as `glassfish` user and install GlassFish into `/opt/app-server/glassfish-v3`. We can do it using the following command:

```
sudo su glassfish
./path-to-glassfish-installer.sh
```

After executing the first command we are logged in as `glassfish` user and can install GlassFish application server either in the headless mode or using the GUI installer.

Restricting access to the filesystem

In this step we are preventing `glassfish` user from accessing any other directories which it is not supposed to access. For example if we need to prevent it from accessing a directory named `/opt/docs` we can use the following command:

```
sudo chmod -R glassfish -rwx /opt/doc/
```

Restricting access to network interfaces

Now it is time to continue with restricting `glassfish` user from accessing the network interfaces that it should not have access to. Basically we can use any firewall operating in layer 2 and layer 3 of TCP/IP stack to prevent different applications from accessing network interfaces or using different ports. In Linux distributions, we have a firewall named **iptables**. We can configure iptables by adding or removing its rules using the `iptables` command. The following snippet shows two command lines which we can use to add new rules to iptables.

```
sudo iptables -A INPUT -i eth2 -m glassfish --uid-owner 1001 -j DROP
sudo iptables -A OUTPUT -o eth2 -m glassfish --uid-owner 1001 -j DROP
```

In the above command we assumed that `glassfish` user does not have the right to access a network interface named `eth2`. So we are simply asking the iptables to prevent `glassfish` user from acting as client or server on this interface. Our policy is to drop any packet without notifying the sender that we dropped the packet. The value we used for `--uid-owner` parameter is the id of `glassfish` user. We can obtain this value using the `id` command when we are logged in as `glassfish` user.

The `id` command simply shows identification information like group ID, user ID, and groups' membership of a given user, assuming that we have the right to see that information. When we use it without any parameters it shows the mentioned information about the current user. It shows something like the following details if we use it when we are logged in as `glassfish` user.

```
masoud@HAL10000: ~
glassfish@HAL10000:/opt$ id
uid=997(glassfish) gid=997(glassfish) groups=997(glassfish)
glassfish@HAL10000:/opt$ ▮
```

Restricting access to ports

Sometimes we only need to prevent the application server from accessing a specific port in a network interface. In these cases, we can again use `iptables` command to add rules for preventing the user from accessing the port as follows:

```
sudo iptables -A INPUT -i eth1 -p tcp --dport 3300 -m owner --uid-owner
glassfish -j DROP
sudo iptables -A INPUT -i eth1 -p udp --dport 3300 -m owner --uid-owner
glassfish -j DROP

sudo iptables -A OUTPUT -o eth1 -p tcp --dport 3300 -m owner --uid-owner
glassfish -j DROP
sudo iptables -A OUTPUT -o eth1 -p udp --dport 3300 -m owner --uid-owner
glassfish -j DROP
```

Each line of the above listing represents one command that we can execute on the terminal window.

You may wonder what all of these parameters we provided for the `iptables` command are. We are simply configuring the firewall to prevent `glassfish` user from acting either a client or server socket for port `3300` of the `eth1` interface. To do so, we are dropping any packet, either TCP or UDP, which `glassfish` user tries to establish.

Enforcing storage usage limitation

And at last, in some cases we may need to implement hard disk usage quota for `glassfish` user to prevent extra hard disk usage in case of a security breach.

The disk usage limitation in Linux can be enforced for a single user or a group of users over different filesystems like `/home`, `/opt` and so on. We can enforce the limitation over a number of consumed **blocks** and **inodes**.

Each block, depending on its size, can contain 4 KB, 16 KB, or any value specified during the filesystem creation. So, limiting the number of blocks limits the amount of data that can be stored in the file system.

Each inode contains a reference to a file or a directory in the file system. So limiting the number of inodes limits the number of files and directories that can be created.

Before we get down to the business, we should understand basics that the disk quota operates on. The following three terms explains these basics.

- **Soft limit**: Maximum amount of disk space that a user or a group of users can use. The disk usage by the user or the group can be exceeded for a certain amount of time. This amount of time is called **grace period.**

- **Grace period**: A period of time that the soft limit may stay exceeded by a user or a group of users. The grace period can be specified in seconds, minutes, hours, days, weeks, or months. This period of time lets the user get below the soft limit.

- **Hard limit:** Specifies a hard limit for the user or group disk usage. This limitation cannot be exceeded in the grace period.

The following instructions show how we can implement quota for `glassfish` user:

1. First we need to install the `quota` package that provides the required utilities and mounting options for defining quota. Package installation can be done using the following command:

```
sudo apt-get install quota
```

The above command will install the quota-related binaries in a Debian-based distribution like Ubuntu. For RPM-based distributions like Fedora and SUSE we can use the following command to install the package.

```
yast -i quota
```

2. Next, we need to enable the file system quota for filesystems. To enable quota on /dev/sda2 we can change or add the following line to the /etc/fstab file.

```
/dev/sda1 /opt ext3 defaults,usrquota,errors=remount 0 1
```

You may ask what these parameters are that we are using in the `fstab`. The following table describes each parameter.

Parameter	Description
/dev/sda1	Identifies the device we want to mount.
/opt	Specifies the mount point or the directory we want to access the filesystem through.
ext3	The file system we want to mount and access the partition using.
defaults	Using default mount options.
usrquota	Enabling the quota for this file system.
errors=remount	If any error occurs regarding the file system, we issue a remount.
0	Specifies whether the dump utility should create backup of this file system or not. Any value other than 0 means it should create the backup.
1	The `fsck` will check this parameter to decide whether it should perform an integrity check for the file system on boot or not. Any value other than 0 means it can check the file system for error if required.

3. We should either restart the system or remount the partitions to make the new options effective. To remount the file systems we can use the following command:

    ```
    sudo mount  -o defaults,remount  -t ext3 /dev/sda1 /opt
    ```

    This command simply mounts the /dev/sda1 partition to /opt directory using the `defaults` options. Specifying the remount options asks the mount command to remount the partition if it is already mounted.

4. Next, we define the quota for `glassfish` user. To do so we should enable the quota using the `quotaon` command. We can use `-av` to enable it for all associated filesystems and also to see a verbose output of the command execution.

    ```
    sudo quotaon -av
    ```

5. We should assign quota on each filesystem for each user we want to limit usage space. To do so we can use the `edquota` command as follows:

```
sudo edquota -u glassfish
```

The above command will open an editor which lets us specify the hard and soft limits for `glassfish` user on any filesystem we want. The default values shown by the command is similar to the following figure:

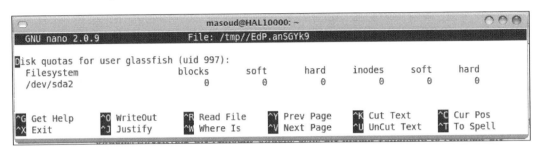

In the figure, the first column shows the filesystem the quota is defined for and the second shows the number of used blocks. The third and the fourth columns identify the soft and hard limit for block usage, the fifth column shows the number of used inodes and the sixth and seventh columns specify the soft and hard limit on inodes usage. Specifying 0 for any numeric column means no quota value for that column.

 To find the block size on a device we can use `dump2fs` or `tune2fs`. For example, to find the disk block size on `/dev/sda1` we can use the following command:

```
sudo dumpe2fs /dev/sda1 | grep 'Block size'
```

Assuming that we want to enforce a soft limit of 2 GB with 4 GB as the hard limit for the `glassfish` user, we can change the values as shown in the following figure. Next we should save the content. To save the changes, press *Ctrl+X*, accept the default name, and type *Yes* to store the changes.

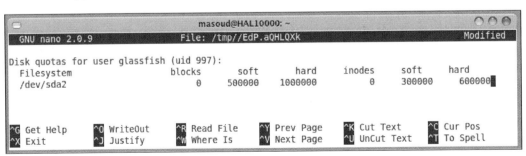

In my case the editor which edquota command uses is **GNU nano**. You can change the editor by exporting EDITOR environment variable to whatever editor you are familiar with. For example, if you want to use **gedit** simply execute the following command in the terminal, then invoke the edquota command:

```
Export EDITOR= /usr/bin/gedit
```

We can manually edit quota definition files with any text editor. The files are located in the root of each file system and are named as follows:

- The quota.user which contains user quotas for the filesystems
- The quota.group which contains group quotas for the filesystems

To specify the grace period we can use edquota -t, which allows us to specify the grace period of the blocks and inodes quota per filesystem. The following figure shows a sample output of edquota -t. As you can see, the grace period for both inodes and blocks is **7days**.

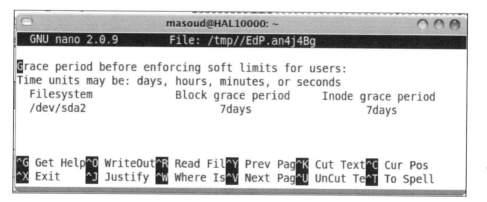

We can change the grace period for both inodes and blocks by changing their values in the editor and then saving it as explained above.

Here we are finished with implementing all required security measures from the operating system side to ensure that if a security breach happens in the application server, our operating system will be at no risk. Using these measures we guarantee that the only endangered resources, in case of a security breach caused by an application hosted in our application server, will be the resources our application server can access. The corporate network interfaces or other files and resources located on the server machine will not be affected. In the next section we will study how we can use Java Security Policy to implement security on the JVM running our GlassFish server instance to prevent the JVM from accessing unnecessary resources. We will also study how we can define security policies in the Application level to implement different levels of restrictions on each application deployed in the GlassFish application server.

Implementing restrictions in the application server level

In the previous section we discussed what we can do to protect operating system from malicious applications which we may host. In this section we will discuss what is provided by GlassFish to protect the operating system from the applications it hosts.

Securing the Java Runtime environment from unprivileged access

Java platform provides a set of infrastructural security measures starting from authentication and authorization standards down to cryptography and bytecode access control. In this section we will review what policy management in Java platform is and how it can be used to secure the Java Runtime environment from unwanted access by the application running inside the runtime.

The whole point of Java policy management is defining which classes or set of classes can or cannot access a specific resource like a directory, a socket, and so on.

 For Java Runtime to check application's actions permissibility it needs the Platform Security Manager to be enabled.

Java Runtime does not enable a security manager by default. We can either enable the security manager when we are initializing the JRE or in our software source code.

The following command line sample shows which parameters are required to enable the security manager from the command line when initializing the JRE:

```
java -Djava.security.manager
  -Djava.security.policy==path/to/policy_definition_file
  -jar path/to/a/jar/file
```

Enabling the security manager from the source code is as easy as calling the `System.setSecurityManager()` method and passing an instance of a security manager implementation to it.

In the command line sample you saw that we passed a policy definition file to the Java command. The policy definition file contains the rules which policy manager will check each invocation against to determine whether the invocation should go through or it should be prevented.

Using a policy definition file lets us use the standard implementation of `SecurityManager`, which reads the policy rules from a plain text file.

Implementing the policy manager

We said that the policy file contains a set of rules that security manager checks against before letting any of our applications actions go through. Syntax of these rules is as follows:

```
grant [signedBy "signer" [,codeBase "code_base_URL"] [, principal
principalClassName "principal Name"] {
 permission "class name"  ["name" [, <action list>]] [,signedBy
"signer names"];
};
```

Following snippet shows a simple rule to let you have a better understanding of the policy syntax.

```
grant codebase "file:${app.home}/lib/-",

        signedBy "kalali",

        principal javax.security.auth.x500.X500Principal
"cn=glassfish" {

    permission java.io.FilePermission "/opt/export", "read, write";

};
```

The above rule allows any code inside the `${app.home}/lib/` directory that is signed by a digital certificate nicknamed `kalali` and currently executed by a user named `glassfish` to have read and write access to a directory named `/opt/export`.

Another sample for a rule that allows everyone and any part of the application code base to have read access to a directory is as follows:

```
grant {
        permission java.io.FilePermission "/opt/configs.properties",
            "read";
    };
```

The following table shows these keywords and their description.

Keyword	Sample and description
grant	Granting a set of permissions to a codebase.

keystore	Digital certificates keystore to check public keys of the singers. A keystore entry must appear in the policy file if any grant entries specify signer aliases, or if any grant entries specify principal aliases. Only one keystore element can appear in a policy file. The syntax is as follows:
	
	`keystore "some_keystore_url", "keystore_type",`
	`"keystore_provider";`
	`keystorePasswordURL "some_password_url";`

permission	Specifies the actions that can be executed on a resource or set of resources.
signedBy	When used with a codebase, it will only allow codes singed by a digital certificate with this alias to pass through the rule and get the chance of being executed.
principal	Specifies the current operating system user. When we use this element we instruct the policy manager to only allow the codebase to pass the rule if it is executed by specified user.
codeBase	A URL to a file or set of files, a website as the source for downloading the files, and so on. This element specifies the set of bytecodes which this rules is applied on.

A sample for a policy file is as follows:

```
grant codeBase "file:${app.home}/lib/main.jar" {
    permission java.security.AllPermission;
};
grant codeBase "file:${app.home}/lib/server.jar" {
    permission java.net.SocketPermission "192.168.1.101:6404",
        "connect,accept,listen,resolve";
  permission java.util.PropertyPermission "*","read";
};
```

This policy definition gives all permissions to the `main.jar` file. Then it defines a rule that permits the `server.jar` to listen on port `6404` and have the permission to read any of the system properties like `user.home`, `java.version`, and so on.

The `192.168.1.101` address can be the IP address of one of our server network interfaces, which we want to allow GlassFish to listen on one of its specific ports. To obtain the server IP addresses we can use `ifconfig` in Linux and UNIX or `ipconfig` in Windows. These commands show a list of network interfaces along with their associated IP addresses. We can use `SocketPermission` policies along with `iptables` rules to ensure our network interfaces security.

We studied a small set of permissions in previous examples; there are many of different permission types which we can use to define policies we need. Some of these permissions are included in the following table.

Permission	Description
`java.security.SecurityPermission`	Controls access to security methods.
`java.io.FilePermission`	Controls read/write/execute access to files and directories.
`java.io.SerializablePermission`	Controls serialization operations.
`java.lang.RuntimePermission`	Controls use of some system/runtime functions like `exit()` and `exec()`. Also controls the package access/definition.
`java.lang.reflect.ReflectPermission`	Controls use of reflection to do class introspection.
`java.net.SocketPermission`	Controls use of network sockets.
`java.net.NetPermission`	Controls use of multicast network connections.
`java.util.PropertyPermission`	Controls read/write access to JVM properties, such as `java.home`.

All of these classes extend `java.security.Permission` or one of its subclasses. Each one of these classes acts differently based on its purpose. To see what set of parameters they accept consult with the Javadoc at `http://java.sun.com/javase/6/docs/api/java/security/Permission.html`.

Enforcing security always has its overhead and enabling the security manager in the platform level is not an exception. When we enable the security manager we are imposing an average overhead of 3%. The overhead varies between different rules definitions. The exact match rules impose the highest overhead while full wildcard matches imposes the smallest amount of overhead.

In addition to rule definition, the amounts of overhead each policy enforcement type impose differs between different permissions. For example the `SocketPermission` imposes the highest overhead. Some permission overheads, like `FilePermission`, do not affect the performance as their overheads are negligible compare to the methods execution themselves.

Securing the GlassFish using security manager

So far we discussed how a policy file can be used to restrict the Java Runtime access to different type of resources like the network sockets and filesystem. Now let's see how this security definition fits in GlassFish architecture and affects its runtime. The Java platform benefits from two policy definition files as follows:

- Global policy file: It's located at `java.home/jre/lib/security/java.policy`. Any policy rule defined here applies to all applications running on top of this JRE.

- User policy file: It's located at `user.home/.java.policy` which we can use to apply more rules for Java application running under this account.

The GlassFish application server itself has two level of policy definition as follows:

- GlassFish policy file: Located at `domain.home/config/server.policy`; we can use this file to define domain-wide policy rules.

- Per application policy file: The GlassFish application server let us define rules for each application separately. We can grant all permissions to GlassFish user and then define restrictive rules based on each application requirement or we can add more rules on top of previous rules for each deployed application. The application's policy files can be found at: `domain.home/generated/policy/<app.name>/<module.name>/granted.policy`.

Now, let's see how we can use this hierarchy of policy files to define a complete security policy for our server system.

Defining security policy in platform policy file

The global security policy file comes bundled with JRE and we should change its rules when we know that all applications that use this JRE will not get affected by our new rules. So, we leave the global policy file in the same state that it is in and define our new policy rules in the GlassFish policy file.

 It is good practice to define less restrictive rules in the more widely applied policy file and define more restrictive rules in policy files that cover smaller scopes.

Introducing the GlassFish policy file

Any rules we define in the `server.policy` file will affect its owner domain and all applications hosted in that domain. Let's analyze one of the rules defined in the default `server.policy` file and see how we can customize it to serve our needs.

```
grant codeBase "file:${com.sun.aas.installRoot}/lib/-" {
    permission java.security.AllPermission;
};
```

As you can see in this rule all permissions are granted to all JAR files located inside the `lib` directory of the domain. We need to restrict these JAR files to only have access to `glassfish` user home and only the network interfaces installed in our system. Applying our customization changes the `grant` permission to:

```
grant codeBase "file:${com.sun.aas.installRoot}/lib/-" {
  permission java.net.SocketPermission "192.168.1.101",
  "connect,accept,listen,resolve";

  permission java.util.PropertyPermission "user.*";
  permission java.io.FilePermission "/home/glassfish", "read,write";

  permission java.io.FilePermission "file:${com.sun.aas.instanceRoot}",
  "read,write";
  permission java.io.SerializablePermission "*";
  permission java.lang.RuntimePermission "*";
};
```

First, we only let GlassFish libraries use the `192.168.1.101` network interface and not any other interface in the system. Then we provide them with a read-only access over any system property starting with user.

The ${com.sun.aas.installRoot} expression points to the GlassFish installation directory. Inside this directory we have the lib directory, which contains different GlassFish libraries.

Coming down to file access permissions, we provide GlassFish with enough access permissions to read and write from the glassfish user home directory and from the domain installation directory.

 The ${com.sun.aas.instanceRoot} expression points to the current domain directory.

Finally we gave GlassFish all kinds of runtime permissions and serialization permissions because it needs those permissions to serve users requests.

Applying policies on deployed applications separately

So far we have defined rules to restrict the whole Java process running GlassFish from accessing specific resources, but what if we need to further restrict an application by applying new rules to prevent the application from opening any network socket? To do this we can edit the policy file generated for our application during the application deployment in GlassFish.

In the previous chapters we developed a secure enterprise application and deployed it into our GlassFish instance. Now let's study the policy file generated for its EJB module and further tune this file to serve our needs. The following snippet shows some part of the granted.policy file, which is located at domain_root/generated/ policy/Conversion/Conversion-ejb_jar/.

As you remember we did not enforce any authentication or access restrictions on toCentimeter method of ConversionBean when we were developing the sample application and therefore, as we can see in the snippet, anyone can access toCentimeter method either in its local or remote interfaces.

```
grant {

  permission javax.security.jacc.EJBMethodPermission
    "ConversionBean", "toCentimeter,Local,int";

  permission javax.security.jacc.EJBMethodPermission
    "ConversionBean", "toCentimeter,Remote,int";

};
```

In contrast with `toCentimeter` we defined some restriction on the `toInch` method, which only allowed the `manager` group to access it. The reflection of that restriction is shown in the following snippet of the policy definition file.

```
grant principal com.sun.enterprise.deployment.Group "manager" {

    permission javax.security.jacc.EJBMethodPermission
      "ConversionBean", "toInch,Local,int";

    permission javax.security.jacc.EJBMethodPermission
      "ConversionBean", "toInch,Remote,int";

};
```

Finally, in the last `grant` statement we can see that `employee` group receives the permission to invoke the `toMillimeter` method.

```
grant principal com.sun.enterprise.deployment.Group "manager" {

    permission javax.security.jacc.EJBMethodPermission
      "ConversionBean", "toMilimeter,Local,int";

    permission javax.security.jacc.EJBMethodPermission
      "ConversionBean", "toMilimeter,Remote,int";

};
```

The above `grant` statement permits the invocation of the `toMilimeter` method to the `manager` group.

```
grant      principal com.sun.enterprise.deployment.Group "employee" {

    permission javax.security.jacc.EJBMethodPermission
      "ConversionBean", "toMilimeter,Local,int";

    permission javax.security.jacc.EJBMethodPermission
      "ConversionBean", "toMilimeter,Remote,int";

};
```

If you look more carefully into this file you can see that the security constraint that we defined in the `ejb-jar.xml` and `sun-ejb-jar.xml` is translated to standard policy rules which are included in this file.

GlassFish performs its container access decisions according to the Java Authorization Contract for Containers (JACC or JSR 115) and JACC mandates using policy decision interfaces of the Standard Edition JRE to determine access rights. Adding the following rule to the `granted.policy` will permit the conversion application access to only `user.home` system properties when the `server.policy` did not allow any `propertypermission` to the running JVM.

```
grant {
        permission java.util.PropertyPermission "user.home";
}
```

Every time we deploy the application, GlassFish will generate a new version of this file, so any change we make to this file will not survive a redeployment of the application.

Only permissions defined by JSR-115 are effective in the application-specific policy file. These policies are enforced by the container irrespective of whether the `SecurityManager` is ON or OFF, whereas all the other permissions defined by Java are enforced only when the `SecurityManager` is ON.

Alternative container policy providers

GlassFish v3 supports two alternative container policy providers. By default, GlassFish is configured to use a file-based provider compatible with `PolicyFile` implementation of the JDK. GlassFish can be configured to use another provider by specifying the provider name in the `jacc` attribute of the `security-service` element in `domain.xml`. The following snippet shows how we can use `jacc` attribute for this.

```
<security-service jacc="simple">
```

The value of this attribute must be the same as the `name` attribute of a `jacc-provider` element. The `security-service` can have one or more `jacc-provider` child elements to define the available providers. The default value of the `jacc` attribute is `default`, which matches the `name` attribute of the file-based `jacc-provider` element. Setting the value of this attribute to `simple` will cause the in-memory provider to be used. The in-memory provider will not generate the per-application policy file and therefore we cannot fine-tune the generated file.

The following snippet shows the definition of bundled policy providers in the `domain.xml`:

```
<jacc-provider policy-provider="com.sun.enterprise.security.
provider.PolicyWrapper" name="default" policy-configuration-
factory-provider="com.sun.enterprise.security.provider.
PolicyConfigurationFactoryImpl">
<property name="repository" value="${com.sun.aas.instanceRoot}/
generated/policy" />
</jacc-provider>
<jacc-provider policy-provider="com.sun.enterprise.security.jacc.
provider.SimplePolicyProvider" name="simple" policy-configuration-
factory-provider="com.sun.enterprise.security.jacc.provider.
SimplePolicyConfigurationFactory" >
</jacc-provider>
```

The admin console may be used to define additional `jacc-provider` configurations in `domain.xml`, and then any such provider can be configured for use by the Glassfish `security-service`, by setting its name as the value of the `jacc` attribute.

Estimating security risks: Auditing

Auditing is an integral part of security measures to track back the events and check the overall health of the system security. Using auditing we can estimate security risks and get a thorough understanding of possible points of intrusions and attacks in the system.

The GlassFish auditing system let administrators audit seven important security events which are included in the following table:

Action	Description
Authentication*	Any authentication attempt can be audited.
Web resource invocation*	Any attempt to access a web resource can be audited.
EJB method invocation*	Any attempt to invoke an EJB method can be audited.
Web service invocation	Any attempt to invoke a web service can be audited.
EJB method as Web service invocation	Any attempt to invoke an EJB method as a web service can be audited.
Server startup	A successful startup can be audited.
Server shutdown	A successful shutdown can be audited.

GlassFish kernel produces the auditing information listed in the above table and channels them to any enabled auditing module by invoking representative methods in the auditing module implementation class.

The auditing information produced by GlassFish kernel carries different levels of details about the event. For example, in the first three events that are marked by a "*" sign the auditing module will receive the username used for the invocation attempt while no username is propagated for other events.

Enabling the default auditing module

If we choose to configure GlassFish auditing, any security-related event will pass through the auditing layer. This layer consists of one or more auditing modules that can react to security events based on their design and purpose. For example, the default auditing module of GlassFish, when enabled, stores all security events listed in the previous table in the `server.log` file, which is located in the `domain.dir/logs/` directory.

To enable the default auditing module we can navigate to **Tree | Configuration | Security | Audit Modules | default** and then enable the module by changing the `auditon` property value to `true`. Now we can check the sever logfile to see auditing information. An example entry for a failed authentication is like the following snippet.

```
[#|2009-10-04T21:43:40.905+0330|INFO|sun-appserver9.1|javax.
enterprise.system.core.security|_ThreadID=15;_ThreadName=httpWork
erThread-4848-1;admin;|SEC5046: Audit: Authentication refused for
[admin].|#]
```

The log message says that the authentication for `admin` user has been refused. But the whole log record contains other information that can help the administrator to track the possible breach by looking at the event time and date, the package which fired the event, and the thread that faced this security event.

One of the main advantages of GlassFish is its modularity and extensibility, which lets administrators and developers add new features or extend its current features to cover their requirements. The GlassFish auditing layer benefits from the same architecture and lets administrators to plug in new auditing modules to treat the security events in different and more suitable ways. In the next section we go through developing a new auditing module.

Developing custom auditing modules

Developing a new auditing module is as easy as extending `com.sun.appserv.` `security.AuditModule`, which is an abstract class, and overriding methods that handle different security events in a way that suits our needs. The following snippet shows methods that we can override to treat security events the way we need.

```
public abstract class AuditModule {
    Properties props = null;
    public void init(Properties props) {
        this.props = props;
    }

    public void authentication(String user, String realm,
      boolean success) {    }
    public void webInvocation(String user, HttpServletRequest req,
      String type, boolean success) {    }
    public void ejbInvocation(String user, String ejb, String method,
      boolean success) {    }
    public void webServiceInvocation(String uri, String endpoint,
      boolean success) {    }
    public void ejbAsWebServiceInvocation(String endpoint,
      boolean success) {    }
    public void serverStarted() {    }
    public void serverShutdown() {    }
}
```

Imagine that we need to get notified when container-managed authentication fails three times in a row. We can override the `authentication` method and send a notification e-mail in the case that we have three failed authentications in matter of five minutes or so.

After we develop the auditing module, which can be as small as a single class or as large as a complete library involving data access, JDBC, **JavaMail**, and so on, we should put related JAR files in the application server, such as inside the `domain_dir/` `lib` directory or by extending the classpath variable from Administration Console at **Application Server | JVM Settings | Path Settings**

After that we can add the module to the set of application server auditing modules. The process is straightforward using the `asadmin` utility of the Administration Console. For example:

```
asadmin create-audit-module --classname

glassfish.book.security.chapter4.SampleAuditModule --property

datasourceName=auditSource SampleAuditor
```

The above command will add an auditing module named `SampleAuditor` based on an auditing module implementation named `book.glassfish.security.chapter4.SampleAuditModule`. We can pass as many initialization properties as required using the standard `asadmin` format. These properties form the `props` object that we can access inside the `init` method.

After we create the new auditing module we should add it to the set of registered auditing modules which receive the security notifications using the `asadmin` or Administration Console. Registering the auditing module using the `asadmin` is as simple as executing the following command:

```
asadmin set server-config.security-service.audit_modules=default,SampleAu
ditor
```

Now we have our auditing installed and activated. We only need to restart the server to make the changes effective.

Summary

In this chapter we covered environment security and security auditing, which are basic parts of application server security. We saw what we need to do at operating system level to ensure that GlassFish installation is isolated from the whole operating system. We later on discussed how we can use the security policy to ensure that GlassFish process and deployed application can only access the resources intended for them. Finally, we learned the importance of auditing and how we can create new auditing modules to customize the security events treatment.

In next chapter we will cover GlassFish administration security tasks like password security and listener security.

5

Securing GlassFish

In the previous chapter we discussed how we should protect the environment from malicious applications, which a user may deploy into our server. We discussed the security of GlassFish installation at the operating system level by using GlassFish exclusive user, filesystem, and network interfaces. In this chapter we will discuss GlassFish security from another perspective — the administration and applications security.

- Overviewing of GlassFish administration
- Learning GlassFish administration security
- Protecting passwords used in GlassFish
- Securing different network listeners
- Using Virtual Server for isolating applications
- Using cross context SSO available in GlassFish

Administrating GlassFish

GlassFish benefits from several different administration channels and each of them provides a unique set of features that ease a set of specific tasks. The following table shows the GlassFish administration channels.

Administration Channel	Description
Java Management Extensions (JMX)	Allows us to interact with the GlassFish administration layer through Java code or using any JMX-capable administration console, like **JConsole** and **VisualVM**, which are bundled with JRE.
Command-Line Interface (CLI)	Command line administration tools to ease terminal-based administration and scripting.

Administration Channel	Description
Web Administration Console	Using a modern GUI to administrate the servers and deployed artefacts.
RESTful Administration interface	A RESTful interface to allow almost any programming language to interact with the GlassFish administration layer.

Using CLI is the preferred approach for experienced administrators who prefer to quickly type a command and see a brief result without waiting for web pages to load. Except for the tasks like `creating`, `removing`, `backing up` and `restoring`, and `starting` a domain, all other administration tasks are possible through all administration channels. So there are no steep differences between these administration interfaces in term of provided capabilities.

Using CLI for administration tasks

GlassFish uses a utility named `asadmin` to provide the command-line interface for the administrator. The `asadmin` utility is located at the `$GF_HOME/bin` directory. It is either a batch file named `asadmin.bat` for Windows or a shell script named `asadmin` for Linux and UNIX.

We can use `asadmin` script by two different methods. The command execution schema for the first method is as follows:

```
./asadmin [ program options] command_name *[[--param] values]
```

This method is more suitable for creating custom scripts or for executing only one command at a time. The following table shows the `asadmin` options and what their usage is.

Option	Description
`--host`	The application server administration listener's IP address or host name.
`--port`	The administration listener port number.
`--user`	A username in `admin` realm.
`--passwordfile`	The password file containing the administrator's password.
`--terse`	Produces output intended for automated parsing.
`--interactive`	If specified, the CLI utility will ask for required parameter in an interactive way.
`--secure`	If specified, the CLI utility will use HTTPS to communicate with the administration application to prevent possible security breach.

The second method of using `asadmin` involves entering the `asadmin` shell and running commands inside it. This is a bit faster than first method because in the first method we need to run the `asadmin` utility each time a command is invoked, which involves some CPU time. To enter the shell and invoke commands, execute the `asadmin` script without any trailing command or parameter.

The `asadmin` utility can execute both local and remote commands. Local commands are commands that should take place locally and in the operating system level like starting and stopping a domain or restoring a domain backup. Remote commands mostly deal with managed objects inside the application server like applications, Java EE resources, application server services like listeners, and so on.

The following figure illustrates how `asadmin` utility can execute remote commands. Local commands mostly deal with filesystem and operating system level commands.

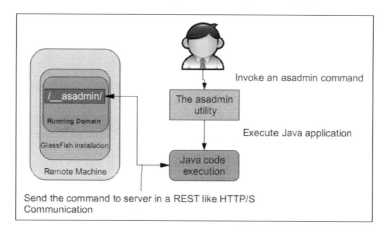

When we issue a command in the CLI, `asadmin` script invokes a Java application and passes all received parameters to it. If all parameters are correct, the Java application sends an HTTP or HTTPS request to the `asadmin` application deployed in the application server. The application server executes the command and either sends back the result or an error message in the case of an incorrect command.

The following figure illustrates some part of an HTTP packet, which is carrying the list authentication realm's command to the server:

```
▽ Hypertext Transfer Protocol
  ▽ POST /web1/remotejmx HTTP/1.1\r\n
    ▽ [Expert Info (Chat/Sequence): POST /web1/remotejmx HTTP/1.1\r\n]
        [Message: POST /web1/remotejmx HTTP/1.1\r\n]
        [Severity level: Chat]
        [Group: Sequence]
      Request Method: POST
      Request URI: /web1/remotejmx
      Request Version: HTTP/1.1
    Content-type: application/octet-stream\r\n
    Connection: Keep-Alive\r\n
  ▽ Authorization: Basic YWRtaW46YWRtaW5hZG1pbg==\r\n
      Credentials: admin:adminadmin
    Cache-Control: no-cache\r\n
    Pragma: no-cache\r\n
    User-Agent: Java/1.6.0_14\r\n
    Host: 127.0.0.1:4848\r\n
    Accept: text/html, image/gif, image/jpeg, *; q=.2, */*; q=.2\r\n
```

If you look closely at the highlighted section you can see that the username and password are passed in clean text, which poses a great risk if someone listens in middle of `asadmin` utility and the application server. We will discuss more about securing `asadmin` in the latter sections.

Implementing security in CLI

The CLI is our means to administrate the application server. It can be very useful for performing daily tasks but it can be catastrophic if we fail to protect it well from unauthorized access. In this section we will discuss CLI security in detail to see how we should keep the CLI secure and what security-related commands it provides.

The asadmin and administration credentials

When administration comes to mind we also think about administrator credentials. The administration credentials are a set of a username and a password. By default, we only have one administrator with `admin/adminadmin` as the credentials. We can add more users when necessary.

When we want to perform administrative tasks we should provide administration credentials and these credentials are sent to the server to perform authentication before the server-side application, which is responsible for executing our commands.

When we execute an `asadmin` command we should either provide the username and password as command options or the `asadmin` utility will ask for username and password interactively. For example, the following command will cause the `asadmin` utility to ask for a username and a password before it continues with execution:

```
./asadmin list-auth-realms --host 127.0.0.1 --port 4848
```

In this method of invoking `asadmin` command, the password is not provided in clean text and later on the `asadmin` utility asks for the password in a secure way, which means entered characters are not shown as we type them. If you are wondering what the above command does, it lists all authentication realms on a server which its administration listener is listening on `127.0.0.1:4848`, provided that we enter a correct administration password.

Sometimes we should not even type the administration password for sake of security. In such conditions we can use a file or any other media containing the required password. The `asadmin` utility provides us with an intuitive way of providing the administration password using a password file containing password. The password file, along with the username, can be passed to the `asadmin` utility using the options showed in the previous table.

For example:

```
./asadmin list-auth-realms --host 127.0.0.1 --port 4848 --user admin --
passwordfile /path/to/passwordfile
```

The password file is a standard property value file with some predefined properties. The following snippet shows a sample password file:

```
AS_ADMIN_PASSWORD=adminadmin
AS_ADMIN_MASTERPASSWORD=changeit
```

As you can see we have more than one property; the first property specifies the administration password for the user that we passed as an option along with the password file to the `asadmin` utility. The second entry specifies the master password, which we are going to discuss shortly.

You may ask why you have never before been asked to provide a password when you were performing administration tasks using the `asadmin`. For example, you may have invoked the following command without the `asadmin` utility asking you for any password:

```
./asadmin list-http-listeners
```

The answer is in the way that you have created the domain or the way that the domain is created for you by the GlassFish installer. It has used the `--savelogin=true` option to save the administration username and password in a default password files, which the `asadmin` utility tries to use when no credentials are provided during the command invocation.

The `--savelogin=true` asks the domain creation command to save the administration password of the domain into a file named `.asadminpass` that is located inside the `$USER.HOME` directory, which we refer to it as `$USER_HOME`. The content of this file is similar to the following snippet:

```
asadmin://admin@localhost:4848 YWRtaW5hZG1pbg==
```

The syntax simply specifies what is the administration username and password for a domain with its administrator listener running on `localhost:4848`. The password is encrypted to prevent anyone learning it without being authorized.

> Using `localhost` and `127.0.0.1` for IPv4 and `::1` for IPv6 refers to the `loopback` network interface of the current computer. Sometimes we use loopback address to name the `127.0.0.1` or `localhost`.

There is an `asadmin` command that performs a similar task to what `--savelogin` does for domains that are already created. We can use this command to save the credentials to prevent the `asadmin` utility from asking for them either in an interactive mode or as `--passwordfile` parameter. The following snippet shows how we can use `login` command:

```
./asadmin login    --host localhost --port 9138
```

This command will interactively ask for administration username and password and after a successful authentication it will save the provided credentials into the `.asadminpass` file. After we execute this command the content of `.asadminpass` will be similar to the following snippet:

```
asadmin://admin@localhost:4848 YWRtaW5hZG1pbg==
asadmin://admin@localhost:9138 YWRtaW5hZG1pbg==
```

The `.asadminpass` contains the **SHA** hashed copy of passwords, therefore it is not possible for anyone to recover the original passwords if he can grasp the file. Using the saved passwords means that anyone with access to the `asadmin` command can execute any command they like. So, protect the operating system password to prevent it from falling into the hands of unauthorized personnel.

The `login` command is very useful when we need to administrate several domains from our administration workstation. We can simply login into each remote or local domain that we need to administrate and then `asadmin` will pick the correct credential from the `.asadminpass` file based on the `--host` and `--port` parameters.

As there is no way to recover the administration password because of one-way hashing mechanism, the only way to administrate a domain with a forgotten password is to create a new domain with `--savelogin=true` option and then copy the content of the `domains/new.domain.dir/config/admin-keyfile` to the `domains/old.domain.dir/config/admin-keyfile`. We can delete the temporary domain after we copy the file. Using this way we can log into our administration console with the password we associated with the new domain. The file we just copied is the credential store for a security realm named `admin-realm`, which GlassFish uses to store the usernames, passwords, and groups of any `admin-realm` member. The `admin-realm` is a file realm.

Protecting GlassFish domain using master password

The master password is designated to protect the domain-encrypted files like digital certificate store from unauthorized access.

When we start a GlassFish domain, the startup process needs to read these certificates and therefore it needs to open the certificates' store files. GlassFish needs the master password to open the store files and therefore we should either provide the master password during the `start-domain` command execution in an interactive way or we should use the `--passwordfile` parameter to provide the process with the master password.

The most common situation for using a previously-saved master password is when we need our application server to start in an unattended environment, like when we make a Windows service or Linux daemon for it.

Again, you may ask how you were starting your default domain without the `asadmin` utility asking for the master password. It is because `--savemasterpassword=true` was used as an option for the domain creation command. When we use this option, the asadmin utility saves the master password into a file named master-password, which resides inside the `$DOMAIN.DIR/config` directory.

 If we forget to save the master password during the domain creation time, we can use the `change-master-password` command to save it as explained in the next section.

Changing passwords

As an administrator we usually like to change our passwords from time to time to ensure keeping a higher level of security precautions. GlassFish lets us simply change the master or administration password using some provided commands.

To change the master password we must be sure that the application server is not running, then we can run `change-master-password` as follows:

```
Change-master-password --domaindir=/opt/dev/apps/domains/ --
savemasterpassword=true GiADomain
```

After executing this command, the `asadmin` utility will interactively ask us for the new master password, which must be at least eight characters. We use the `--savemasterpassword` to ensure that the master password is saved and during the domain startup we do not need to provide the `asadmin` with it. We need to change the password file if we are using it to feed the `asadmin` utility with the master password.

 If we use the `change-master-password` without the `--savemasterpassword=true` the current password file will be deleted if it exists.

To change the administration password we can use `change-admin-password`, which is a remote command, and needs the application server to be running. The following snippet shows how we can change the administration password for a given username:

```
change-admin-password --host 127.0.0.1 --port 4747 --user admin
```

After executing this command in which we should replace the `port` and `host` parameter to reflect our administration listener, `asadmin` will ask for the administration password and then change the password of the given user. If we change the password for a user, we will need to log into that domain again if we need to use automatic login. Also, we need to change the password file if we are using it to feed the `asadmin` utility with its required passwords.

Protecting passwords with encryption

We have many places in any application server that need some username and passwords which the application server will use to communicate with external systems like JMS brokers and databases. Usually each part of the overall infrastructure has its own level of policy and permission set, which leads us to the fact that we should protect these passwords and avoid leaving them in plain text format in any place, even in the application server configuration files, which can be opened using any text editor.

GlassFish provides a very elegant way for protecting these passwords, by providing us with the required commands and infrastructure to encrypt the passwords and use an encrypted password's assigned alias in the application server configuration files. The encrypted passwords are stored inside an encrypted file named `domain-passwords`, which resides inside the domain's `config` directory. The `domain-passwords` file is encrypted using the master password and if the master password is compromised then these file can be decrypted.

The command for creating password aliases is a remote command named `create-password-alias` and a sample usage is shown in the following snippet:

```
create-password-alias --user admin --host localhost --port 4747
GiA_Derby_Pool_Alias
```

After we execute this command `asadmin` utility will ask for the password that we want this alias to hold, although `asadmin` may ask for administration credentials if we are not logged in.

Now that we created the alias we can access it by using the alias accessing syntax which follows the `${ALIAS=password-alias-password}` format. For example, if we want to create the JDBC connection pool using the newly-created alias as the connection password we can do it as follows:

```
create-jdbc-connection-pool --user admin  --host localhost --port 4747
--datasourceclassname org.apache.derby.jdbc.ClientDataSource --restype
javax.sql.XADataSource --property portNumber=1527:password=${ALIAS= GiA_
Derby_Pool_Alias}:user=APP:serverName=localhost:databaseName=GiADatabase:
create=true GiA_Derby_Pool
```

Password aliasing is not present just for external resources, but it can be used to protect the content of the password file, which contains the administration and master passwords to be used, instead of typing the password when the `asadmin` interactively asks for it. We can simply create a password alias for the administration password and for the master password and use them in password file. Sample content for a password file with aliased password is like this.

```
AS_ADMIN_PASSWORD=${ALIAS=admin-alias}
AS_ADMIN_MAPPEDPASSWORD=${ALIAS=master-alias}
```

Like all other administration commands, the alias administration commands set has some other commands which help with commands administration. Other commands in this set are shown in the following table.

Command	Description
`delete-password-alias`	We can delete an alias when we are sure we are no longer using it.
`list-password-aliases`	We can get a list of all aliases that we have in our `domain-password` file.
`update-password-alias`	We can update an alias by changing the password that it holds.

Password aliasing is very helpful when we do not want to give our passwords to the personal in charge of application server management or administration tasks. Instead we can provide them with an aliased password, which they can use.

Securing the CLI communication channel

So far we have discussed how we can protect the CLI passwords locally, but a more important aspect of security is guaranteeing the transmission security. In the second figure of this chapter we saw how administration credentials are transmitted over the wire in plain text, which will create a golden opportunity for a malicious person to sniff the data and extract the administration credentials. To prevent a big risk like this we can enable the security of `admin-listener`, which is fully explained in the next section.

The `asadmin` utility can verify the certificate provided by the server by validating it against a trust store dedicated for the `asadmin` utility. The trust store file that the `asadmin` utility uses is named `.asadmintruststore` and is located inside the `$USER.HOME` directory. We can manage the certificates in the `.asadmintruststore` using the well-known `keytool` that we used in *Chapter 2* of this book to import digital certificates into the application server's keystore and trust store.

The `asadmin` utility does not support mutual authentication using digital certificates. So if we enable the **Client Authentication** in the administration listener, we won't be able to use the `asadmin` utility. To disable the mutual authentication we need to use the web administration console and disable the mutual authentication. Mutual authentications is explained in the following section.

Securing different network listeners

Everything an application server offers to the users is accessible by a listener. Basically each listener is assigned a server socket that handles requests placed on the socket it listens on. For example, by default the `admin-listener` listens on `0.0.0.0:4848`, which means it listens on all available network addresses on port `4848`.

Because of the diversity of Java EE platform and application servers, different application servers have multiple types of listeners which administrators can use to configure the application server to listen on different port and addresses for handling different set of protocols.

In GlassFish we have three types of listeners and for each type we have one or more instance configured by default. The following table shows these listeners.

Listener type	Description
HTTP listener	Serves HTTP requests for admin, user, and `asadmin` requests. There are three different instances configured by default.
JMX listener	Serves JMX requests. Usually for administration purposes.
IIOP Listener	Server requests for accessing managed objects like EJBs, JMS connection factories, and so on.

When we have all of these listeners exposed, a user may access an accounting application or he may try to interact with the application server's core using JMX interface, which normal users are not usually permitted to do. So listeners should be protected in different levels using different set of protection layers, which starts by proper configuration of firewalls and network router to only allow certain traffic for each listener.

Each listener in the application server can listen on as many network addresses as required. By default all listeners listen on `0.0.0.0` and their dedicated ports. It means that clients can connect to the application server using any of the network addresses assigned to the server machine. Although it is useful when we are developing applications, it can pose security risks in the production environment when we only need a certain set of inbound traffic to hit each listener. For example, we should configure the admin listener to listen on the network interface accessible through our LAN and not through the WAN to prevent any security breach over the administration console.

Securing HTTP listeners

Using HTTP is the most common way of communication between an application server and its clients. Securing HTTP listeners is the first step in configuring a secure installation of an application server. In GlassFish we can secure HTTP listeners using the asadmin utility or using the administration console as the easiest ways.

To configure the HTTP listeners' security we will use the administration console. To get started, log into the administration console by navigating to your GlassFish administration console, which by default is accessible at http://127.0.0.1:4848 if you are on the server machine, and then from the right-side tree navigate to **Configuration | Network Config | Network Listeners**. A list of default listeners similar to following figure will appear in the browser:

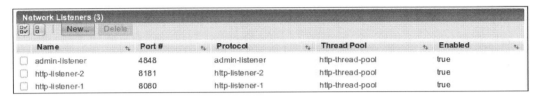

These are default HTTP listeners which serve administration requests—HTTPS and HTTP requests hitting the application server. After clicking on **http-listener-2**, which by default serves all HTTPS requests, a page with all information and settings related to **http-listener-2** will open. The page is similar to the following figure:

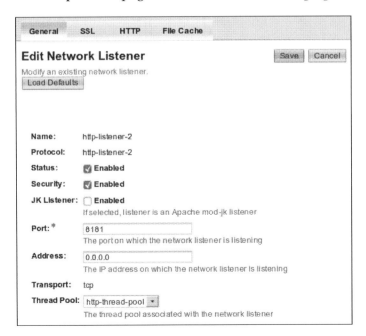

First thing that we need to change is the **Address**. The default 0.0.0.0 means that this listener will listen on any interface available to the Java runtime, which we usually do not need, so we should change it to the IP address of network interface that our clients have access to.

We can assign multiple network interfaces to a listener if needed. We have multiple network interfaces on our server machine to serve requests coming from internal and external networks by entering their IP addresses separated by a comma, such as 192.168.1.121, 74.34.21.12. In this sample, the first IP can be the address of the internal network interface and the second one can be the external network interface address.

As mentioned earlier, this listener is the default HTTPS listener and for that to work the **Security** checkbox is checked to enable HTTPS support. To view and change the SSL configuration click on the **SSL** tab, which opens a page similar to the following figure in the browser.

The options, along with the descriptions are included in the following table.

Option	Description
SSL3	Enabling it means that we want the listener to support legacy client's which uses SSL3 protocol instead of TLS.
TLS	It must be enabled if the listener is meant to interact with modern browsers or clients. Nowadays all major web browsers and network frameworks support TLS.
Client Authentication	Enabling this option will enforce a mutual authentication in which the client needs to provide a verifiable digital certificate to the server, in addition to the server providing its digital certificate to the client.
Certificate Nickname	The value of this option must be a valid certificate name in the keystore we provide in the next option. The default self-signed digital certificate nickname is `s1as` and we should replace it with a legally-signed digital certificate for production use.
Key Store	Its value should either be empty (meaning the default key store file) or path to a valid keystore file (jks) containing the certificate with the given nickname.
Trust Algorithm	It should be left empty or filed with SRP, PKIX, or any other supported algorithm for checking the certificate chain for certificates provided by client.
Max Certificate Length	It specifies the maximum number of intermediate certificate issuers between the client's provided certificate and a root certificate in the trust store. Imagine that we want to only trust certificates issued directly by a root certificate authority. In that case the number should be 0. Usually we accept certificates issued by certificate authorities five levels deep in the chain from a root certificate. This option affects the way that listeners verify client's certificates when we use PKIX as the verification algorithm.
Trust Store	It should be empty to use the default trust store or it should point to a valid trust store file. Any certificate included in the trust store will result in the listener's confirmation of client's certificate signed by them.

We can specify the cipher suites in the same page. Using the **Cipher Suites** sections we can specify which cryptography algorithms with what level of strength we want our listener to use when negotiating the secure communication configuration. By default all cipher suites are supported for different algorithms. We should only enable the cipher suites that are legally allowed in the host and client countries because different countries have different policies in permitting the use of cipher suites and key lengths for inbound and outbound communications.

We can create as many listeners as we need to support different clients connecting to our application server in order to serve each set of clients with the level of demanded security based on the sensitivity of their work.

 Digital certificates and using them for security purpose has become very common in recent years as the processing power of servers has increased and handling the related load is much easier than compared to the past. There is open source certificate authority software named **EJBCA** (http://ejbca.sourceforge.net/) which we can use to create a small CA. We can use it for SSL mutual authentication without need to pay for digital certificates for our controlled client and server applications. The following article fully discusses using EJBCA with GlassFish to have a fully-controlled setup of mutual authentication between clients and GlassFish: http://weblogs.java.net/blog/kalali/archive/2010/02/06/glassfish-v3-and-ejbca-394-fair-couple-mutual-ssl-authentication.

Securing ORB listeners

ORB listeners serve remote clients who want to use Java EE managed objects such as JMS connection factories, EJB methods, and so on. The ORB listeners handle these types of requests and if necessary, authenticating, conducting an SSL session, and performing a mutual authentication via digital certificates is also done.

We can view and configure ORB listeners by navigating to **Configuration | ORB | IIOP Listeners**, which will show a list of current IIOP listeners similar to following figure:

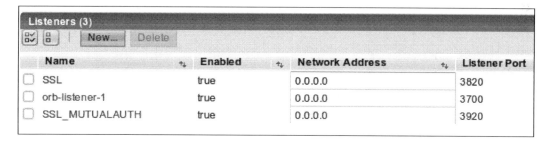

Name	Enabled	Network Address	Listener Port
SSL	true	0.0.0.0	3820
orb-listener-1	true	0.0.0.0	3700
SSL_MUTUALAUTH	true	0.0.0.0	3920

As you can see, there are three preconfigured listeners present in the list of IIOP listeners. All of them are listening on all available network addresses, so we should change the network address according to our needs.

Clicking on any of these listeners will open a listener configuration page similar to the HTTP listeners' configuration page. All elements are similar and security considerations for them are the same as HTTP listeners.

 The only difference between configuring IIOP listeners and HTTP listeners is the SSL3 requirement in the IIOP listeners because of legacy systems that interact with EJB layer over IIOP.

Securing JMX listeners

The JMX communication channel is another means of interaction with GlassFish administration and management. Using JMX we can virtually do anything we do with CLI and administration console.

To view and change the configuration of the JMX listener, we can navigate to **Configuration | Admin Service**, which will open a page similar to the following figure:

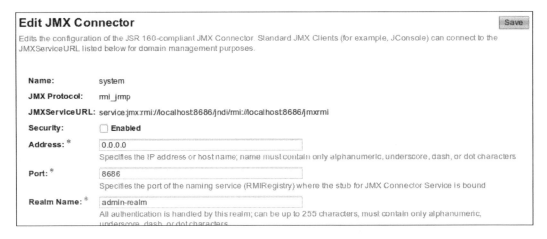

You can see similar attributes like **Security**, **Address**, and **Port** which we already know how to use along with the **SSL** tab that let us change the JMX listener's SSL support, which is similar to HTTP and IIOP listener.

You can see one additional option named **Realm Name**, which we can use to specify which security realm we want to use for authenticating the JMX connections. The presence of username and password authentication lets us authenticate users using classic tokens and meanwhile enable SSL to ensure data integrity and confidentiality. In special cases when we need maximum security on the JMX listener we can enable **Client Authentication** in the **SSL** tab to enforce mutual SSL authentication before letting a client use JMX to interact with the application server.

Hosting multiple domains using one IP

Virtual hosts or virtual servers are basically the feature that made it possible for web hosting providers to host multiple domains using one IP and one physical machine. For example, two domains like www.domain5.com and www.domain6.com can be hosted on one physical machine having one IP address.

In such cases, the name server translates both addresses to one IP address and later on the web server or application server directs the requests to a correct virtual server based on the domain name or the URL pattern.

For GlassFish, the story is a bit different because GlassFish gives more flexibility and isolation compared to Tomcat or other application servers.

> To see how virtual host configuration works on different application server, take a look at the following references:
>
> - Virtual hosting and Tomcat: http://tomcat.apache.org/tomcat-6.0-doc/virtual-hosting-howto.html
> - Configuring virtual host on Geronimo: http://cwiki.apache.org/GMOxDOC22/configuring-virtual-host.html
> - JBoss and virtual hosting: http://community.jboss.org/wiki/VirtualHostswithJBossAS

When we install Glassfish, the installer creates two virtual servers—one for user applications and one for administration applications. The following figure shows a list of virtual servers, which are created by default.

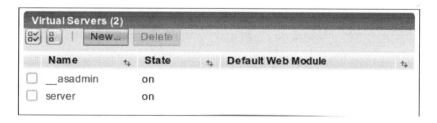

Both virtual servers are enabled and neither of them has a default web application to handle requests that do not match any of the deployed web applications. Creating a new virtual server will be straightforward after we study one of the preconfigured virtual servers and learn what the properties of each virtual server are.

Let's click on the __asadmin virtual server and see its current configuration. Clicking on __asadmin will open a page similar to the following figure:

Id:	__asadmin
Hosts: *	${com.sun.aas.hostName}
	Comma-separated list of hosts or IP addresses
State:	⦿ **On - Virtual server active**
	○ **Off - Virtual server inactive; return code 404 (resource not available)**
	○ **Disabled – Virtual server inactive; return code 403 (refused to fulfill the request)**
SSO:	⦿ **Controlled by HTTP Service**
	○ **Enabled**
	○ **Disabled**
Network Listeners:	admin-listener http-listener-2 http-listener-1
	Comma-separated list of network listeners
Default Web Module:	[▾]
	Module to use if requests to other modules are not resolved
Log File:	${com.sun.aas.instanceRoot}/logs/server.log
	Default is the log-root attribute of the domain
Docroot:	${com.sun.aas.instanceRoot}/docroot
	Absolute path to root document directory for server

Access Log

Access Logging:	⦿ **Controlled by HTTP Service**
	○ **Enabled**
	○ **Disabled**
Directory:	${com.sun.aas.instanceRoot}/logs/access
	Absolute path to server access logs

The following table shows the options we have in the virtual host creating page along with a description for each one of them.

Option	Description
Id	It is a unique ID that we specify when we create each virtual host.
Hosts	This is a comma-separated set of IP addresses or domain names, which the DNS server will resolve to the IP address this virtual host's HTTP listeners listen on.
State	It lets us specify whether the virtual host is active or inactive.
SSO	This option specifies whether we want to have single sign-on between all applications deployed in this virtual host using a similar security realm or not. If we choose to have SSO, users will only need to login once and stay authenticated for all applications deployed in the same virtual host and using the same security realm. Specifying the SSO state in the virtual server level will override the specified value in the HTTP service level.
Network Listeners	This element allows us to select one or more HTTP/S listeners to receive requests for applications deployed in this virtual server.
Default Web Module	The default web module will handle requests that do not match any of the deployed applications.
Log File	This element specifies where this virtual server should write the log entries. By default all virtual servers use the server logfile.
Docroot	This element specifies the document root for this virtual server.
Access Log	When enabled, any access to any resource in the server will be logged. Specifying the access log state in the virtual server level will override the specified value in the HTTP service level.

When we deploy applications in GlassFish we can choose which virtual server we want to use for that application. In the CLI mode, we can specify the target virtual host using the `--virtualservers` and in the case where we use Administration Console we can select the target virtual host in the first step of application deployment wizard.

Sharing security context between different applications using SSO

The most basic task of single sign-on is saving users from entering their username and passwords when there are different applications which are related. GlassFish supports SSO between web applications deployed in the same virtual server. When we enable SSO for a virtual server, any user authenticated in one of the applications deployed in that server will stay authenticated for all applications deployed in the same virtual server. There are only two conditions that our server-side applications and the client must have to use this SSO capability:

- The applications deployed in the same virtual host must use the same security realm, same value for the `realm-name` of `web.xml`, to make it possible for GlassFish to verify the authentication token

- The client-side application must support cookies because the authentication token acquired after client authenticates against one web application will be carried on to other applications when user tries to access them

When a user authenticates against one web application, a cookie will be set in the client side which contains the authentication token and when the user tries to access a protected resource on any one of the other applications, GlassFish will verify the cookie and then check their access rights against the requested resource. If the user has permission to access the resource, the request will go through; if they do not have the access rights they will get an HTTP 403 error message or equivalent as defined in the `web.xml`.

Enabling SSO in virtual server

To enable SSO in the virtual server we can navigate to the **Edit Virtual Server** section and tick the corresponding checkbox as shown in the following figure:

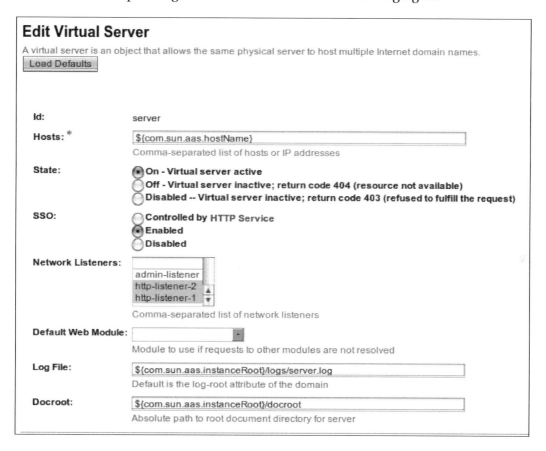

We have two other options besides leaving the **SSO** option **Disabled**, which are as follows:

- **Enabled**: Enabling the SSO for this virtual server, all applications will share the authentication token.

- **Controlled by HTTP Service**: Inheriting the SSO state from the HTTP service configuration, if it is enabled in the HTTP service level it will be enabled for the virtual server and vice versa.

In the **Additional Properties** section of the same page we can add two extra properties as follows:

- The `sso-max-inactive-seconds` property specifies the amount of time that a user's single sign-on record can stay inactive before it becomes eligible for purging. The value is specified in seconds and any request placed on any of the applications deployed in the virtual server will renew the period. Specifying a longer time will allows users to stay authenticated longer at the expense of using more of the server machine's memory. The default value for `sso-max-inactive-seconds` is 300 seconds.

- The `sso-reap-interval-seconds` property specifies the interval between expired token sweeps, with the default value as 60 seconds. Specifying a smaller interval involves more CPU time for sweeps while specifying a longer interval will leave expired tokens in the memory.

We should tune these two properties based on our user load, amount of memory, and the CPU time we can devote to SSO. The best approach is to leave the tokens valid for long as it poses no security threat. We should not let a large number of expired tokens on the server as it will increase the CPU time for purging them.

Summary

In this chapter we discussed more about GlassFish security by examining the administration security, password protection, network listener security, and by discussing the benefits of virtual servers for isolating different applications deployed in the a single machine with a single IP address. We also looked at the SSO capability of GlassFish and discussed how we can configure it to our advantage to take away from our clients the burden of going through authentication for each one of the related applications deployed in the application server.

In the next three chapters we will dig into OpenAM to further facilitate the Java EE applications and Web Services security in conjunction with providing SSO across several domains using OpenAM.

6
Introducing OpenDS: Open Source Directory Service

During the development of enterprise applications, many different requirements arise which can be addressed with a limited set of base software, but using one tool for all tasks will not result in an acceptable outcome in terms of performance, availability, end user's experience, maintenance costs, security, and so on.

One area of wide misuse is placing a database system to perform a task when a directory server can do much better. Tasks that need to share semi-static information in the enterprise can be considered tasks that a directory server performs better than a database server. Examples of these types of data can be an organization chart, subscribers, services, devices, entitlements, preferences, and so on.

This chapter covers the following topics about OpenDS:

- What a directory service is
- What OpenDS is
- Installing and administrating OpenDS
- Using OpenDS in embedded mode
- Setting up an OpenDS replication topology

Storing hierarchical information: Directory services

A **directory service** is a software system for storing directory information, which basically maps names to values. In a directory, a name can be mapped to multiple values like a word in a dictionary, which can have multiple definitions associated with it. Imagine a person in a company information book. The person may have multiple attributes to be identified, such as name, business description, phone numbers, roles, and so on. Such information is best suited to be stored in a directory service.

Back to the person's directory; each piece of information we store for a person represents an attribute of the person such as his job, address, organization, and so on. Directory services can store information in a hierarchical way, something like a tree. In this tree the person can be a leaf and the country the person is living in can be the root of the tree, while each branch of the tree represents a city and each small branch represents a street, and so on.

 We call this tree-like structure of information stored in a directory service a **Directory Information Tree (DIT)**.

Directory services are developed around the requirement of storing a set of attributes for an object in a tree system optimized for read operations. Directory services use these attributes to associate different objects to each other, like associating a set of people to an organization or a department of an organization.

Each record has a unique identifier called **Distinguished Name (DN)**. The DN is constructed from one or more of the object attributes—**Relative Distinguished Name (RDN)**, followed by its parent object DN. So, the distinguished name of an object can have one or more of its own attributes and one or more of its parent object attributes. A full path to a file represents that file's DN, while the file name or a directory name is the RDN because it is identifying the file or the directory related to its parent.

The following snippet shows how employee information is stored in a directory service:

```
dn: cn=John Doe,dc=example,dc=com
cn: John Doe
givenName: John
sn: Doe
mail: john.doe@example.com
mail: john.doe2@example.com
```

```
manager: cn=Barbara Doe,dc=example,dc=com
objectClass: inetOrgPerson
objectClass: organizationalPerson
objectClass: person
objectClass: top
```

As you can see, in the first line we have the DN of the employee, which is composed of some of his own attributes in addition to the domain name of the employer company. We also have two values for the e-mail attribute.

The `objectClass` attribute specifies which class this object belongs to so the directory server can effectively find the object, identify which attributes it has, and also check whether or not the object conforms with schema it belongs to.

In directory services, each object belongs to one or more classes. These classes are defined in schemas known to the directory server. Each class definition in the schema specifies what attributes the object must have and what are the optional attributes of the object.

Many different schemas have been defined for different industries over the years and all major directory services come bundled with important schemas. Almost all major directory services provide administration capabilities for importing new schemas and applying them on the DIT. Some example of directory services schemas are DNS, DHCP, NIS, white pages schema, and so on.

The role of directory services in IT has become bolder over the years and the standard organizations decided to define a protocol to let software systems access all directory services in a standard and unified way. So the **Internet Engineering Task Force (IETF)** and **OASIS** defined several **RFCs** and standards for making directory services compliant with each other. These standards include RFCs for **Lightweight Directory Access Protocol (LDAP, RFC 4510)**, **Data Interchange Format (RFC 2849)**, OASIS specification for **Service Provisioning Markup Language (SPML)**, **Directory Services Markup Language (DSML)**, and standard schemas which represent different types of information that can be stored in directory services.

Connecting directory services to software systems

When it become apparent that software systems need a comprehensive and yet simple way to access directory service information, LDAP standard introduced a concept letting software systems access directory service information over TCP/IP.

The LDAP standard lets client applications use directory services by asking the server to perform an operation. By default, LDAP servers accept the operation requests on port 389. The following table shows the list of mandatory operations that each LDAP server needs to implement in order to cover LDAP v3 standard operations.

Operation	Description
StartTLS	Using Transport Layer Security (TLS) extension for a secure connection.
Bind	Authenticating and specifying LDAP protocol version.
Search	Searching for and/or retrieving directory entries.
Compare	Checking whether an object contains a given attribute value.
Add, Delete, Modify an object	Adding, deleting, and modifying an object.
Modify Distinguished Name (DN)	Moving an object in the tree or modifying its DN.
Abandon	Aborting the previous operation.
Extended Operation	A generic operation to define other possible operations.
Unbind	Closing the current connection.

The operation invocation is not synchronous and clients can send multiple requests without receiving any response to the previous requests. It is not mandatory for the LDAP server to send back the responses in the same order it received the requests.

Introducing OpenDS

In the chapter introduction we saw that a directory server can be used to store hierarchical information with high number of read and small number of write or updates. Samples of these types of information can be company employees or telecom subscribers. You know that the data models for each of the mentioned items differ from each other and so there should be a way to imply some standardization on these data models to introduce some level of interoperability between directory servers. In order to provide some level of interoperability in data model level, some standards define data models for directory servers' data, for example RFC 4512 and RFC 4519.

These standard data models are called **Directory Information Tree's (DIT)** schemas and some of the popular schemas are already defined and standardized. Directory schemas are defined as object classes which can have attributes, name bindings, and namespaces. Attributes of an object class can be required or optional—the required attributes must be present in each object entry in the directory server while optional attributes can be present or not. Each object class inherits from its parent object class (and ultimately from the root of the hierarchy) which leads to adding attributes to the required/optional list of the descendant objects.

LDAP is the accepted communication protocol between a directory server and its clients. LDAP can be considered a lightweight TCP/IP-based variation of **Directory Access Protocol (DAP)** which was and is in use with OSI-layered networks in telecom systems. Interaction between client and directory server over LDAP is based on operations that the client asks the server to perform, which includes search, add, remove, bind, and so on.

OpenDS, hosted at `http://www.opends.org`, is an open source project initiated by Sun Microsystems (now sponsored by Oracle), implementing a high-end open source directory service available under CDDL license. OpenDS is heavily under development and implements all LDAP standard RFCs, plus numerous extensions (standard and experimental) in addition to secure communication, information replication, plug-ability, and DSML gateway

 We will discuss OpenDS version 2.2 in this chapter, which fully supports LDAP v3 and DSML version 2.0.

You may know that there are already some other open source directory servers available for the community, including OpenLDAP, ApacheDS, and Port 389 (formally known as **Fedora Directory Server)**, which can be used at no cost for both commercial and non-commercial deployments. Although Sun Microsystems itself has an advanced directory server product, they initiated OpenDS in August 2006 with the following goals:

- Implementing a pure Java directory service to further facilitate the platform independency and ease the maintenance

- Achieving higher performance levels required by modern applications, for both reading and writing data

- Providing commercial support for the open source product

- Using OpenDS as next version of Sun Directory Server Enterprise Edition core

- Simplifying the transition between open source products and its commercial sibling for customers

OpenDS has well designed extensibility points which lets the developers extend the functionality of the directory service in different points—from intercepting and processing the LDAP operations before they are executed by the directory server and post processing the result of an operation to adding new services in order to support a new interaction channel between OpenDS and its clients.

OpenDS supports **Simple Network Monitoring Protocol (SNMP)** in order to let system administrators monitor OpenDS in the same console that they monitor other network infrastructure. It also supports JMX to let any JMX-capable console monitor OpenDS in runtime with a very low overhead. Support for running in embedded mode, in addition to standalone mode is another nameable feature.

When we deploy a directory server in standalone mode, we usually need the directory server to be always available and disaster-proof. OpenDS **Multi-Master Replication** helps us to set up a highly available directory service, which guarantees the availability of service and integrity of data. The following table shows some other outstanding OpenDS features and a brief explanation of each feature.

Feature	Explanation
LDAP v3 support for core operations.	Support for all core LDAP v3 operations, including search, bind, modify, add, delete, modify DN, compare, abandon, and extended operations.
Support for a number of standards or experimental controls. Controls can be included in requests to ask the server for additional processing. Each additional processing capability is called a **control**.	Including proxied authorization, persistent search, LDAP pre-read and post-read controls, LDAP assertions, retrieving matched values, paged results, authorization identity request, password policy controls, and account usability controls.
Support for some of **Simple Authentication and Security Layer (SASL)** authentication mechanism with possibility to add other mechanisms.	Supported mechanisms include: **ANONYMOUS, CRAM-MD5, DIGEST-MD5, EXTERNAL, GSSAPI**, and **PLAIN**.
Server extendibility and plugability.	It is possible to extend the server capability by: • Adding new schema and data types. • Pre- and post-processing of the operations and their results. • Password-related operations and functionalities. • Adding new services for new types of communication protocols.

Feature	Explanation
Recurring tasks.	Recurring tasks allow an administrator to schedule repeated tasks such as backup.
OpenDS complies with password policy implementation draft.	Some of OpenDS supported policies are: • Password complexity requirements. • Password history and age. • Account lockout conditions.
Already implemented and possibility to add more Extended operations.	Implemented passwords modify, and cancel extended operations.
Support for StartTLS and SASL encryption.	Possibility to use X.509 certificate for client and server authentication and SSL for a transport security, StartTLS is an extended operation.
Access Controls using **ACL**.	**Access Control Lists (ACL)** in OpenDS allow controlling who has access to what, from a subtree, down to specific values of an attribute, and the kind of access—read, search, write, and so on.
Fractional replication.	Possibility to specify which attributes to include or exclude in replication.
The binary transfer option is now supported.	Supports binary transport option for transporting binary data.

Understanding OpenDS backend and services

Directory services need to store their data into some kind of storage that is fast to read, filter, and locate operations based on the hierarchical nature of directory services' stored data. This storage usually consists of several sections which are called **backend** and each backend is target storage for a specific prefix of data hierarchy. By default OpenDS uses **Berkeley DB Java Edition** (http://www.oracle. com/database/berkeley-db.html) as a data store and retrieval framework because of its good write performance characteristics, high granularity of record locking, and efficiency in reading, filtering, and locating data.

OpenDS is a directory service implementation and based on the vast use cases of directory services it needs to be highly flexible in the way that it communicates with its clients. To address this requirement OpenDS uses an extendable architecture for handling client connections. OpenDS architecture allows adding new connection handlers in order to support new communication protocols. So far OpenDS supports LDAP for accessing the directory information and JMX, and SNMP for monitoring and administration purposes. There are some SPIs available for adding new communication protocols. For example, we can develop a connection handler for DNS, which will access the directory tree information to perform a DNS search.

Installing and administrating OpenDS

The first step in using any server-side software is knowledge of the installation procedure and some basic administration experience, which helps in performing certain tasks to keep a test server up and running.

Installing OpenDS and DSML gateway

In this section we will look at OpenDS and DSML gateway system requirements and the installation process. I have concisely described the installation process in order to have enough space for more advanced topics.

Understanding the system requirements

The OpenDS system requirements may amaze you as they are the minimal requirement for a Java application. The requirements are as follows:

- Any operating system with at least JRE 1.5.8. The latest version of Java 6 JRE is recommended for better performances.

- For replicated topologies high speed, and low latency network can further accelerate the operations.

Downloading and installing OpenDS server

OpenDS installation is possible using Java Web Start enabled setup program but we manually download and install the ZIP file to lift the Internet connection requirement for later installation. Installing OpenDS server requires some steps as follows:

1. Download `OpenDS-2.2.0.zip` from `https://www.opends.org/promoted-builds/2.2.0/OpenDS-2.2.0.zip`, and extract it in a directory for which you have execute permission over.

2. Open a shell window (cmd in Windows or a terminal instance in Unix-based systems) and switch to the directory that you extracted the OpenDS archive file. Execute ./setup or setup.bat depending on your operating system.

3. Bypass the **Welcome** screen, the real installation process begins where we provide basic information like hostname, LDAP communication port, Distinguished Names (DN) for root user who administrate the directory server, and its password. You can use following information to ensure that all sample commands work without any change.

   ○ **Root user DN**: cn=gf admin
   ○ **Password**: admin
   ○ **LDAP listener port**: 1389

 Using admin as the password is only for the sake of simplicity. In a production environment it is better to use a complex password which has at least six alphanumeric and some special characters like @#$%^&*.

LDAP **well-known** port is 389 (and 636 for LDAPS). However, since these ports are under 1024 and considered privileged ports they can only be opened and used by applications with specific privileges, for example the Unix root user, or Windows Administrator. For developers, the use of these ports is cumbersome and OpenDS detects the lack of privileges and offers by default to use ports 1389 and 1636. Note that 389 is also often used on Windows by Active Directory and installing OpenDS on this port is not possible in default Windows Server installations.

4. Now we need to configure the LDAP to enable the secure communication using SSL or TLS, so press the **Configure** button and select the following:

   ○ **Enable SSL on port 1636**
   ○ **Enable StartTLS for LDAP**
   ○ **Generate Self Signed certificate**

5 In the **Directory Data** page just make sure to use dc=glassfish,dc=book as the **Directory Base DN** and also make sure to check **Only Create the Base Entry** option. When installation finishes, the installer will show a report page containing information related to the installation. Here we can click on the **Launch Control Panel** button to open the OpenDS control panel. A dialog will ask you for the **Bind DN** and **Password**, which we specified in the installation process as cn=gf admin and admin.

Differences between X.509 certificate stores

Whenever we use SSL or TLS we need to provide a digital certificate, which will be used during the handshake, self-identification, and encryption of shared secret. Usually when we work in development stage we use self-signed certificates which are stored in Java keystore (jks) file and are not signed by any certificate authority. But in a production environment we should not use JKS files as it is a proprietary Java format and not a standard file format. Instead we should use **PKCS** #12-compliant certification storage file or **PKCS #11** hardware token to provide the server with the required certificate.

Usually in production either we use an internal certificate authority which can be an installation of EJBCA for all digital certificate required functionalities of the enterprise or we can buy required digital certificates from other CAs.

The installation can also be done from the command line. Invoke the following command where we extracted OpenDS ZIP file to install the directory server and start it afterward.

```
./setup --cli -n -b "dc=glassfish,dc=book" -a -p 1389  --
adminConnectorPort 4444 -D "cn=gf admin"  -w "admin" -q -Z 1636 --
generateSelfSignedCertificate
```

The following figure shows the OpenDS control panel. This panel can be used for managing OpenDS to some extent. As you can see both LDAP and LDAPS are enabled based on our configuration in previous steps. SNMP and JMX Connection Handlers are disabled; we will discuss enabling JMX Connection Handlers in subsequent sections of this chapter.

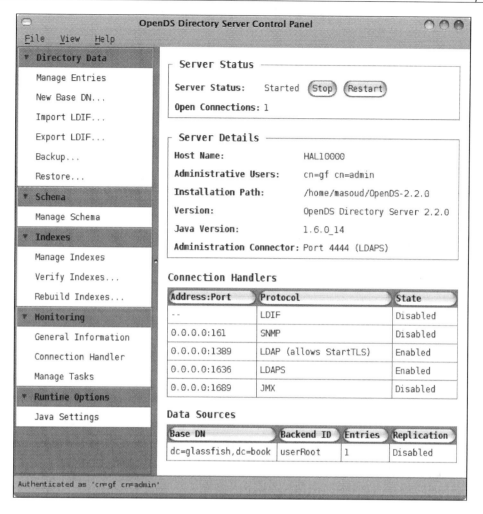

As you can see in the above figure, the control panel provides a rich set of administration and management functionalities including but not limited to:

- Creating backups and restoring them
- Starting and stopping the server
- Importing and exporting compressed and uncompressed LDIF files
- Managing directory server's data
- Schema management
- Index management

We can use the control panel to connect to remote OpenDS servers for administrating and managing the remote servers.

Studying the OpenDS directory structure

Inside the OpenDS installation directory there are several subdirectories that we need to know in order to get better understanding of OpenDS. The following table shows important directories that reside inside the installation directory of OpenDS, along with a concise description about them.

Directory name	Directory description
bin	Contains scripts for performing daily tasks like starting the directory server. It's target users are Unix-based users.
bat	Contains batch files for performing daily tasks like starting the directory server. It's target users are Windows users.
db	Contains all default backend data files.
logs	All logs including error, access, and so on are stored in this directory.
config	All configuration-related files and folders are stored in this directory.
changelogDb	If the installation acts as a replication server then this directory contains replication-related database files.

To summon the control panel mentioned in the previous section we can execute control panel script, from one of bin or bat directories according to our operating system.

Installing and configuring the DSML gateway

As you already know, we can interact with OpenDS using DSML which defined an XML schema for sending operations to directory servers and getting the operation result back as an XML document.

To interact with OpenDS by using DSML we need to deploy and configure a gateway which acts as an XML to LDAP converter. This converter is called DSML gateway and is a web application available at https://www.opends.org/promoted-builds/2.2.0/OpenDS-2.2.0-DSML.war. To deploy the application you can use the following command when GlassFish is running:

```
./asadmin deploy --port 4848 --host 127.0.0.1 --user admin OpenDS-2.2.0-
DSML.war
```

After you deploy the web application, you will need to configure it to connect to OpenDS instance that you want to communicate with using DSML. For configuring the DSML gateway you need to change the values of `ldap.host` and `ldap.port` in the DSML web application's `web.xml` file. The designated `web.xml` file is located at `domain_dir/applications/OpenDS-2.2.0-DSML/WEB-INF`. To change the values, just open the file and change them with your OpenDS installation details.

Testing the DSML Gateway

To test the DSML gateway we can use any DSML-compliant console, such as **JXplorer** which is available at `http://www.jxplorer.org`. The following figure shows what connection attributes we should use to connect to the DSML gateway using JXplorer:

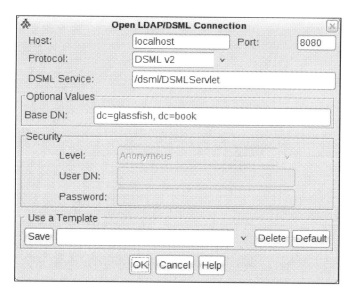

We cannot add new entries to directory server or update any object as the connected user (`anonymous`) does not have the privileges required to update the directory server content. DSML has no restrictions over the useable operations, but JXplorer 3.2.1 does not support authentication over DSML, which leads to using `anonymous` user who has no privileges.

Some other DSML tools are as follows:

- The DSML Tools suite hosted at `http://www.dsmltools.org/`
- Sun **Directory Server Resource Kit (DSRK)** available at: `http://www.sun.com/software/products/directory_srvr_ee/resource_kit/index.xml`
- The `dsmlsearch` and `dsmlmodify` utilities of OpenDS

Administrating and managing OpenDS

OpenDS provides many useful scripts and utilities that help us with the administrative tasks. One set of these scripts deal with tasks related to server lifecycle management. The following table includes this set of commands along with their explanation.

Command script file	Description
status	A console that shows server status along with some useful details. It can be executed in both interactive or script-friendly mode which allows its inclusion inside other scripts.
start-ds	Starting the directory service, provides some flexibility switches like -N.
stop-ds	Stopping the directory service, provides some flexibility switches like -Q.
ldapsearch	Searching the OpenDS tree for specific entries.
backup	Creating backup from one or more backend. These backups can be restored using the restore command.
restore	Restoring a backend backup created with the backup command.
dsconfig	We can define the configuration for the directory server.
control-panel	Launch the OpenDS control panel.
dsreplication	Setting up, managing, and monitoring replications topologies.

To run a script in Unix and Linux use a terminal and navigate to the bin directory inside the installation folder and use ./command_name to execute the command. For Windows, open a command window, navigate to the bat directory, and execute the batch files by calling them. There are several other utilities present in the bin or bat directories, you can try them with -h or --help to see what you can do with them, and what parameters they take.

Importing and exporting data

Usually we import information into the directory server from another source, which can be an LDIF file exported from another directory server. In this section, we will see how easily we can import an LDIF file into the OpenDS database and later on export a subsequent of the directory server database into an LDIF file. In order to be able to import an LDIF file into the directory server we should have some basic information about LDIF file content's format. The following listing shows a sample LDIF file content:

```
dn: dc=glassfish,dc=book
objectClass: top
objectClass: domain
dc: glassfish

dn: cn=Thomas Quist,dc=glassfish,dc=book
objectclass: person
objectclass: organizationalPerson
objectclass: inetOrgPerson
objectclass: top
cn: Thomas Quist
description: Seaman Quist
givenname: Thomas
mail: tquist@royalnavy.mod.uk
manager: cn=Horatio Hornblower,ou=people,dc=glassfish,dc=book
sn: Quist
uid: tquist
userpassword:: myPassWord
```

As you can see, the content of LDIF file is plain text attribute, value pairs. At the first highlighted line we define root DN, then we have a blank line which indicates that the current object is finished and another object is going to begin in the next line. Later on at the second highlighted line we have a second-level object, which is going to be inserted as an immediate child of the root object. Finally, at the last highlighted line we have the userpassword attribute whose value is expressed in plain text; later on we will see that OpenDS stores a hashed representation of this plain text value for increased security.

Having users' password in plain text in a file (LDIF for that matter) is not a good security practice. OpenDS can accept hashed representations with some configuration tuning. Generally setting clear text passwords in LDIF should only be used for demo purpose or for setting an initial passwords to users who MUST change it as soon as possible. For more information about using hashed password in LDIF files check `http://blogs.sun.com/Ludo/entry/opends_tips_importing_ldif_with`.

The above listing includes an entry for adding new root DN. If we try to import this listing into our OpenDS instance we will face an error indicating that the entry `dc=glassfish, dc=book` cannot be added because an object with that name already exists and duplication is not allowed in directory servers. LDIF files can become complex when we use them to change attributes' values, add new attributes, remove object or attributes, and so on.

Importing LDIF files

In the archive file containing sample code for this book you can find an LDIF file located inside the `chapter06` directory. The file name is `import.ldif` and we can import it into our OpenDS installation by invoking the following command when we are in the `bin` directory of OpenDS installation:

```
./import-ldif -h localhost -p 4444 -D "cn=gf admin" -w admin -b
dc=glassfish,dc=book -n userRoot --trustAll  -l /path/to/import.ldif -R
/path/to/rejects.ldif
```

All three lines indicate one single command for importing an LDIF file into an OpenDS instance with its administration handler listening on `localhost:4444` with `cn=gf admin` as its administration DN and `admin` as its administration password. If any entry gets rejected, the rejected entries will be stored inside `rejects.ldif` file. The `import-ldif` command accepts many parameters and has many features like scheduled import, filtered import, headless import using a properties file, and so on.

Note with the `import.ldif` file you should not have any entry rejected. So the `rejects.ldif` should remain empty.

There is an alternative way which we can use for loading a high volume of data in offline mode. The command usage is as follows:

```
./import-ldif -b dc=glassfish,dc=book -n userRoot -l /path/to/import.ldif
```

Exporting database content into LDIF file

Exporting database content is as simple as importing it. The following command shows how we export the content of the OpenDS database:

```
./export-ldif -h 127.0.0.1 -p 4444 -D "cn=gf admin" -w admin -b
dc=glassfish,dc=book -n userRoot --trustAll  -l export.ldif
```

If you open the exported file and take a closer look you can see that the `userpassword` attribute is not the same as what we provided and instead they are hashed and the hash value is stored in the directory server database. This command has the same flexibilities that `import-ldif` command has, with functionalities like scheduled export, filtered export, and so on.

Backing up and restoring data

When we are dealing with a mass of data, we should have some plans which guarantee the availability of our system to its clients in case of any failure on the server side. With LDAP directory servers in general, and OpenDS in particular, this is achieved using Multi-Master Replication. The disaster recovery plans usually have at least two sub-plans including:

1. Backup strategy that includes a schedule for creating backups, type of backup (full, incremental, and so on), schedule for checking backup copies, purging strategy for old backups, and so on.

2. Disaster recovery plan which includes two sub-plans, including disaster recovery itself and a database restore plan. The former describes how to quickly set up another data center and the later one describe how to restore the data center's state to what it was before the disaster.

Defining these strategies is out of this chapter's scope because many factors like redundancy of the infrastructure, replication topology, number of slaves and masters in the topology, amount of traffic on the topology instance, storage type, and many more affect the backup strategy and recovery plans. However, we will discuss how we can create full and incremental backups and how we can recover the state of the server using these backups.

Creating a backup of OpenDS data

Here we will discuss which parts of OpenDS need to be backed up, what the reason for creating the backup is, and how we can create the backup. The following table shows what should be backed up and why.

Data stores	Backup
Backend	All directory service information is stored in backend (refer to the table on the next page). Backend resides in db directory which is mentioned in table (as mentioned in the table under *Studying OpenDS directory structure* section).
Configurations, including server settings that are stored in config. ldif, which reside inside the config directory, schemas that the directory supports, and so on.	All OpenDS configurations including security settings, replication, supported schemas, and so on are stored inside the config.ldif file and config folder.
Tasks	All scheduled tasks need to be backed up, in order to make it possible to restore the directory server to its backup time state. Tasks are stored in a designated backend mentioned in table (refer to the table on the next page).

The above table describes data stores that should be backed up in order to be able to recover a single server's state in case of a disaster. At least creating two types of backups should be supported by any software that acts as data storage, full and incremental. The full backup creates a backup from the entire database, which can be resource consuming in term of the time that the operation takes and required space that it needs to store the backups. The other type is incremental backup, which is from all data we saved after the last backup operation.

 OpenDS has an automated archival for the config.ldif files whenever there is a change in the configuration. Take a look at the config/archived-configs/ folder to see all previous instances of the file. This mechanism provides an auditing log of the changes in the config, and allows us to restore a known working configuration at any point.

To perform a full backup, with compression enabled to reduce the backup size and encryption enabled to make backups secure, we can issue a command like:

```
./backup -h localhost -p 1389 -D "cn=gf admin" -w admin --backUpAll --
compress --hash --signHash --encrypt --backupID first-backup-after-data-
load-091231 --backupDirectory /path/to/backups/directory
```

The simplest command to create a backup is:
`./backup -a -d /path/to/backups/directory`

This command creates a backup of all backend of the directory server running on `localhost`, which can be replaced by the corresponding server's IP address; it encrypts the backup information and gives the backup our designated ID. Backup IDs can be used to simply ask the `restore` script to restore the system to a state equal with the given ID's backup state.

To create an incremental backup we should let the backup script have access to latest backup we, created to make it possible for it to determine which portions of data has changed since the previous backup. A sample command for creating an incremental backup can be similar to:

```
./backup --backUpAll --incremental  --incrementalBaseID first-backup-
after-data-load-091231 --compress --backupDirectory /path/to/backups/
directory
```

These two commands create backups from all available backend. For creating a backup from one backend we can replace `--backUpAll` switch with `--backendID backend_ID`. Creating incremental backup from a single backend requires at least one full or incremental backup from the same backend to be available in the backups directory.

OpenDS installation creates seven different backend which are described in the following table.

Back-end	Description
userRoot	User entered information.
adminRoot	Administration-related information, like privileged users and so on.
monitor	Monitoring information is stored in this backend. This backend is accessible by SNMP and JMX clients in read-only mode.
task	Scheduled tasks like backup, restore, and so on are stored in this backend.
ads-truststore	X.509 certificates are stored in this backend.
backup	Information about backups are stored in this backend.
schema	All supported and available schema information is stored here.

The `backup` command is flexible enough to let us perform a variety of tasks like listing, compressing, encrypting the backup content, scheduling the backup operations, and many others. To see the full list of backup utility functionalities take a look at the result of executing the `./backup --help` command.

Restoring server state using backups

Restoring backup is a bit more complex because we simply cannot restore all backend at the same time. The `restore` command can be used to see information about the available backups in the backup directory. Usually we check available backups to decide which backup we should use before we commence with a restore operation. The following command shows how we check for available backups. The command which can be used to view available backups for `userRoot` backend is similar to:

```
./restore --listBackups --backupDirectory path/to/backups/directory/
userRoot
```

The following figure shows what can be a possible outcome of querying the list of available backups:

```
Backup ID:            first-backup-after-data-load-091231
Backup Date:          01/Jan/2010:02:20:39 +0330
Is Incremental:       false
Is Compressed:        true
Is Encrypted:         true
Has Unsigned Hash:    true
Has Signed Hash:      false
Dependent Upon:       none

Backup ID:            201001010022045
Backup Date:          01/Jan/2010:02:21:18 +0330
Is Incremental:       true
Is Compressed:        true
Is Encrypted:         false
Has Unsigned Hash:    false
Has Signed Hash:      false
Dependent Upon:       first-backup-after-data-load-091231
```

You can see that we made two backups with different attributes:

- The first one is a full backup and is encrypted, compressed, and carries a hash digest for its integrity checking.
- The last one is incremental and compressed, but not encrypted. The incremental backup is based on the full backup I made earlier.

For the first backup we used a manually assigned backup ID, which can help us determine the database state when we performed the backup. In the second backup we can see an automatically assigned backup ID, which is hard to use to deduce anything about the backup content. The first backup ID is the result of using `--backupID` when we were performing the full backup.

In the previous command we added the backend name after the backup directory name. It means that we need to see information about the backups available for this backend, which are stored in a directory with the same name in the `backups` directory.

After looking at available backups we can select one and restore the backend information to the state stored in that particular backup. The following command restores `userRoot` backend to the state stored in before upgrade backup.

```
./restore  --backupID first-backup-after-data-load-091231--
backupDirectory backup/path/to/backups/directory/userRoot
```

 Best option is to restore all backend to the same states in order to prevent any conflict between the way that data is stored and the way that OpenDS is configured to deal with the data.

Enabling JMX Connection Handler

We saw that OpenDS is an extensible directory service implementation. One extensibility point of OpenDS is Connection Handlers, which lets developers develop their own channel of communication with OpenDS core. There are several Connection Handlers already included in OpenDS. To see included Connection Handlers, open the OpenDS control panel by executing the `control-panel` script which is available in the `bin` directory of OpenDS installation.

We can also use the `status cli` to view the status information as follows:

```
./status -n
```

This command shows the same information as in main screen of the control panel. A sample output for this command is shown in the following figure:

```
masoud@HAL10000: ~/C
masoud@HAL10000: ~/OpenDS-2.2.0
masoud@HAL10000: ~/
masoud@HAL10000:~/OpenDS-2.2.0/bin$ ./status -n

          --- Server Status ---
Server Run Status:      Started
Open Connections:       0

          --- Server Details ---
Host Name:              HAL10000
Administrative Users:   cn=gf admin
Installation Path:      /home/masoud/OpenDS-2.2.0
Version:                OpenDS Directory Server 2.2.0
Java Version:           <not available> (*)
Administration Connector: Port 4444 (LDAPS)

          --- Connection Handlers ---
Address:Port : Protocol                : State
-------------:------------------------:---------
--           : LDIF                    : Disabled
0.0.0.0:161  : SNMP                    : Disabled
0.0.0.0:1389 : LDAP (allows StartTLS)  : Enabled
0.0.0.0:1636 : LDAPS                   : Enabled
0.0.0.0:1689 : JMX                     : Disabled

          --- Data Sources ---
Base DN:     dc=gf,dc=book
Backend ID:  userRoot
Entries:     <not available> (*)
Replication: Disabled

* Information only available if you provide valid authentication information
when launching the status command.
```

By looking at the above figure you can see that the only enabled Connection Handlers are LDAP and LDAPS. Now to enable the JMX Connection Handler we can use the following command:

```
./dsconfig set-connection-handler-prop -D "cn=gf admin" -w admin --
handler-name "JMX Connection Handler" --set enabled:true --set listen-
port:1689 -n
```

This command will simply enable and configure the JMX Connection Handler, which lets JMX-enabled applications connect to OpenDS to view monitoring statistics. Monitoring statistics are stored in the `monitor` backend which is the only backend that JMX client can access. In order to access this backend we should define a user with required permissions. For example the following command grants the read, write, and notify privileges to root DN such as `cn=gf admin`.

```
./dsconfig set-root-dn-prop  -D "cn=gf admin" -w admin --add default-
root-privilege-name:jmx-read --add default-root-privilege-name:jmx-write
--add default-root-privilege-name:jmx-notify -n
```

Now we can use JConsole (included with JDK) to monitor a running OpenDS instance. Username and password would be the same as root DN and its password. The JMX URL is `service:jmx:rmi:///jndi/rmi://127.0.0.1:1689/org.opends.server.protocols.jmx.client-unknown`

The following figure shows the JConsole connected to OpenDS server:

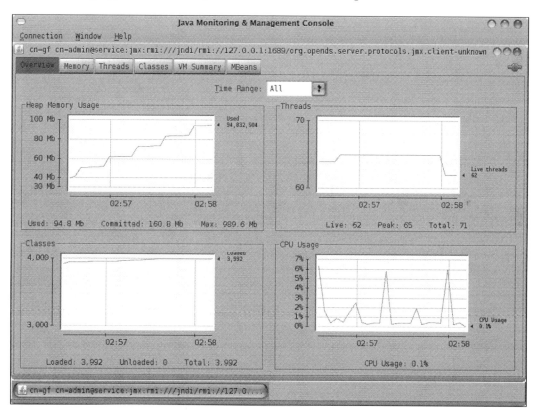

VisualVM can also be used to manage and monitor OpenDS using JMX; check VisualVM at `http://visualvm.dev.java.net/` or just try to execute it by finding it inside your JDK `bin` directory.

 VisualVM is bundled with JDK since JDK 6 update 10. If you have an older JDK version you should either update to the new version or you can download the VisualVM from its website.

Embedding OpenDS

A Java application can embed the OpenDS JAR files and thus run the service in the same JVM. When doing so, the client application is also in charge of the OpenDS directory server lifecycle. We discussed benefits and possible reasons for using embedded software in the first section of this chapter. So let's go straight into the details of running OpenDS in embedded mode.

Benefits of embedded mode capability of OpenDS

Being able to run OpenDS in embedded mode means the client application and the directory server are running within the same JVM which leads to the possibility of having specific kinds of use cases, along with many benefits including:

1. Developing an LDAP-dependent packaged application without need to install a directory service in the user environment.

2. Making the installation easy by removing the configuration required for the software to interact with an external directory server.

3. Providing users with default configuration and dataset right after installation for testing purposes or for providing default operational configuration and dataset.

4. Using less memory by utilizing the same JVM by application and directory server.

5. Providing LDAP directory services as a web application, allowing deployment like the other elements of the J2EE applications.

Preparing the environment

Before we can use any Java framework or application, we should let JVM have access to that particular application's libraries (simple JAR files or classless packages) and some required configuration files and operational directories, which will be used by the software.

Using embedded OpenDS in any standard, web, or enterprise application, requires two needs to be satisfied. These needs are:

- We should add the JAR files included in the OpenDS `lib` folder to our class path.

- We should copy locks, logs, db, and `config` directories from the OpenDS installation directory to our application root directory. These directories are discussed in the second table of this chapter.

It is better that you copy these folders from a newly-installed OpenDS instance to avoid copying inappropriate configuration and dependencies such as replication settings. If you are installing a new OpenDS instance make sure that you import the LDIF file mentioned in the first section of this chapter in order to be able to run the sample embedded core successfully. The following listing shows how we can use embedded OpenDS in our Java application.

The first step of using embedded is specifying the path to the root directory of designated OpenDS installation, in the following snippet it is `/home/masoud/ EmOpenDS`. Then we need to specify the path to `config.ldif` file, and we want to use to bootstrap the embedded instance using it. We should also deactivate the Connection Handlers. The directory server can then only be used from within this application and no connection will be accepted over network.

```
String projectRootDirectory = System.getProperty("/home/masoud/
EmOpenDS");
DirectoryEnvironmentConfig envConfig = new
DirectoryEnvironmentConfig();
envConfig.setServerRoot(new File(projectRootDirectory));
envConfig.setConfigFile(new File("config", "config.ldif"));
envConfig.setDisableConnectionHandlers(true);
```

Later on we can use some provided utility class to check the instance status and start it if it was not already started using the same environment that we described above.

```
if (!EmbeddedUtils.isRunning()) {
    EmbeddedUtils.startServer(envConfig);
}
```

After starting the server we can either get a connection using the root DN or any other DN which is authorized to connect to directory server. Now having an authorized connection, we can perform any LDAP operation that we need. Our sample code performs a search operation using the `uid` attribute.

```
InternalClientConnection IConn = InternalClientConnection.
getRootConnection();
InternalSearchOperation searchOperation = IConn.processSearch("dc=glas
sfish,dc=book", SearchScope.WHOLE_SUBTREE, "(uid=tquist)");

   for (SearchResultEntry matchingEntry :
     searchOperation.getSearchEntries()) {
       for (Attribute attr : matchingEntry.getAttributes()) {
           System.out.println(attr.getName() + ":" +
             attr.getValues().toString());
       }
   }
```

Finally we should stop the embedded server if we do not need it anymore.

```
if(EmbeddedUtils.isRunning())
EmbeddedUtils.stopServer("glassfish.book.ch06.EmbeddedOpenDS", "We are
finished with demo");
```

We are passing two informative parameters to the `stopServer` method. The first parameter is name of the class that stopped the server and the second parameter is a string representing the reason for stopping it.

The following figure shows what the result of executing the above listing is. As you can see we printed all the attributes of an LDAP object.

```
givenName:[Thomas]
uid:[tquist]
description:[Seaman Quist]
cn:[Thomas Quist]
sn:[Quist]
userPassword:[{SSHA}rHXb0KFvwLfERWn5qFzpx1fES3UVx0tmdFF8hg==]
mail:[tquist@royalnavy.mod.uk]
manager:[cn=Horatio Hornblower,ou=people,o=sevenSeas]
```

This example uses the OpenDS internal APIs. It is possible to use JNDI or Netscape LDAP SDK to embed OpenDS. For more information look at:
- `http://java.sun.com/products/jndi/tutorial/`
- `http://www.mozilla.org/directory/`

Some attributes have multiple values, which is one of directory services features. OpenDS default access control rules only allows the root DN and the user himself to read the `userPassword` attribute.

In the embedded mode, we start the instance when we start the application and we do not stop it until we are sure that we do not use it anymore. OpenDS might be in use by multiple services in our application or it might be configured to replicate the data tree with some other instances, which requires it to be running to keep it synchronized with other instances. Another reason can be the amount of time required for starting the embedded OpenDS instance, which is relatively long and can introduce delays in our application routines.

Replicating Directory Information Tree (DIT)

Directory servers are used to share semi-static information across the enterprise and they should be reliable during peak times and possible disaster. OpenDS is equipped with Multi-Master Replication capability, which lets the directory service infrastructure have multiple **read and write** instances.

In directory servers' world we have both partitioning and replication concepts, which are similar to the concepts available in the relational database world. In the world of directory servers, partitioning concept is called **distribution**. The term replication is used to indicate that the same DIT is copied to another directory server for redundancy and throughput improvement. The term distribution is used to indicate that multiple directory servers, that hold different subtrees of the entire DIT, are running to form a distributed directory service. Directory instances that form the distributed directory server can be governed by different authority. A sample of distributed directory service is **Domain Name System (DNS)** itself.

OpenDS provides the possibility to form both distributed directory service and replicated directory service infrastructure. In this section we briefly discuss how its replication system works and how we can set up a replicated directory service infrastructure.

OpenDS replication mechanism

A sample schema showing OpenDS replication infrastructure is shown in the following figure. As you can see in the figure, three directory servers replicate information between each other while a load balancer balances the incoming requests between them. OpenDS replication's internal mechanism is a bit more complex because OpenDS servers may act as directory servers, replication servers, or as both. In the figure below all server instances are working both as replication server and directory server.

A replication topology requires each replication topology member to perform certain tasks. The important tasks each member should perform are as follows:

- Forwarding changes from one directory server to all other connected directory and replication servers
- Keeping each newly-joined or failed and rejoined directory server or replication server information up-to-date with the current state or database

The **load balancer** can be any **layer four** load balancer, which can simply distribute the incoming requests between different server instances to ensure that all healthy servers receive as many requests as they can handle.

 Some vendors such as Oracle/Sun have directory proxy server products that are able to provide Application level (LDAP) load balancing and advanced LDAP routing capabilities. More information is available at `http://www.sun.com/software/products/directory_srvr_ ee/dir_proxy/index.xml`.

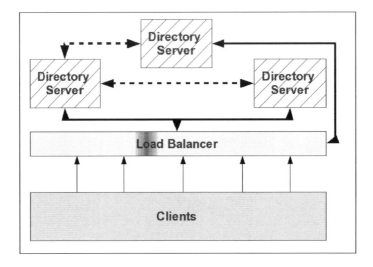

OpenDS replication operates in two different modes, which are as follows:

- **Asynchronous replication**: Clients receive acknowledgements as soon as the server that they are connected to persists the changes made by the client in its backend. The server will send the change notifications to other members of the replication topology asynchronously.

- **Assured replication**: Assured replication guarantees that the changes are propagated to a predefined number of servers or all servers in the replication group before the client receives an acknowledgement confirming the change it made. The assured replication mode mimics the synchronous replication model to some extent. Note that assured replication is not fully transactional.

Setting up an Asynchronous replication infrastructure

To setup a directory server infrastructure we can use a graphical installer or the `dsreplication` command, which is more flexible in term of turning a standalone server to a replication infrastructure's member.

We have already installed one instance of OpenDS. Install another instance in the same machine or any other machine with network access to the first machine and start it using either control panel or `start-ds` script. I assume that we installed the second instance in the same machine that we have the first instance and the second instance administration is `2444`, its root DN is `cn=gf admin`, and its password is `admin`.

Open a console (`gnome-terminal`, `cmd`) window and navigate to the `bin` directory of the OpenDS instance which we installed first. For creating an infrastructure of two directory server's, use following steps:

1. We need to set up the replication, so execute the following command in the terminal window:

```
./dsreplication enable   --host1 127.0.0.1 --port1 4444 --
bindDN1 "cn=gf admin"   --bindPassword1 admin --replicationPort1
18989   --host2 127.0.0.1 --port2 2444 --bindDN2 "cn=gf admin" --
bindPassword2 admin  --replicationPort2 28989  --adminUID admin --
adminPassword admin --baseDN "dc=glassfish,dc=book"
```

The command will start an interactive script which will ask for some configuration information like whether we need cryptography over our replication communication or not. Make sure that you can remember the global administration password; for the sake of simplicity enter `admin` as the password and continue with the script until the script execution finishes. The global administrative account created when setting up a replication topology is replicated and shared across all instances in that topology and can be used to apply commands to multiple servers (or the whole set of servers), like `initialize`.

> When setting the replication topology on our desktop machine we can use `127.0.0.1` to test the replication but when we are setting up a production replication we need to replace the `127.0.0.1` or `localhost` with the actual IP addresses or names of the server on which OpenDS instances are running.

2. Now we need to initialize the new member of our replication infrastructure with all the data that the old server has; just run the following command and initialization of new server will be done:

```
./dsreplication initialize --baseDN "dc=glassfish,dc=book" --
adminUID admin    --adminPassword admin --hostSource 127.0.0.1 --
portSource 4444    --hostDestination 127.0.0.1 --portDestination
2444
```

In the above command we only initialized one instance by using the `initialize` subcommand and providing the destination instance connection information. If we set up a large replication topology we can use the `initialize-all` command to initialize all of the replication members with the information stored in the current instance's backend.

To monitor the replication infrastructure we can use the `dsreplication` command. It lets us see which servers are up, and what is the status of each server. A sample command for viewing the servers' status can be similar to:

```
./dsreplication status -h 127.0.0.1 -p 4444 --adminUID admin --
adminPassword admin
```

Testing the replication setup is very easy. In order to test your replication installation and configuration you can connect to one of the replication members using JXplorer and remove or update an object in that directory server instance, and then after you connect to the other replication member you will see the change.

You can also shut down a replication member and change some entries in other members. After you start the unavailable member of the replication you can see that all changes will propagate to the newly-started member.

There are two interactive commands in OpenDS which can help administrators in many ways. These commands are `dsreplication` for helping administrators with replication-related configuration and tasks and `dsconfig` for general configuration of an OpenDS installation.

Now you are ready to start your exploration in the OpenDS world, as there are many configuration parameters and helper scripts available in the `bin` directory of your OpenDS installation. You already know how to install, administrate, manage, and set up a replication infrastructure for OpenDS.

Summary

OpenDS is one of the most ambitious directory service projects because of its fast development, versatile features, and full compliance with LDAPv3 directory server, implementing all standards along with experimental RFCs and extensions. In addition to being standard-compliant it provides lots of very useful features and a promising roadmap towards new features which can be another reason for using it in our infrastructure.

Installing OpenDS is possible using a Java Web Start-enabled installer or by using the provided ZIP bundle when there is no Internet connection present. OpenDS provides lots of very useful features which can help developers and administrators realize their infrastructure topology easier than compared to using similar products. In this chapter we learned what a directory service is and what set of features OpenDS provides us. We studied installing, administrating, and monitoring OpenDS. Finally, we discussed how we can use OpenDS in embedded mode and set up a replication topology to ensure the service and data availability in the case of unpredicted disasters like hard disk breakdown.

7
OpenSSO, the Single sign-on Solution

OpenSSO is the answer to many complexities that have emerged during recent years because of the complexity and dynamicity of the security functionality required for software systems. The complexity in software security increases as a result of the increase in complexity of security requirements of the target business that the software should drive and diversity in the integration between different partner's software systems that collaborate to complete a client request.

An example of such system is integration between an online shopping system, the product provider who actually produces the goods, the insurance company that provides insurance on purchases, and finally the shipping company that delivers the goods to the consumers' hand. All of these systems access some parts of the data, which flows into the other software to perform its job in an efficient way. All the employees can benefit from a **single sign-on** solution, which keeps them free from having to authenticate themselves multiple times during the working day.

Another example can be a travel portal, whose clients need to communicate with many other systems to plan their traveling. Integration between an in-house system and external partners can happen in different levels, from communication protocol and data format to security policies, authentication, and authorization. Because of the variety of communication models, policies, and client types that each partner may use, unifying the security model is almost impossible and the urge for some kind of integration mechanism shows itself bolder and bolder.

SSO as a concept and OpenSSO as a product address this urge for integrating the systems' security together. In this chapter we are going to learn the following topics:

- What SSO is
- What OpenSSO is
- Installing and configuring OpenSSO
- Understanding different methods of using OpenSSO
- Using Identity Services for authentication, authorization, and SSO

Let's begin with learning more about SSO in general.

What is SSO

The urge for security integration solutions resulted in different concepts for resolving different parts of the problem:

- **Single sign-on (SSO)**: Introduced to provide the required mechanisms for letting users sign-on into one system and stay authenticated between circles of different software systems, which have agreed upon accepting each others' users identity. The SSO server just provides the authentication header which confirms that the user is authenticated. The following figure further describes the SSO concept.

In conjunction with SSO you may see or hear the cross domain SSO or simply **CDSSO**, which refers to using the same authentication token across multiple security domains—for example, between www.domain2.com and www.domain2.com.

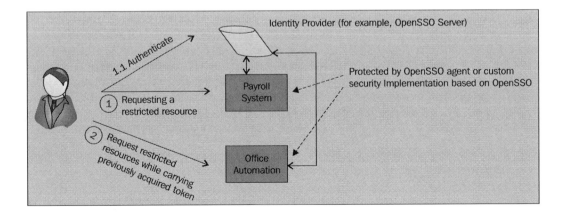

- **Identity federation**: Introduced to provide the required specification, mechanism, and enabler products for letting user's identity information along with, or without, some additional information. It will be carried from one security domain (enterprise) to another security domain without the presence of the same software or same user information storage in both enterprises.

Many standards like **WS-Security** and its family, **WS-Federation**, and **Security Assertion Markup Language** (**SAML**) were introduced to ease the task on integrating disparate security domains where Web Services are going to be dominant business components and web browsers will dominate the user interface and interaction means of users with systems.

Open Web Single Sign-On (OpenSSO) is a pioneer in the access management solutions world by providing support for bleeding edge standards, large scale deployment, compatibility with all major Java EE application servers, and so on.

What is OpenSSO

OpenSSO, hosted at `http://opensso.dev.java.net`, is a Sun Microsystems-sponsored open source project started in 2005 for providing core identity services such as single sign-on (SSO), federation, and Web Services security. The project is based on the code base of Sun Java System Access Manager 7.0 and Sun Java System Federation Manager 7.0, which are previous versions of Sun Microsystems commercial, closed source products. OpenSSO provides support for industry-accepted standards like SAML 2.0, **eXtensible Access Control Markup Language** (**XACML**), WS-Federation, **Liberty Alliance**, **OpenID**, **Information Card**, and so on. These functionalities are either in the main code base or through its extensions.

After Oracle took over Sun Microsystems, they decided to take back the latest release of the OpenSSO and only provide the enterprise release available for download. A company named ForgeRock (`http://www.forgerock.com/`), decided to stand behind the project and continue its development in the same open source mode that Sun was developing the product. The only different is that the project and product names are changed to OpenAM instead of OpenSSO. Latest version of nightly and stable builds of OpenAM are available in the ForgeRock website. In this book, both OpenAM and OpenSSO are referring to the version available in the ForgeRock website.

Using OpenSSO you can manage securing access to resources hosted in any of its wide range of supported containers, which includes GlassFish, Tomcat, WebLogic Server, IIS, Apache Web server, and so on. Accessing the container can be either within the enterprise or between the enterprise and its circles of partners. OpenSSO can act as a single point of security enforcement including entity authentication and access management based on the defined rules for protecting different assets from unauthorized access. You can use OpenSSO to integrate different security domains and web applications using its federation management capabilities. This will ease the navigation of your customers, partners, and employees between a set of heterogeneous environments and web applications within your enterprise or between your enterprise and your circle of partners. OpenSSO is an umbrella project for several components or set of components including:

- **OpenSSO Server** which provides the core functionalities for access management and federated identity management.

- **OpenSSO Policy Agents** police the container where resources are hosted by intercepting the incoming requests for valid authentication headers. Policy agents are in direct contact with the OpenSSO server for performing the authentication and retrieving permissions of an authenticated user. Agents can either protect the URLs or they can integrate with the Java EE security model to act as constraint enforcement entity. Several agents are provided for integration with different application servers like GlassFish, IIS, WebLogic; Servlet containers like Tomcat; and web servers like Apache HTTPD, and so on.

- **OpenSSO Extensions** provides support for other languages like PHP, for direct communication with the OpenSSO core framework. Some products that utilize OpenSSO extensions include **Spring Security framework**, some **OpenID** implementation, and identity provider hardware like Hitachi Finger Vein Biometric.

- **OpenSSO Client SDKs** for directly communicating with OpenSSO from Java, C++, and .Net. Each client SDK provides support for some of the core functionalities. The highest level of support is devoted to Java SDK, which lets the SDK developers perform all operations using it.

OpenSSO can be counted as the most comprehensive open source web access management, federation, and Web Services security provider. Some other web security frameworks are listed below:

- **Java Open Single Sign-On (JOSSO)** hosted at http://www.josso.org/
- **Central Authentication Service (CAS)** located at http://www.jasig.org
- **JBoss SSO** available at http://www.jboss.org/jbosssso
- **Enterprise Sign On-Engine (ESOE)** hosted at http://esoeproject.org/

Different frameworks and products provide a variety of functionalities and selecting a product requires us to study all available options before proceeding with the selection.

OpenSSO functionalities

OpenSSO is a large project with a whole lot of functionalities ranging from integration with Java EE security model for access management, generating and processing SAML assertions for authentication and authorization, Web Services security enforcement, integration with diverse set of user information repository, and so on. The following figure shows OpenSSO from 10000 feet above in architecture, which utilizes all of its functionalities.

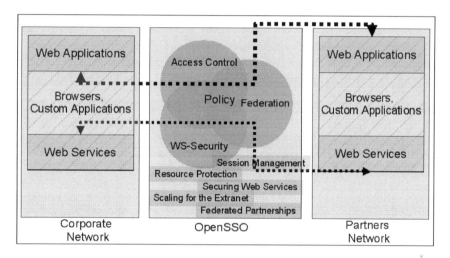

OpenSSO functionalities fall under three major categories including Access Control, Federation Management, and Web Services security. Each one of these categories covers some part of the requirement for access control management and federation identity management.

Controlling user access

Access Control must proceed before letting a request reach its destination service or resource. So before any client can access a resource, OpenSSO policy agents intercept the request to determine whether the user is authenticated or not. If not authenticated, the authentication process will start and after successful authentication the user's permission for accessing the resource will be determined by comparing the permitted roles against the roles assigned to the user. If user has the right to access the resource, the request will go through, otherwise it will fail with a 403 Exception.

If the request does not contain the authentication token, it will be directed to the authentication interface to provide credentials to be authenticated and after a successful authentication the authorization process will commence. We can use **OpenSSO Identity Web Services** or any of the client SDKs to conduct the authentication and authorization process without using policy agents.

OpenSSO benefits from a standards-based, extensible authentication framework, which supports several authentication mechanisms out of the box with the possibility to extend it by including new modules. The provided authentication mechanisms are LDAP, **RADIUS**, Certificate, **SafeWord**, **RSA SecurID**, UNIX, Windows NT, Windows Desktop SSO (Kerberos), and so on. OpenSSO uses JAAS and provides **Service Provider Interface (SPI)** for developing new authentication modules. In OpenSSO we can configure authentication to happen using a chain of different modules for additional security. OpenSSO lets us define a specific authentication mechanism for each set of resources. Therefore, we can ensure that highly-sensitive resources will be protected by multiple authentication phases and each phase can be based on one authentication factor. For example, a chain of biometric and digital certificate authentication in addition to username and password token can protect the OpenSSO administration console.

Authorization in OpenSSO commences by applying policies. A **policy** is a set including Rules, Subjects, Conditions, and Response Provider. Each segment of the policy has a description as follows:

- **Rules**: The resource to be protected, for example a URL.
- **Subjects**: Who is allowed to access the protected resource. Subjects can be a user, a role, or a group.
- **Conditions**: Extra constraints that limit the accessing by environmental restrictions, like IP address, time, date, and so on.
- **Response Provider**: Additional response data to be sent back to resource after the authentication is completed.

With such complex authentication and authorization we can ensure that our system will stay safe behind the guards of OpenSSO, if we configure it appropriately.

Federation Management

The whole story behind Federation Management is communication of user information, including authorization and authentication information, which are parts of the Access Control process between security domains. Identities which users have in the local identity store will federate with other partners' identity store systems and allow the user to authenticate with one of the identity providers and stay authenticated (logged in) on any other affiliated service provider system. It simply means that we have SSO over a federation of service providers that agreed to share and accept identity information and the authenticated identity of each other.

OpenSSO Enterprise supports several open federation technologies including the SAML versions 1 and 2, WS-Federation, and the **Liberty Alliance Project Identity Federation Framework (Liberty ID-FF)**, therefore encouraging an interoperable infrastructure among providers.

Securing Web Services were introduced to make flexible integration and interaction between different software easier and more accessible. This flexibility and exposing of the functionalities through the web or between partners can lead to security risks if these interaction interfaces are left unprotected. So, there should be some security measure in place to ensure the integrity, confidentiality, and security of Web Services.

Openness and flexibility caused several standards to emerge in order to keep the flexibility and interoperability for security measures between different software providers. These standards include:

- **Liberty Alliance Project Identity Web Services Framework** (Liberty ID-WSF)
- **WS-I Basic Security Profile**
- **WS-Trust** (from which the Security Token Service was developed)

OpenSSO fully supports these standards, which lets web service developers focus on the business functionality and leave the security and quality of service (QoS) to OpenSSO. We will discuss the Web Services security in more detail in *Chapter 8*.

Identity Web Services

To use OpenSSO in an easier way and let a broader range of developers benefit from its capabilities, OpenSSO exposes a set of required functionalities as Web Services. When we say Web Services we are not referring only to SOAP-based Web Services but also to **RESTful** services. Provided functionalities of RESTful services include:

- Authentication to validate user credentials
- Authorization to permit access to protected resources
- Provisioning for user attribute management and self-registration
- Logging to keep track of activities for later audition

The following figure shows the IWS features along with the information on what each group of the services requires. You can see list of all services in detail in last table included in this chapter.

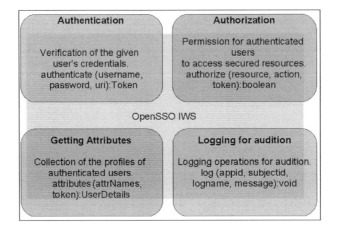

There are some other functionalities embedded in OpenSSO to ease its usage, administration, development, and deployment. These functionalities are listed in the following table.

Feature	Description
Ease of deployment	OpenSSO web application can be deployed into any Servlet container or Java EE application server in virtually any operating system.
Configuration data store	OpenSSO stores all the configuration information in an embedded OpenDS instance. It can also use Sun Java System Directory Server as its data store.
Ease of administration	By using CLI and graphical web-based administration console, OpenSSO administration is very easy and accessible.
User data store independence	OpenSSO allows you to view and retrieve user information without making changes to the existing database. Supported directory servers include Directory Server 5.1, 5.2, and 6.2, IBM Tivoli Directory 6.1, and Microsoft Active Directory 2003.
Web and non-web-based resources	The core design of OpenSSO caters to SSO for both web and non-web applications though the client SDK.
Performance, scalability, and availability	OpenSSO can be scaled horizontally and vertically to handle increased workloads.
Flexibility and extensibility	Many OpenSSO services expose a Service Provider Interface (SPI) allowing expansion of the framework to provide for specific deployment needs.
Internationalization	OpenSSO contains a framework for multiple language support. Customer facing messages, API, command-line interfaces, and user interfaces are localized in the supported languages.

OpenSSO architecture

OpenSSO is a large project with a complicated architecture designed to address all functionalities that it should provide. OpenSSO benefits from a layered architecture with extensibility in its authentication, authorization, identity storage, and so on. You can see a brief model of OpenSSO architecture in the following figure.

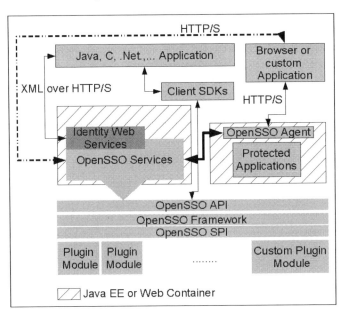

As you can see in the figure, all of the lower-level blocks are running inside an application server or a Servlet container. You can see that multiple types of client applications may interact with the OpenSSO server. These applications can be one of the following types:

- Web applications running inside a Servlet container or Java EE application server, Web Services running inside a Servlet container, or an application server

- OpenSSO agents

- .NET-based Web Services or web applications communicating with OpenSSO using the IDS or .Net SDK

- Standalone applications developed using different programming languages like Java, Ruby, Perl, and C++.

Several programming languages are natively supported by the provided client SDKs, which were discussed in the OpenSSO functionalities section. In addition to client SDKs, OpenSSO provides the possibility for applications to use **SAML assertion** and **Liberty tokens** to communicate with OpenSSO. Using these two methods is well suited for integration and compatibility issues. Another way of interacting with OpenSSO core services is using the Identity Web Services, which greatly suits scripting languages.

Under client SDKs and Identity Web Services layers we have the actual OpenSSO services, which act as the running wheel of OpenSSO interaction with clients. These services provide the authentication, federation, **Liberty ID-WSF**, and **Security Token Service (STS)**. All services available in these layers work on top of the OpenSSO framework and the configuration which we provide the OpenSSO on how different components should run to provide different services. This configuration determines how OpenSSO should deal with tokens, how the identity federation trust circle is configured, how the authentication process should happen, how the policy enforcement should commence, and so on, and they are stored in OpenSSO configuration storage. The configuration store is either an embedded version of OpenDS or a full-blown Sun Java System Directory Server.

Under the framework layer, we have a well designed SPI, which makes it possible for us to develop new modules for OpenSSO. Such modules are already under development as part of the OpenSSO extensions project located at `https://opensso.dev.java.net/public/extensions/`.

OpenSSO, like GlassFish, benefits from different administration channels, including the OpenSSO CLI and web-based administration console. The web-based administration console uses OpenSSO Java SDK to communicate with the core OpenSSO services and OpenSSO CLI uses XML over HTTP to communicate with the OpenSSO framework.

Each one of the OpenSSO-supported programming languages or communication methods can interact with a selected set of OpenSSO services.

Service	Simple XML request and response Java Client SDK	C and .Net Client SDK	SPI	Standards
Authentication	x	x	x	
Authorization (Policy)	x	x	x	
Session (SSO)	x	x	x	
Auditing/Logging	x		x	
Web Services Security			x	x
Federation			x	x

SAML, Liberty Alliance, WS-Security, WS-Trust, and WS-Federation are the supported standards in the Web Services security layer of OpenSSO.

OpenSSO realms

OpenSSO benefits from the realms concept which lets one OpenSSO installation handle multiple applications with a variety of different configurations. Creating multiple realms in OpenSSO lets us provide multiple applications with security definition without requiring us to install multiple copies of OpenSSO. For each realm we can define Agents, authorization, authentication, identity storage, custom login pages, and so on without affecting other realm functionalities.

Installing OpenSSO in GlassFish

OpenSSO Server is a web application, which can be deployed into any J2EE 1.4 Servlet container or application server. We will continue by downloading and deploying OpenSSO release 9, which is available under OpenAM release 9 name on the ForgeRock website and is the same as OpenSSO Enterprise 8.

> Although GlassFish is the preferred container for deploying OpenSSO, you will find the complete list of supported platforms amazing. The list is available at: `http://wikis.sun.com/display/OpenSSO/Support+Dashboard`.

1. Download the latest version of OpenAM which is the same as OpenSSO from `http://www.forgerock.com/downloads.html` and unzip it.

2. Inside the directory that you unzipped you should have a directory named `deployable-war`, inside which you should see `opensso.war`. Deploy the WAR file into your GlassFish application server instance either using CLI, Web administration console, or the auto-deploy directory.

3. Before continuing with other OpenSSO related steps, we need to ensure that our host machine has a fully-qualified domain name. If you have a single PC then it is less likely that it has one; otherwise, if you are a domain member, your machine should have a FQDN.

4. In order to configure the host with a FQDN in Windows we should edit `win_dir\system32\drivers\etc\hosts` and add a new line similar to `127.0.0.1 localhost gfbook.pcname.com` at the beginning of the file, and in Linux and UNIX we can add the same line in the beginning of the `/etc/hosts` file (you will need root permission to edit the file in Linux and Unix).

> The `hosts` file is used to map a name to an IP address to let the system access a remote machine using its name instead of using its IP address. When we are installing the OpenSSO on our local machine for test and development purposes we are not a domain member to have a fully-qualified name and OpenSSO needs a fully-qualified name for the installation process to commence.
>
> To address this requirement we are mapping our loopback address, which is `127.0.0.1`, to a fully-qualified name to continue with the OpenSSO installation.

5. Now that we are ensured the host has a FQDN, we can navigate to `http://FQDN:PORT/opensso` in order to see the OpenSSO management console. The port number is your GlassFish instance port number and `opensso` is the default context name for the OpenSSO web application.

6. Upon first visit to the OpenSSO administration console we need to proceed with the installation process. OpenSSO lets us choose one of **Default Configuration** or **Custom Configuration** models. The first one is useful for development and demonstration purposes and just asks for minimal information like administrators credentials and credentials that policy agents will use to connect to OpenSSO. We will proceed with the custom installation.

7. Selecting the **Custom Configuration** opens a wizard that will guide us through the installation process. In the first step it asks for the administration password. Enter `adminadmin` as administration password and press **Next**.

8. In the **Server Settings** step make sure that you use a server URL with the following pattern: `http://FQDN:SERVER_PORT`, and use `.pcname.com` as the cookie domain. The **Platform Locale** and **Configuration Directory** can be left as they are. The following figure shows the **Server Settings** step.

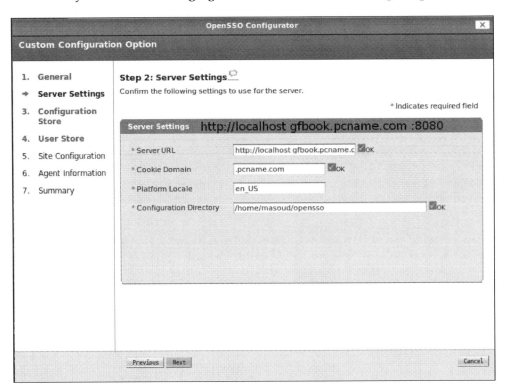

 The domain name should represent the domain that we want OpenSSO to secure resources on with the container running on its member servers.

After the **Server Settings** step we should specify the **Configuration Store**. In this step we are going to specify which storage type OpenSSO should use to store its configuration. We use **Add to Existing Deployment** to let this newly configured instance bear some load or we can set it up as the **First Instance** (a standalone instance). We will go with **the First Instance** mode. We can use an instance of **Sun Java System Directory Server** to store the OpenSSO configuration (suitable for production environment) or we can use the OpenSSO embedded OpenDS to store the configuration. We choose the later one, which is suitable for development purposes. Leave all attributes as they are and proceed to the next step which is the **User Store** step.

Remember that if you are deploying a multi-instance OpenSSO infrastructure all of the instances should use the same encryption key, and use the same certificate for HTTPS.

9. In the **User Store** step select **OpenSSO User Data Store** as we are going to use it for test and development purposes. In a production environment user data store should be separated from the configuration store.

 A step-by-step guide to use OpenDS as the data store for OpenSSO is available at: `http://wikis.sun.com/display/OpenSSO/Using+OpenDS+as+a+User+Data+Store+for+OpenSSO+Enterprise+8.0+Update+1`. I suggest you review it if you want to use OpenSSO in a production environment with OpenDS as the user data store.

10. For step 5, which is the **Site Configuration step**, select **No** and continue to the next step.

 We can use the **Site Configuration** step to configure a load balancer for a set of multiple OpenSSO servers joined together. If you want to learn more about the load balanced deployment of OpenSSO refer to `http://dlc.sun.com/pdf/820-3320/820-3320.pdf`, which is the Sun OpenSSO Enterprise 8.0 Installation and Configuration Guide

11. For **Default Policy Agent User** provide the password that policy agents will use to connect to the OpenSSO server. I specified `agentpass` as the password. Proceed to the **Summary** page and click on the **Create Configuration** button to finish the installation task.

Now that the installation is finished, log into OpenSSO administration console by navigating to `http://FQDN:SERVER_PORT/opnesso/` and using your administration username and password (`amAdmin` and `adminadmin`).

Configuring OpenSSO for authentication and authorization

OpenSSO supports many protocols and services, which leads to a handful of a job for the administrators to configure, administrate, and maintain it. In this section we will just take a look at how we can add some configuration in order to demonstrate authentication, authorization, and single sign-on operations.

After you log into the OpenSSO administration console, you will find yourself in an environment partly similar to the GlassFish administration console. If you do not grasp the meaning of each part don't get disappointed because OpenSSO can be considered one of the most advanced open source projects in the identity management realm. The following figure shows a screenshot of the OpenSSO administration console homepage:

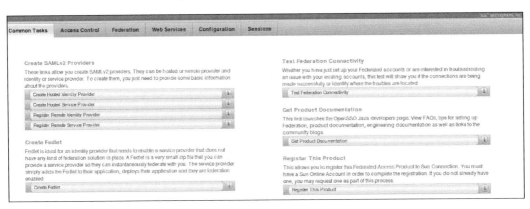

Before we do anything else we need to define what the authentication source is or list the subjects (users) that our access control management software knows. OpenSSO can use Active directory, Sun Java Directory Server, and IBM Tivoli as its user information repository or it can use its own embedded OpenSSO to store user information.

To define some users:

1. Click on the **Access Control** tab, then click on the **opensso** realm.

2. A new set of tabs will appear, go to the **Subjects** tab, and add two users with the following properties:

James	James	Smith	James Smith	james	*Active*
meera	Meera	Spencer	Meera Spencer	meera	*Active*

After we add these users we need to define a group and assign the group to these two users. In the **Subjects** tab switch to the **Groups** tab and add two new groups named employee and manager.

Go back to the **User** tab. Clicking on any of the created users (james, meera) will open a new set of tabs directly related to the user attributes. In these tabs we can add a different group membership for each user. Assign both employee and manager groups to james and assign the employee group to meera. To assign a group membership to a user just add the available list of groups to the selected list.

So far we added some users and groups to the OpenSSO identity storage. We can authenticate users against these identities. We discussed that OpenSSO uses policies and rules to perform authorization. Now we will add some policies and rules to check authenticated user permissions against them before letting its request goes through.

To define a new rule in the **Access Control** tab, select the **Policies** tab and click on the **New Policy** button to create a new policy.

1. Give the policy a name like GlassFish Book Policy and in the **Rules** table click on **New** to create a rule for this policy.

2. Select **URL Policy Agent** as the policy type and specify a name for it—something like localhost Protector and a resource (a URL) which it will police like http://127.0.0.1:38080/Conversion-war/. I entered the link to our Conversion application that we created in *Chapter 3*. You can enter any URL, valid or not valid.

> The rules we define are evaluated by OpenSSO authentication and authorization services when we place any request on the URL it's configured to protect. The resource URL can be anything expressible in the form of a URL.

3. Finally, we should select what possible actions are allowed or denied by this policy. We select both GET and POST and mark both of them as allowed by this policy.

4. By saving the changes we will get back to our policy definition page.

Now we need to add some subjects which are going to be affected by this policy, so:

1. In the **Subject** section click **New** and in the first page of the two-page wizard select **Access Manager Identity Subject**.

2. Click **Next** to see the second page. In this page give the subject a name like `GlassFish Book User Group`.

3. In the **Filter** section search for all groups and add `employee` and `manager` to get the list of selected groups.

4. Click **Finish** and we are done with the required configuration.

In next section we will use these configurations to demonstrate how OpenSSO can manage authentication, authorization, and SSO.

Authentication chaining

We can configure OpenSSO to authenticate the users by different authentication types. The default level that we used in the previous section when we defined the users is the basic authentication configuration, referred to as Realm Authentication.

Before we dig deep into the details of these authentication methods we need to know few basic related terms like **Module Instance**, and **Authentication Service**.

- **Module instance**: An authentication module instance collects user credentials such as a username and password, checks the information against entries in its related storage, and determines whether the credentials are correct or not. There are more than 10 different authentication modules provided out of the box with OpenSSO, some of which are listed below:
    - Active Directory
    - Authentication Configuration
    - Data Store
    - HTTP Basic
    - JDBC
    - LDAP
    - SAE
    - Windows Desktop SSO

 For description of these modules take a look at `http://docs.sun.com/app/docs/doc/820-3886/ghthd?a=view`.

- **Authentication level**: Each module in a realm has an authentication level assigned to it. This authentication level specifies the importance of the module in realm, meaning that when a user is authenticated with a level 5 module it is considered authenticated for any level 3 restrictions.

- **Authentication Service**: An authentication service is a combination of one or more authentication modules forming an authentication chain. A user specified to authenticate against the service will need to provide authentication information for any of the required module in that service. Each module in the service has its own criteria specifying the role of the module in the service with regards to the user's provided information. A module can be OPTIONAL, REQUISITE, REQUIRED, or SUFFICIENT. A user is considered authenticated for the service if the the relevant REQUIRED, REQUISITE, SUFFICIENT and OPTIONAL modules succeed.

    - REQUIRED indicates that the success of the module is required for the Authentication Service to succeed, failure of a REQUIRED module will not end the authentication immediately.

    - REQUISITE is like REQUIRED but if a user fails to authenticate against this module, the authentication fails immediately.

    - SUFFICIENT indicates that success of this module is sufficient to for the service to consider the user as authenticated. However if any of the previous modules marked as REQUIRED fails, the authentication fails, otherwise the authentication ends with success.

    - OPTIONAL indicates that successful authentication for this module is not required but it can affect the authentication level.

The following figure shows a sample authentication service with three module instances configured in its chain.

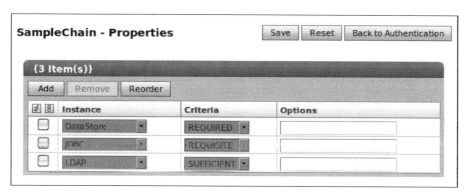

In the following sections we will study some of the authentication type available in OpenSSO.

Realm Authentication

This is the default authentication type that authenticates the realm members with the default authentication type specified for the realm or the su-realm. The default authentication service for realms is ldapService, which only uses one authentication module named Data Store. To configure a realm authentication type and service we can use the administration console. The following steps shows the way for changing the authentication service and module instances:

- Login to administration console,

- Select Access Control tab.

- Select the realm from the realm list.

- Select the **Authentication** tab.

Now we can add more module instances to the realm from the same page or we can further customize the **ldapService** to use more than one module instance or we can change the current module instance to suit our needs. The following figure shows list of modules configured for the default realm out of the box:

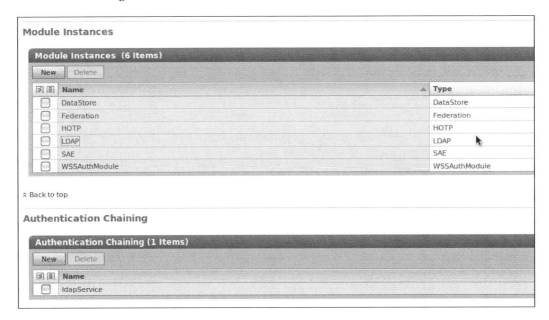

User Authentication

The User Authentication type allows us to have more fine-grained control over what authentication service a user should be authenticated with. This gives us the flexibility to specify more complex and secure authentication service for privileged users like administrators.

We can specify the authentication service for a subject in the subject edit pages. We just need to create the user and then specify its authentication service using the **User Authentication Configuration** element in the **General** tab when we are editing a subject.

To learn more about authentication types refer to Sun OpenSSO Enterprise 8.0 Administration Guide available at `http://docs.sun.com/app/docs/doc/820-3885/gimxg?a=view`.

Securing our applications using OpenSSO

We discussed that OpenSSO provides developers with several client interfaces to interact with OpenSSO to perform authentication, authorization, session and identity management, and audition. These interfaces include Client SDK for different programming languages and using standards including:

- Liberty Alliance Project and Security Assertion Markup Language (SAML) for authentication and single sign-on (SSO)

- XML Access Control Markup Language (XACML) for authorization functions

- Service Provisioning Markup Language (SPML) for identity management functions. Using the client SDKs and standards mentioned above are suitable when we are developing custom solutions or integrating our system with partners, which are already using them in their security infrastructure. For any other scenario these methods are overkill for developers. To make it easier for the developers to interact with OpenSSO core services the Identity Web Services are provided. We discussed IWS briefly in *OpenSSO functionalities* section. The IWS are included in OpenSSO to perform the tasks included in the following table.

Task	Description
Authentication and Single sign-on	Verifying the user credentials or its authentication token.
Authorization	Checking the authenticated user's permissions for accessing a resource.
Provisioning	Creating, deleting, searching, and editing users.
Logging	Ability to audit and record operations.

IWS are exposed in two models—the first model is the WS-* compliant SOAP-based Web Services and the second model is a very simple but elegant RESTful set of services based on HTTP and REST principles.

Finally, the third way of using OpenSSO is deploying the policy agents to protect the resources available in a container. We will discuss policy agents' installation, configuration, and usage in the next chapter.

In the following section we will use RESTful interface to perform authentication, authorization, and SSO.

Authenticating users by the RESTful interface

Performing authentication using the RESTful Web Services interface is very simple as it is just like performing a pure HTTP communication with an HTTP server. For each type of operation there is one URL, which may have some required parameters and the output is what we can expect from that operation. The URL for authentication operation along with its parameters is as follows:

- **Operation**: Authentication
- **Operation URL**: `http://host:port/OpenSSOContext/identity/authenticate`
- **Parameters**: `username`, `password`, `uri`
- **Output**: `subjectid`

The Operation URL specifies the address of a Servlet which will receive the required parameters, perform the operation, and write back the result. In the template included above we have the `host`, `port`, and `OpenSSOContext` which are things we already know. After the context we have the path to the RESTful service we want to invoke. The path includes the task type, which can be one of the tasks included in the IWS task lists table and the operation we want to invoke.

All parameters are self-descriptive except the `uri`. We pass a URL to have our users redirected to it after the authentication is performed. This URL can include information related to the user or the original resource which the user has requested.

In the case of successful authentication we will receive a `subjectid`, which we can use in any other RESTful operation like authorization, to log in, log out, and so on. If you remember session ID from your web development experience, subjected is the same as session ID. You can view all sessions along with related information from the OpenSSO administration console homepage under the `Sessions` tab. The following listing shows a sample JSP page which performs a RESTful call over OpenSSO to authenticate a user and obtain a session ID for the user if they get authenticated.

```
<%
try {
    String operationURL =
       "http://gfbook.pcname.com:8080/opensso/identity/authenticate";
    String username = "james";
    String password = "james";
    username = java.net.URLEncoder.encode(username, "UTF-8");
    password = java.net.URLEncoder.encode(password, "UTF-8");
    String operationString = operationURL + "?username=" +
       username +"&password=" + password;
    java.net.URL Operation = new java.net.URL(operationString);
    java.net.HttpURLConnection connection =
       (java.net.HttpURLConnection)Operation.openConnection();
    int responseCode = connection.getResponseCode();
    if (responseCode == java.net.HttpURLConnection.HTTP_OK) {
      java.io.BufferedReader reader = new java.io.BufferedReader(
       new java.io.InputStreamReader(
          (java.io.InputStream) connection.getContent()));
      out.println("<h2>Subject ID</h2>");
    String line = reader.readLine();

    out.println(line);
    }
} catch (Exception e) {
    e.printStackTrace();
}
%>
```

REST made straightforward tasks easier than ever. Without using REST we would have dealt with complexity of SOAP and WSDL and so on but with REST you can understand the whole code with the first scan.

Beginning from the top, we define the REST operation URL, which is assembled using the operation URL and appending the required parameters using the parameters name and the parameters value. The URL that we will connect to it will be something like:

```
http://gfbook.pcname.com:8080/opensso/identity/authenticate?userna
me=james&password=james
```

After assembling the URL we open a network connection to authenticate it. After opening the connection we can check to see whether we received an `HTTP_OK` response from the server or not. Receiving the `HTTP_OK` means that the authentication was successful and we can read the `subjectid` from the socket. The connection may result in other response codes like `HTTP_UNAUTHORIZED` (HTTP Error code 401) when the credentials are not valid. A complete list of possible return values can be found at `http://java.sun.com/javase/6/docs/api/java/net/HttpURLConnection.html`.

Authorizing using REST

If you remember in *Configuring OpenSSO for authentication and authorization* section we defined a rule that was set to police `http://gfbook.pcname.com:8080/` URL for us. And later on we applied the policy rule to a group of users that we created; now we want to check and see how our policy works. In every security system, before any authorization process, an authentication process should compete with a positive result. In our case the result for the authentication is `subjectid`, which the authorization process will use to check whether the authenticated entity is allowed to perform the action or not. The URL for the authorization operation along with its parameters is as follows:

- **Operation**: Authorization
- **Operation URL**: `http://host:port/OpenSSOContext/identity/authorize`
- **Parameters**: `uri`, `action`, `subjectid`
- **Output**: True or false based on the permission of subject over the entity and given action

The combination of `uri`, `action`, and `subjectid` specifies that we want to check our client, identified by `subjectid`, permission for performing the specified `action` on the resource identified by the `uri`. The output of the service invocation is either `true` or `false`.

The following listing shows how we can check whether an authenticated user has access to a certain resource or not. In the sample code we are checking james, identified by his subjectid we acquired by executing the previous code snippet, against the localhost Protector rule we defined earlier.

```
<%
try {
    String operationURL =
        "http://gfbook.pcname.com:8080/opensso/identity/authorize";
    String protectecUrl = " http://127.0.0.1:38080/Conversion-war/";
    String subjectId =
    "AQIC5wM2LY4SfcyemVIZX6qBGdyH7b8C5KFJjuuMbw4oj24=@AAJTSQACMDE=#";
     String action = "POST";
    protectecUrl = java.net.URLEncoder.encode(protectecUrl, "UTF-8");
    subjectId = java.net.URLEncoder.encode(subjectId, "UTF-8");
    String operationString = operationURL + "?uri=" + protectecUrl +
        "&action=" + action + "&subjectid=" + subjectId;
    java.net.URL Operation = new java.net.URL(operationString);
    java.net.HttpURLConnection connection =
        (java.net.HttpURLConnection) Operation.openConnection();
    int responseCode = connection.getResponseCode();
    if (responseCode == java.net.HttpURLConnection.HTTP_OK) {
        java.io.BufferedReader reader = new java.io.BufferedReader(
            new java.io.InputStreamReader(
                (java.io.InputStream) connection.getContent()));
        out.println("<h2>authorization Result</h2>");
        String line = reader.readLine();
        out.println(line);
    }
} catch (Exception e) {
    e.printStackTrace();
}
%>
```

For this listing everything is the same as the authentication process in terms of initializing objects and calling methods, except that in the beginning we define the protected URL string, then we include the subjectid, which is result of our previous authentication. Later on we define the action that we need to check the permission of our authenticated user over it and finally we read the result of authorization. The complete operation after including all parameters is similar to the following snippet:

```
http://gfbook.pcname.com:8080/opensso/identity/authorize?uri=http:
//127.0.0.1:38080/Conversion-war/&action=POST&subjectid=subjectId
```

Pay attention that two `subjectid` elements cannot be similar even for the same user on the same machine and same OpenSSO installation. So, before running this code, make sure that you perform the authentication process and include the `subjectid` resulted from your authentication with the `subjectid` we specified previously.

SSO using REST

Usually in big enterprise systems there is one single server that performs all types of authentication required in the enterprise, including a simple username-password authentication to authenticate based on OpenID or X.509 digital certificates.

In our simple scenario we have a Servlet filter that checks all incoming requests for valid authentication token. It will either find that the request is already authenticated (presence of the `subjectid`) or it redirects the user to OpenSSO server for authentication. The filter appends a redirection URL when it forwards the user to OpenSSO for authentication to let OpenSSO redirect the user to that URL after a successful authentication.

In this application, our protected resource is the `restricted.jsp` file on the same context that the Servlet filter is present, and we just check for the authentication token in our filter and no authorization process will commence. In real world example we may define some policies in OpenSSO and check incoming request both for authenticated token and perform authorization after the authentication is completed to see whether we should allow the request to reach the target or should redirect it to an informative page about the requester's access level and why he cannot access the requested resource. The following listing shows the `restricted.jsp` file.

```
<form name="attributes" action="logout.jsp" method="post">
    <b>You are logged in so you can access this restricted page</b>
    <br>
    <input name="logout" value="Logout" type="submit">
</form>
```

The restricted page just shows a welcome message along with a button, which invokes another JSP page for logout operation. Logout operation can be performed using the REST interface. The operation parameters and URL are as follows:

- **Operation**: Logout.
- **Operation URL**: `http://host:port/OpenSSOContext/identity/logout`.
- **Parameters**: `subjectid`.
- **Output**: No specific output. We can check whether the operation is performed correctly or not using HTTP response codes.

The following listing shows how we can invoke the logout operation using REST.

```
<%
  try {
        String serviceUrl =
           "http://gfbook.pcname.com:8080/opensso/identity/logout";
        String subjectid = null;
        javax.servlet.http.Cookie[] cookies = request.getCookies();
        cookies = cookies == null ? new Cookie[0] : cookies;
          for (Cookie cookie : cookies) {
              String cookieName = cookie.getName();
              if ("iPlanetDirectoryPro".equals(cookieName)) {
                  subjectid = cookie.getValue();
              }
          }
        String url = serviceUrl + "?subjectid=" +
           java.net.URLEncoder.encode(subjectid, "UTF-8");
        System.out.println("Opening the Connection");
        java.net.URL Operation = new java.net.URL(url);
        java.net.HttpURLConnection connection =
           (java.net.HttpURLConnection)Operation.openConnection();
        int responseCode = connection.getResponseCode();
        if (responseCode == java.net.HttpURLConnection.HTTP_OK) {
            out.println("<h2>Logged out</h2>");
        }
  } catch (Exception ex) {
      ex.printStackTrace();
  }
%>
```

We start by defining the SSO server URL, and then we extract all cookies from the request in order to find the cookie associated with the SSO `subjectid`. This cookie's name is `iPlanetDirectoryPro` and we need its value to perform the logout. Then we encode the parameters part of logout operation URL and finally open the URL, which is equal to calling the REST operation. We can check the HTTP response code to ensure that our operation has performed with no error and in case that we get an error code we can redirect the user to the appropriate pages.

Now we need to implement the Servlet filter. The filter should be able to check whether the user is authenticated; if not, redirect him to the authentication server for authentication. The following listing shows the Servlet filter's doFilter method.

```
public void doFilter(ServletRequest request,
                ServletResponse response, FilterChain chain)
        throws IOException, ServletException {
    if (isAuthenticated((HttpServletRequest) request)) {
        //perform the authorization if required.
        chain.doFilter(request, response);
    } else {
        ((HttpServletResponse)
            response).sendRedirect(ssoServerURL +
            "/UI/Login?goto=" +((HttpServletRequest)
            request).getRequestURL().toString());
    }
}
```

The doFilter method is implemented in a very simple manner to shows the basics. In the beginning we check to see whether our user is authenticated or not. Later on we redirect the user to the SSO server for authentication; the SSO server will redirect the user to their destination page after the authentication is successfully completed.

The first unknown method in the previous listing is the isAuthenticated method. To keep it simple this method checks to see whether the presented subjectid in the request is valid or not. The isAuthenticated method uses a REST operation to check the subjectid or so-called token; specification of this operation is as follow:

- **Operation**: isAuthenticated
- **Operation URL**: http://host:port/OpenSSOContext/identity/ isAuthenticated
- **Parameters**: subjectid
- **Output**: boolean

The following listing shows the isAuthenticated method implementation. We used the method in our Servlet filter.

```
private boolean isAuthenticated(HttpServletRequest request)
    throws IOException {
        boolean authenticated = false;
        String operationURL = ssoServerURL +
            "/identity/isTokenValid";
        HttpURLConnection connection =
            (HttpURLConnection) (new
            URL(operationURL).openConnection());
        connection.setDoOutput(true);
        connection.setRequestMethod("POST");
```

```
forwardCookies(request, connection,
  getCookieNamesToForward());
int responseCode = connection.getResponseCode();
if (responseCode == HttpURLConnection.HTTP_OK) {
    InputStream in_buf = connection.getInputStream();
    StringBuffer inbuf = new StringBuffer();
    String line;
    BufferedReader reader = new BufferedReader(new
      InputStreamReader(in_buf, "UTF-8"));
    while ((line = reader.readLine()) != null) {
        inbuf.append(line).append("\n");
    }
    String data = new String(inbuf);
    if (data.toLowerCase().indexOf("boolean=true") != -1) {
        authenticated = true;
    }
}
return authenticated;
}
```

You should be familiar with how we assemble the `operationURL` except that this time we passed no parameters while the operation, as mentioned, needs `subjectid` to be passed as its parameter. OpenSSO is smart enough to find its own cookie in the incoming request if we do not provide it as an explicit query parameter. So this time instead of extracting the `subjectid` value we are going to let OpenSSO extract the cookie from our request, so we add required cookies to the request that we are sending to OpenSSO Identity Web Services. Later on, we just change the GET method to POST for more security. And finally we are checking to see the result of the `isTokenValid` operation which as mentioned is Boolean; either the token is correct or not. The first unfamiliar method that we may see is `forwardCookies`, this method simply extracts the required request cookies and adds them to the given connection. We use it to set cookies instead of sending them as query parameters. The following listing shows the `forwardCookies` method.

```
private void forwardCookies(HttpServletRequest request,
        HttpURLConnection connection, Set<String> cookieNames) {
    StringBuilder sb = new StringBuilder();
    Cookie[] cookies = request.getCookies();
    cookies = cookies == null ? new Cookie[0] : cookies;
    for (Cookie cookie : cookies) {
        String cookieName = cookie.getName();
        if (cookieNames.contains(cookieName)) {
            String cookieValue = cookie.getValue();
            sb.append(cookieName);
            sb.append("=");
```

```
                    sb.append(cookieValue);
                    sb.append(";");
            }
        }
        System.out.println(sb.toString());
        if (sb.length() > 0) {
            connection.setRequestProperty("Cookie", sb.toString());
        }
    }
}
```

This method, as we can see, gets a collection of cookies as input parameter. It tries to extract them from the given request, and include them in the given connection request. But how does it know which cookies it should extract from the request? Which cookies don't belong to OpenSSO so our filter should not touch them?

To get this problem solved we use another method to get the list of cookies that belongs to OpenSSO and then we just extract those cookies from the original request header and include them in the request that we are sending to OpenSSO Identity Web Services. There is a REST operation to get the list of OpenSSO cookie names with the following specification:

- **Operation**: getCookieNamesToForward
- **URL**: http://host:port/OpenSSOContext/identity/ getCookieNamesToForward
- **Parameters**: Accepts no parameter
- **Output**: List of all OpenSSO cookie names

The following snippet shows how we can use the getCookieNamesToForward operation in our Java code:

```
private Set getCookieNamesToForward() throws IOException {
    Set nameSet = new HashSet();
    String url = ssoServerURL +
      "/identity/getCookieNamesToForward";
    HttpURLConnection connection =
      (HttpURLConnection) (new URL(url).openConnection());
    BufferedReader br = new BufferedReader(
      new InputStreamReader((InputStream)
      connection.getContent()));
    if (connection.getResponseCode() ==
      HttpURLConnection.HTTP_OK) {
        String line = null;
        while ((line = br.readLine()) != null) {
            if (line.startsWith("string=")) {
                line = line.replaceFirst("string=", "");
                nameSet.add(line);
```

```
                }
            }
        }
    }
    return nameSet;
}
```

You should be completely familiar with the purpose of each code line in the above listing. The method gets a list of all OpenSSO cookie names and returns it as a set to let `forwardCookies` send only the cookies belonging to OpenSSO to the OpenSSO server.

You may ask what is the `ssoServerURL` variable content. I would say that we need to either use a Servlet initializing parameter or a class-level property to provide our filter with the SSO server URL. We also need to add the filter definition to our `web. xml` file. In the sample code available at `https://www.packtpub.com//sites/default/files/downloads/9386_Code.zip` which includes the complete web application for this chapter, the sample application includes complete source code with configure `web.xml` file for initialization parameter.

The following table shows a complete list of other REST operations that are provided by OpenSSO Identity Services.

Operation	URL	Parameters	Response content

Perform logging	`/identity/`
	`log`
		`appid, subjectid`
		
		`logname, message1`
			No output

Search for identities	`/search`	`flter, attributes_names1`
		
		`attribute_values_`
		`attributename1`
			`identitydetails`
			Attributes

Getting subject attributes	`/attributes`	`attributes_names1,` `subjectid`	`userdetails` Read
Reading details of a user	`/identity/` `read`	`name, attributes_names1,` `admin`	`identitydetails` Creation

Creating an identity	`/identity/`
	`create`
		`identity_name, identity_`
		`attribute_names`
		
		`identity_attribute_values_`
		`attributename`
		
		`admin`
			No output

Updating identity details	`/identity/`
	`update`
		`identity_name, identity_`
		`attribute_names`
		
		`identity_attribute_values_`
		`attributename`
		
		`admin`
			No output

Removing an Identity	`/identity/` `delete`	`identity_name,admin`	No output

All of the URLs should be prefixed with OpenSSO server URL, for example `http://localhost:8080/opensso` or `http://gfbook.pcname.com:8080/opensso`.

Summary

In this chapter, we looked at security from an integration point of view. Security, most of the time, is the only subject which developers leave for the later development stages, which is a dire pitfall. Security integration is a very broad topic and this chapter only introduces the OpenSSO server briefly to give you a broader perspective about security integration in general and OpenSSO security in particular. We also discussed what SSO is, what Federation is, how OpenSSO works, how it is architected, and what communication channels it provides for us to interact with its provided services. We saw how we can install OpenSSO, configure it, and perform basic administration tasks like subject and policy management. We learned how we can use OpenSSO RESTful Web Services for authentication, authorization, and SSO token acquiring.

In the next chapters we will study the more advanced topics of securing Java EE applications using OpenSSO policy agents, by looking at the OpenSSO policy agents' features and installation, down to securing the sample application using the policy agents.

More information about OpenSSO is available at the OpenSSO Resource Center `http://wikis.sun.com/display/OpenSSO/OpenSSO+Resource+Center`.

8
Securing Java EE Applications using OpenSSO

Securing a software system is one of the top-level concerns for software architects and project managers. Because of its importance, many standards, frameworks, and products are introduced to help the architects and system designers address the security requirement effectively. Emerging out of different standards, the security integration issue came into focus and led to big vendors jumping into the area to provide better, easier, and more complete solutions for addressing security.

In the age of the Internet and Web 2.0 integration, methods between software systems are rapidly evolving, and there is constant need to change a software system to interact with a partner system. Software architects and designers tend to use products and frameworks that provide plugability features for addressing orthogonal concerns, like security to have the freedom of switching from one product to another if required.

Non-intrusive integration is one of the top-level topics that software architects are involved with and due to market demand many small and large companies are working on the integration issues. One aspect of the software integration is security integration, in which different software developed using diverse technologies will share the same security infrastructure, including authentication, access management, user provisioning, SSO, and so on.

The Java EE security model provides the basics for designing and implementing a fully-configurable security model as we discussed in the first two chapters. Although the Java EE security model can completely address all needs of a software system, for systems with specific requirements, like a wide range of interactions with other partners and software systems and a complex rule based access model, we should look at additional features that are provided by a line of software called **Identity Management (IDM)** or access management systems.

The identity management systems covers all security-related requirements starting with user definition, authentication, complex access rule definition, audition, Web Services security, and so on.

In previous chapters we discussed both the installation and configuration of OpenSSO in order to use it with the provided REST APIs and its Java SDK. In this chapter we will look at OpenSSO security agents, which are interceptors that can intercept requests placed on different types of web and application servers. Agents are like a protector filter that only allows authorized requests to pass and redirects unauthorized requests to appropriate pages, such as a login page, defined by the administrators.

Understanding Policy Agents

As we discussed, **OpenSSO Policy Agents** or simply OpenSSO agents are provided to secure different kinds of resources without an intensive change in the structure of the resource or the resource container, which can be a Web server, Java EE server, proxy server, and so on. In this section, we discuss Policy Agents in general before we get down to the business of securing applications using OpenSSO agents.

In brief, as you can see in the following figure, a policy agent is an entity that sits in front of a server like a Java EE or a Web server and intercepts any request headed towards that server. After intercepting the request, the OpenSSO agent consults with the OpenSSO server whether or not to allow the request to go through.

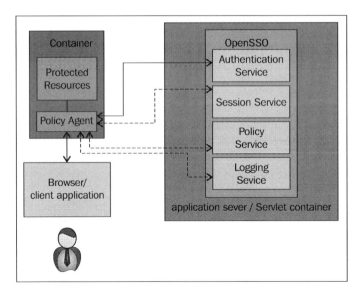

In detail, for an OpenSSO agent configuration we should at least have the following elements:

- An installed and working OpenSSO server. Our server should have some subjects and policies defined to let the agent use them in governing the application's security.

- An agent profile, which is the agent installed in the server we want to protect. This agent interacts with the OpenSSO server to decide whether a request should go through or the request should be denied.

- The agent should be installed in a compatible server, for example the agent should be installed on a Java EE server like GlassFish or a Web server like Apache HTTP server and so on. Resources deployed on this server can be placed under the installed agent protection.

Specifying access privileges by defining policies

A policy defines rules that specify access privileges to protected resources. The policy uses the following items to define the access privileges:

- **Rules**: A rule contains a service type, like a URL, which needs protection, one or more actions that are executable on the resource like GET and POST actions in HTTP, and permissions for those actions like Deny and Allow.

- **Subjects**: A subject defines the user or collection of users (for instance, a group or those who possess a specific role) that the owner policy affects. A policy can apply on a user if and only if the user is in one of the policy subjects. The most widely used type of subject is Authenticated Users, which includes any known user with a valid SSO token.

- **Conditions**: A condition lets us define constraints on the policy. For example, we can use conditions to limit the access to a resource to subjects coming from a specific IP range. The following list shows important condition types we can specify for a policy:
    - Does the subject IP address belong to a specific range?
    - What is the time and date, and which time zone does the user belong to?
    - What is the specific property in the subject's session?
    - Is session activation time less than a threshold?
    - Is subject authentication level more than a specific level?
    - Is subject authenticated through a specific authentication chain?

Besides the ones mentioned you can also think up your own conditions.

- **Response Providers**: Response providers are plugins that provide policy-based response attributes. They can be used to send specific properties back to the agent, and further back to the application for customized uses. For example if a policy named `policy_3` is successfully evaluated for the request and we need the client application or the agent to know that this particular policy has evaluated successfully, we can add a property to the response specifying that the `policy_3` has successfully evaluated.

Protecting diverse types of containers using Policy Agents

We said that there are different types of agents to protect different kind of servers. The following table shows a list of agent types along with a basic description about each type.

Agent	Description
J2EE Agent 3.0 for GlassFish/Sun Application Server	We can use it to protect GlassFish and Sun Java Application Server both in URL and Java EE mode.
J2EE Agent 3.0 for WebLogic 10	Protecting applications deployed in WebLogic Application Server.
Web Agent 3.0 for Webserver 7	Protecting Sun Java Web Server 7.x.
J2EE Agent 3.0 for WebSphere	Protecting applications deployed in WebSphere Application Server.
J2EE Agent 3.0 for Tomcat 6	Protecting web applications deployed in Tomcat 6.
J2EE Agent 3.0 for Jetty 6.1	Protecting resources deployed in Jetty 6.1.
Web Agent 3.0 for Apache 2.0.x, 2.2.x	Protecting URLs in Apache Web server 2.0 and 2.2.x.
Web Agent 3.0 for Proxy Server 4.0	Protecting Sun Proxy Server 7 resources.
Web Agent 3.0 for Microsoft IIS 6, 7.0	Protecting applications deployed in Microsoft IIS 6.0 and 7.0.
J2EE Agent 3.0 for JBoss 4.x, 5.x	Protecting Java EE applications deployed in JBoss 4 and JBoss 5.

These agents are available for different operating systems including Windows, Linux, and Unix variants.

The above table shows an extensive list of supported servers which itself means that OpenSSO agents should work with a broad range of modes to integrate with different types of servers and protect different types of resources on those servers.

The most basic task for an OpenSSO agent is enforcing the specified rules on the web resources identified with their URLs. When the OpenSSO agent is configured to protect resources based on their URLs, the Agent intercepts any request and only allows certain groups of users to access the resource when certain conditions are met. Some of these conditions are as follows:

- Controlling access based on the client IP address
- Controlling access based on the specific time of the day or day of the week

The users who are permitted to access each resource and the condition that should be met before the users or group of users can access the resource are defined by the system administrator using OpenSSO administration console.

Working of OpenSSO agents

When an agent needs to protect a Java EE application or resource deployed on a Web server, it needs to intercept the incoming requests and determine whether it should allow the requests to go through or should redirect the user to another page, such as a login page. To accomplish this task, the agent must be able to see all incoming requests and also the incoming requests the agent should integrate with the application server or the Web server.

To further scrutinize the way that an agent works, let's see what changes are applied on the application server during the agent installation, what kind of configuration is required for the agent to protect the application, and finally changes that should be applied on the applications we need to place under the agent protection. Installing a Policy Agent into a container introduces the following changes into the host container:

1. The Java EE agent uses Servlet filters to intercept all requests and then interact with the OpenSSO server, so it needs some classes to be available in the runtime. So during the agent installation, it adds all required JAR files to the target application server instance classpath.
2. The Java EE security model is based on security realms; the OpenSSO agent installation adds the required security realm to the set of application server realms. This realm represents the groups and subjects we defined in the OpenSSO server and lets the Java EE application server security integrate with OpenSSO.
3. The installation process also adds the Agent realm and JAAS modules to the `domain_dir/config/login.conf` file.
4. Deploying a web application into the server for housekeeping tasks like cross domain SSO and notification processing. We need to install the agent application manually.

The following tasks are required to protect an application using OpenSSO agent:

- Adding the agent filter to the `web.xml` file so the agent filter can intercept incoming requests for the protected application
- Changing the roles mapping to map the Java EE application roles to OpenSSO groups

And finally, the following configurations are required for the agent and OpenSSO server so we can have the basic security for our application:

- Defining users and putting them into appropriate groups according to the security requirements and security schema of the application.
- Defining the login and logout URLs.
- Defining the URL patterns that do not need protection, for example content of the `/styles/`, `/images/` paths may not need protection. So we should define them as non-protected URLs.
- Defining required policies to protect the resource in our application.

As you can see we have a small to-do list to place an application under the agent protection. In the meantime we can enforce sophisticated policies and benefit from user provisioning, audition, and SSO without introducing dependencies in our application source code to the OpenSSO libraries.

Protecting different types of resources

We said that OpenSSO provides different agent types and each agent can operate on different modes to address the requirements. The GlassFish policy agent can operate in three modes to address variety of requirements. These modes are as follows:

Operating mode	Description
NONE	In this mode the Policy Agent does nothing and it appears as though no agent is active. Basically this mode deactivates the Servlet filter. When the Agent filter is operating in this mode, any declarative J2EE security policy or programmatic J2EE security API calls will return a negative result regardless of the user.
SSO_ONLY	This is the least restrictive mode for OpenSSO agent as the Agent filter only ensures that users are authenticated using OpenSSO authentication service. In this mode any declarative J2EE security policy or programmatic J2EE security API calls evaluated for the application will result in a negative evaluation.
URL_POLICY	In the URL_POLICY mode, the Agent filter enforces the URL policies that are defined in OpenSSO Enterprise, similar to the two previous modes. Any declarative J2EE security policy or programmatic J2EE security API calls evaluated for the application will result in negative evaluation.

Operating mode	Description
J2EE_POLICY	In this mode, the Agent filter and agent realm work together with various OpenSSO services to ensure the correct evaluation of J2EE policies. In contrast with previous modes, using this mode guarantees that any declarative J2EE security policy or programmatic J2EE security API calls evaluated for the application result in the correct values based on the security annotations and declarations in the deployment descriptors.
ALL	This is the most restrictive mode of the Agent filter. In this mode, the filter enforces both J2EE policies and URL policies as defined in OpenSSO Enterprise. By default OpenSSO agents operates in ALL mode.

From the five mentioned modes of operation for the Java EE agent, the SSO_ONLY and URL_POLICY modes are also available for the Web agents.

Exploring outstanding features of Policy Agents

The current version of OpenSSO policy agent is version 3, which has some significant improvement over the previous version to further ease the installation process, manage of larger deployments of OpenSSO agents, improve the system uptime, and so on. Some of these new features are as follows:

Managing Centralized Agent Configuration

In the previous version OpenSSO Policy Agent, all agent configurations were stored in the agent machine and managing those configurations required the administrator to access the agent machine to change a configuration value. In version 3 of OpenSSO Policy Agents, most of the configuration properties are moved to the OpenSSO central data repository instead of to a local file.

In the local mode, all of the agent configuration is stored locally in a configuration file named OpenSSOAgentConfiguration.properties in the same machine that the agent runs on while in the centralized mode; most of the configurations are stored in OpenSSO storage and the agent uses a bootstrap file named OpenSSOAgentBootstrap.properties to locate the OpenSSO server and retrieve the configuration from it.

Managing agents in groups

Agent groups are introduced to let administrators group agents of the same type together and manage them as a single entity. This feature reduces the amount of time administrators need to spend on agent configuration. Although all agents in a group share most of the configuration properties, they have some individual properties which are unique for each agent, like the notification URL for the agent application, and so on.

Applying agents configuration on-the-fly

Prior to the version 3 of Policy Agents we needed to restart the agent container after changing the configuration by applying new configurations. In version 3 more hot-swappable configuration properties are introduced to increase the uptime of the agent application server. For example, all logout-related properties and user-mapping properties are hot-swappable and we can change them and expect the changes to be effective immediately without a container restart.

Having more control over the installation process

In version 3, we have more features included in the installation application to let administrators have more control or an easier installation process. The default installation method asks less configuration questions compared to previous versions and the customer installation method provides more installation options, like creating the agent profile on the OpenSSO server during the agent installation.

Now that we have a basic understanding about how OpenSSO agents and especially GlassFish agent works, we can dirty our hands and install the agent.

Installing J2EE Agent 3.0 for GlassFish

Installing the J2EE agent is easy and straight forward once you understand the information you should provide during the installation. The first step in installing the agent is downloading the appropriate version from OpenSSO agent's page located at: `http://forgerock.com/downloads.html`. Currently the latest version, which is J2EE Agent 3.0 for GlassFish, can be downloaded from `http://www.forgerock.com/downloads.html`.

The downloadable package directory structure is similar to the following figure:

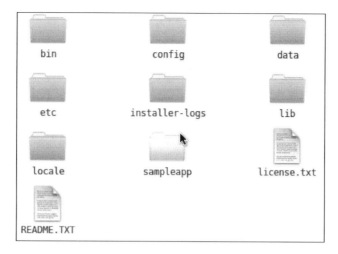

The following table briefly explains the directories and their contents.

Directory	Description
bin	Contains the administration and installation scripts.
config	Templates for configuration files.
data	Will contain a license agreement-related file, which indicates we agreed to the licensing term. The file will be created after we create the first agent profile.
etc	The agent application is located inside this folder. The application must be installed in the GlassFish agent server. The file name should be agentapp.war.
installer-logs	Logfiles related to creating and installing an agent profile. Using these logs we can track possible installation problems.
lib	Contains the JAR files required for the agent to operate. These JAR files will be added to the agent server classpath by the agent installer.
locale	Contains the localization information.
sampleapp	Sample applications that can help you understand the agent and its functionalities better.

Now that we understand the basics of the agent it's time to get our hands dirty and install and configure the agent.

We should not install the agent in the same GlassFish instance that we are deploying OpenSSO server. If we do so, the classpath collision between agent and OpenSSO libraries will prevent them from functioning properly.

1. We can create a new domain and install the agent into this new domain. The following command shows how we can create a new domain. We assume that we are inside the `glassfish_dir` /bin folder.

    ```
    ./asadmin create-domain --domaindir /opt/dev/apps/glassfish-2.1.1/
    domains --adminuser admin --adminport 34848
        --instanceport 38080 --domainproperties jms.port=37676:domain.
    jmxPort=30001:orb.listener.port=30002:orb.ssl.port=30003:orb.
    mutualauth.port=30004:http.ssl.port=38443
      --savemasterpassword=true --savelogin=true   domain2
    ```

    The above command will create a domain named `domain2` in the default domains directory. All port numbers for the new domains are `30000` more than the default port numbers. For example, the administration port is `34848`.

2. Now start the domain using the following command:

    ```
    ./asadmin start-domain domain2
    ```

3. Now deploy the `agentapp.war` file, which is located inside the `agent_dir/etc` directory and which we can deploy using the following command:

    ```
    ./asadmin deploy -host 127.0.0.1 -port 34848 agent_dir/etc/
    agentapp.war domain2
    ```

Make sure that `domain2` is down and proceed to the next step, which is agent installation.

 To stop the domain you can use the following command:
```
./asadmin stop-domain domain2
```

During agent installation we need a password file, which includes the agent password. The password file contains single line of text, which is the password in clear text. Agent installation will encrypt the password during the installation. The following snippet shows the password file named `password.pwd`.

```
adminadmin
```

I assume the following is our current configuration for the installation process.

Configuration item	Description
OpenSSO server	We assume that OpenSSO is running on `http://127.0.0.1:8080/opensso`
Agent server	We assume that agent server ports are as stated above
Password file	We assume that we have the password file created and it is located at `/opt/password.pwd`
Agent application (agentapp)	We assume that it is deployed or will be deployed in the agent server as follows: `http://127.0.0.1:38080/agentapp`

Now navigate to `agent_dir/bin` and get ready to install the agent into the agent server.

 If you are on a Linux or Unix platform you need to give the execution permission to the `agentadmin` file. You can do it using the following command:

chmod +x agentadmin

Start the installation with the following command:

./agentadmin --install --saveRespose /opt/response.resp

We used two parameters for the `agentadmin` command. The first parameter tells the `agentadmin` that we want to install a new agent and the second parameter asks the `agentadmin` to save our responses to the `agentadmin` configuration questions in file for later use. We will discuss all `agentadmin` parameters in the next table.

After we execute the command, it will show a license agreement that we should accept. After accepting the license, `agentadmin` will ask a series of questions included in the following table:

Question	Description and our answer
Enter the application server config directory path	We should provide a path like `domains_dir/domain2/config`.
OpenSSO server URL	We should provide a fully-qualified name if we need SSO and its features (discussed in the previous chapter) or a plain URL similar to `http://127.0.0.1:8080/opensso` if we do not need SSO features.
Agent URL	We should provide a fully-qualified URL if we need SSO and its features (discussed in the previous chapter) or a plain URL similar to `http://127.0.0.1:38080/agentapp` if we do not need SSO features.
Enter the agent profile name	A unique name for this agent, something like `gfbook_agent`.
Enter the path to the password file	Full path to the password file we created in the previous step.

The configuration-related questions are over, now agent installation will ask to confirm the configuration. After this step the agent installation is over.

We will need to add the agent profile to our OpenSSO server. To add the agent profile to the OpenSSO server we should:

1. Log in to the OpenSSO administration console, which by default is located at `http://127.0.0.1:8080/opensso`.

2. Now in the first page, select the **Access Control** tab and then select the **Top Level Realm** or any other realm which you want the agent to be activated in. Now select the **Agent** tab and then select the **J2EE** tab. Click on the **New** button.

3. Now, we should provide the **Agent Name** and **Password**. In our configuration, the **Agent Name** is `gfbook_agent` and the password `adminadmin` which we provided during the installation using the `password.pwd` file. We should provide two URLs and then we are done with creating the agent profile in the server.

4. For the **configuration** item we can either use localized or centralized mode. The local mode is kept for backward compatibility of OpenSSO server with older versions of OpenSSO agents and using centralized mode is recommended for OpenSSO agent's version 3 and above.

In the local mode, all of the agent configuration is stored locally in a configuration file named OpenSSOAgentConfiguration.properties in the same machine that the agent runs on while in the centralized mode. Almost all of the configurations are stored in OpenSSO storage and the agent uses a bootstrap file named OpenSSOAgentBootstrap.properties to locate the OpenSSO server and retrieve the configuration from it.

5. The next two fields are links to the OpenSSO server and the agent application. For our configuration we should specify them as follow:

   ○ **Server URL**: http://127.0.0.1:8080/opensso

   ○ **Agent URL**: http://127.0.0.1:38080/agentapp

6. Now that we have specified all of the properties we can click on the **Create** button to create the agent profile and finish the creating agent profile steps.

7. After we have created the agent profile we can select it from the agents list and customize its configuration in areas like SSO, the application that it protects, the OpenSSO services that the agent is using, and so on.

Let's go back and check what happened when we created the agent in the agent machine. When we create an agent, the agentadmin utility creates a directory named Agent_NNN in the agent directory. The NNN is a sequential number assigned to each agent after we create it. For example, the first agent is located inside Agent_001, the second one inside Agent_002, and so on.

Inside the agent directory we have two other directories as follows:

- The config contains the configuration files for the agent instance, including OpenSSOAgentBootstrap.properties and OpenSSOAgentConfiguration.properties

- The logs directory contains the following subdirectories:

   ○ The audit directory contains local audit trail for the agent instance

   ○ The debug directory contains the debug files for the agent instance when the agent runs in debug mode

The following table shows a list of all `agentadmin` commands along with a basic description about them.

Commands	Description
`--install`	Installs a new agent instance.
`--custom-install`	Installs a new agent instance.
`--uninstall`	Uninstalls an existing agent instance.
`--listAgents`	Displays details of all the configured agents.
`--agentInfo`	Displays details of the agent corresponding to the specified agent IDs.
`--version`	Displays the version information.
`--getEncryptKey`	Generates an Agent Encryption key.
`--encrypt`	Encrypts a given string.
`--uninstallAll`	Uninstalls all agent instances.
`--migrate`	Migrates the agent to a newer version.
`--usage`	Displays the usage message.
`--help`	Displays a brief help message.

Each command has one or more options, which you can see by issuing the following command:

```
agentadmin --help
```

Now that we installed OpenSSO agent in the system, we can take our *Chapter 2* samples and configure the system so it can be protected by the agent instead of using the built-in functionalities of Java EE security.

Placing the sample application under OpenSSO protection

So far, we installed the agent and we created the agent profile in the OpenSSO but this agent does nothing unless we configure it to protect an application and also change the application to use agent protection instead of the default Java EE security provided by GlassFish.

Changing sample application descriptor files

Let's see what changes we should introduce in our conversion application to place it under the agent protection. You can create a copy of the application and change it to later on compare two applications and further understand the changes we made to put it under the agent protection.

First we need to add the agent filter to the `web.xml` file of our conversion application's web module. To do so, open the `web.xml` file and add the following snippet immediately inside the `web-app` node.

```
<filter>
    <filter-name>Agent</filter-name>
    <filter-class> com.sun.identity.agents.filter.AmAgentFilter
        </filter-class>
</filter>
<filter-mapping>
    <filter-name>Agent</filter-name>
    <url-pattern>/*</url-pattern>
    <dispatcher>REQUEST</dispatcher>
    <dispatcher>INCLUDE</dispatcher>
    <dispatcher>FORWARD</dispatcher>
    <dispatcher>ERROR</dispatcher>
</filter-mapping>
```

Now, we do not need to have an authentication realm in place, so find the following line in the `web.xml` and delete it.

```
<realm-name>ConversionRealm</realm-name>
```

We are done with our changes to this file. Now we should change the roles to groups mapping because starting from now on we are mapping our roles to groups we defined in the OpenSSO server.

As you may remember we used `sun-application.xml` for role mapping to lift the need to define the role mappings in both `sun-web.xml` and `sun-ejb-jar.xml`. Now just open the `sun-application.xml` and replace the group names as shown in the following table.

Old Group Name	New Group Name
manager	id=manager, ou=group, dc=opensso, dc=java, dc=net
employee	id=employee, ou=group, dc=opensso, dc=java, dc=net

These are all the changes we needed to introduce to switch from plain GlassFish security to agent protection.

Now our application is under protection of the agent but the agent does not know anything about the application. The agent does not know which section of the application should be protected, which sections need no protection, and so on.

Configuring the agent to protect the sample application

In this section we should let agent know what kind of security measures we need to be applied on our resources, which set of subjects and groups are known to the agent, and so on.

To configure the agent, log in to the OpenSSO administration console and do as follows:

1. Navigate to **Access Control | Realm Name | Agents | J2EE** as shown in the following figure.

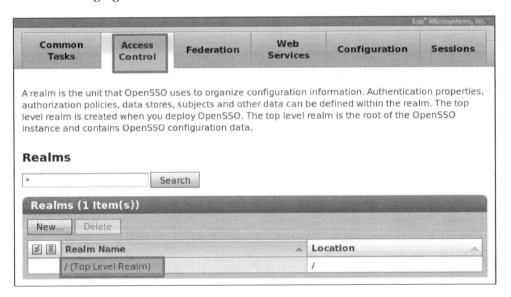

2. Click on the **gfbook_agent** link; the **Global** tab of the agent configuration pages shows up as demonstrated in the following figure.

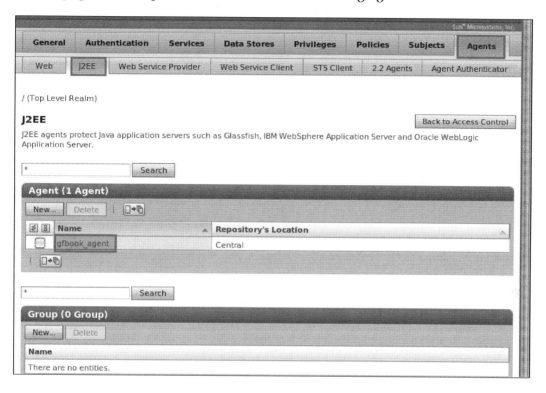

3. Now click on the **Login Processing** link to configure the login page, and enter `/Conversion-war/auth/login.html` in the **New Value** box and click on the **Add** button.

4. Navigate to the top the page and click on the **Logout Processing** link to configure the logout page. In the **Application Logout URI**, enter `Conversion-war` in the **Map Key** field and enter the `/Conversion-war/auth/logout.jsp` in the **Corresponding Map Value**.

5. Navigate to the top the page and select the **Application** tab and click on the **Access Denied URI Processing** to configure the agent to show an information page about user being denied access to a URL. In the **Map Key** enter `Conversion-war` and in the **Corresponding Map Value** enter `/Conversion-war/auth/AccessRestricted.html`.

6. Click on **Not Enforced URI Processing** and enter the following items one by one using the **New Value** box and the **Add** button.

   ° /Conversion-war/Converted

   ° /Conversion-war/public/*

   ° /Conversion-war/jsp/toCenti.jsp

   ° /Conversion-war/index.jsp

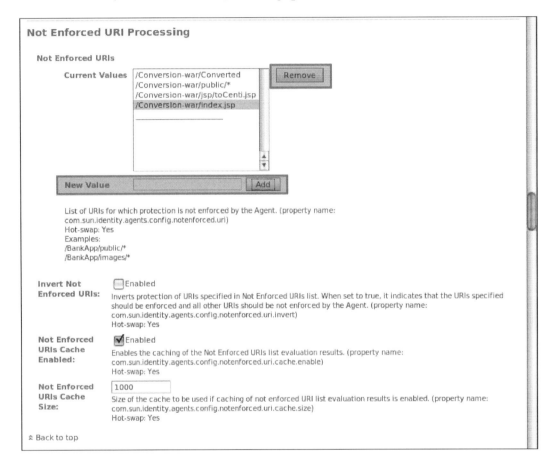

7. Navigate to top of the page and then click on the **Save** button to have all these configuration saved.

What we did so far is place the application under the agent protection and let the agent know which page is our login page, which page is the logout page, and which set of resources do not need any protection and can be viewed by any user, either authenticated or not.

Defining access rules

Now we need to define some rules to let the agent and OpenSSO server determine which users can access which set of resources in the conversion application. As you remember we have already defined our users and user groups in the previous chapter and we should now only define security rules that governs relation between our conversion application and those users. To do so:

1. Navigate back to the OpenSSO administration console main page and select **Access Control**, click on **/ (Top Level Realm)** and then click on the **Policies** tab.

2. Click on the **New Policy** button and in the **Name** field type gfbook_P1 and make sure that **Active** checkbox is ticked.

3. Now in the **Rules** section click on the **New** button, select **URL Policy Agent (with resource name)** and click on **Next** button.

4. Now, for the **Name** field use gfbook_R1 and for the **Resource Name** field use http://127.0.0.1:38443/Conversion-war/* or the corresponding URL based on our server configuration and sample application context.

   Make sure that both **POST** and **GET** actions are selected, then select **Allow** as both actions' value. As illustrated in the following figure, click on the **Finish** button and it will navigate back to the **New Policy** page.

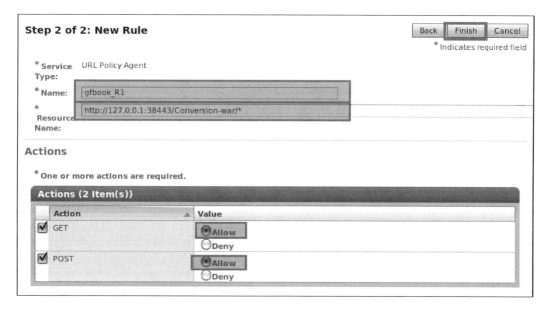

5. In the **Subjects** section click on the **New** button. Now select the **OpenSSO Identity Subject** from the tree possibilities and then click on the **Next** button.

6. Enter a name like **gfbook_S1** as the subject name and use the filtering capabilities and add `employee` and `manager` group to the list of selected subjects.

7. Now click on the **Finish** button and then click on the **Save** button to save the policy.

If required, we can define constraint on the policy by adding access conditions that can conditionally allow or deny access to the resource by evaluating access conditions like time of the day or the required origination network address.

Now that we have defined the effective policies we can test the application. To test the applications navigate to `http://127.0.0.1:38080/Conversion-war/index.jsp` or the corresponding URL in your configuration and try accessing different conversion methods.

If we try to access centimeter conversion by hitting `http://127.0.0.1:38080/Conversion-war/jsp/toCenti.jsp` we will be able to access it. It is possible because we place it in the **Not Enforced URI Processing** list. If we try to use any other conversion pages like `http://127.0.0.1:38080/Conversion-war/jsp/toInch.jsp` or `http://127.0.0.1:38080/Conversion-war/jsp/toMilli.jsp` it will trigger the authentication and authorization process because those two resources are protected by the agent.

If we try to access any of those two restricted URLs we will be redirected to the OpenSSO login page, which we will need to provide a valid username and password to log in.

For using the `toMilli.jsp`, we should authenticate as an employee because in the `web.xml` we granted anyone with `employee` role to have access to this URL.

You should remember that in the previous chapter, when we defined two users in the OpenSSO administration console, we created a user named `meera`, identified with `meera` as password, as a member of `employee` group. We also created a user identified as `james/james` and gave him the `manager` group membership. So, to access the `toMilli.jsp` we will need to login with `meera/meera` and to access the `toInch.jsp` we will need to login with `james/james`.

When we are logged in as a user with lower permission level, for example we are logged in as an employee, and we try to access a resource restricted to our user, such as a resource only available to the manager, we will be redirected to the `AccessRestricted.html`, which we defined in the agent's application **Configuration** section.

Usually, the `AccessRestricted.html` page includes a link to log out from the system and information about the resource we just tried to access, such as the required access level to inform the user which resource they were trying to access and what access level they must have before they can access it.

To access `toInch.jsp`, log out by hitting the logout page which is located at `http://127.0.0.1:38080/Conversion-war/auth/logout.jsp`. After logging out, any effort to view the `toInch.jsp` page will result in the kick-start of an authentication process which shows the OpenSSO login page, which is similar to the following figure:

You may ask, how we can customize the login page of OpenSSO to tailor our needs, the answer lies in editing a few XML and JSP files. For more information about customizing the login and logout pages you can check the following pages:

- `http://docs.sun.com/app/docs/doc/820-3320/ghlfa?a=view`
- `http://blogs.sun.com/bouyges/entry/opesso_customizing_login_page`

Now, take a look at the following figure to further understand what happens in the background when we place a request on a resource which is protected by the OpenSSO agent.

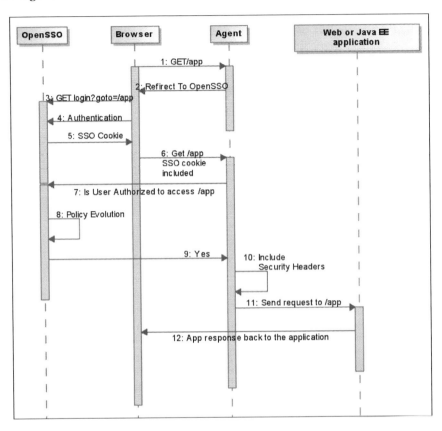

As you can see, the OpenSSO agent intercepts any request made to the protected applications, then it consults with the OpenSSO server to check whether the requested resource is under protection or if it is in the list of Not Enforced URIs. If the resource is protected, OpenSSO will check to see whether the user is authenticated or not by examining the presence of OpenSSO cookie. If the user is not authenticated he will be asked to provide authentication tokens, which can be username/password or any other type of authentication tokens. After the user is successfully logged in, OpenSSO sets the required security attributes in the HTTP header. Now it is time to evaluate different policies to see whether the user is authorized to access the required page or not. If authorized his request will go through and if not authorized he will be redirected to the Access Denied URI, which is defined in the Application section of the agent configuration.

Log in using one of our defined users, for example meera/meera, and then navigate to http://127.0.0.1:8080/opensso to see what happens. Each OpenSSO user can edit his profile by logging in and navigating to the OpenSSO home page.

Now that we have enough knowledge and experience regarding using OpenSSO policy agents, it's time to see how we can use OpenSSO and OpenSSO agents to secure our Web Services.

Summary

In this chapter, we discussed OpenSSO policy agents that let us as architects, system designers, and developers secure a Java EE application using OpenSSO without changing the application source code. We discussed the policy agents, policy agent installation, and administration along with changing our sample application to place it under agent protection instead of using plain Java EE protection.

In the next chapter we will discuss Web Services security and how we can use OpenSSO and OpenSSO agents to secure our Web Services deployed in GlassFish.

9
Securing Web Services by OpenSSO

The need for integration and interoperability is growing exponentially and any new platform and standard should be introduced with these factors in mind. Not only do we need data and process integration but we also need to be able to integrate our security schemas and policies to make as smooth an interaction between our systems possible. Several attempts were made in the past to address the interoperability problem — IIOP is one of those attempts that gained enough attention and success to let it be in use years after its introduction.

Introducing Web Services is the new attempt to tackle the same problem that IIOP tackled years ago. We take into consideration all new innovations and changes in the software development landscape, like the possibility for using Web Services independent of the platform and the programming language, easier development, using new standards and protocols in different layers, and the possibility to use it in the old software development platform as well as the new one.

In this chapter we are going to learn about the following topics:

- Learning how to apply authentication and authorization on Web Services
- Learning the standards involved in Web Services security
- Applying the standards in developing a secured Web service
- Using OpenSSO to secure the sample Web service developed previously

Java EE and Web Services security

Java EE by itself does not provide anything specific for Web Services security but rather different vendors implement some basic security measures to protect Web Services with basic authentication and authorization.

Securing Web Services in a Web module

In the Web module we can protect a Web service endpoint the same way we protect any other resource. We can define a resource collection and enforce access management and authentication on it. The most common form of protecting a Web service is using the HTTP Basic or Client Certificate.

For example, if we use the HTTP basic authentication and our Web service client uses the Dispatch client API to access the Web service. We can use an snippet like the following one to include the username and password with the right access role to invoke a Web service.

```
sourceDispatch.getRequestContext().put(Dispatch.USERNAME_
PROPERTY,"user");
sourceDispatch.getRequestContext().put(Dispatch.PASSWORD_
PROPERTY,"password");
```

The `user` and the `password` should be valid in the security realm we configured for the Web application and should have access right to the endpoint URL.

> Another way of authenticating the client to the server in HTTP level is using the `Authenticator` class, which provides more functionalities and flexibilities. For more information about the `Authenticator` class check http://java.sun.com/javase/6/docs/technotes/guides/net/http-auth.html.

Web Services security in EJB modules

We can expose a Stateless Session Bean as a Web service and therefore we can use all security annotations like `@RolesAllowed`, `@PermitAll` and their corresponding deployment descriptor elements to define its security plan. But enforcing authentication for Web Services is vendor-specific and each vendor uses its own method to define the security realm, authentication, and so on.

EJB-based Web Services authentication in GlassFish

To apply access control on a Web service developed using a Session Bean and deployed either as an EJB module or as a part of an enterprise application we can use the `sun-ejb-jar.xml` to include the role mapping, and the security realm.

Lets see how we can develop restricted EJB based Web service and enable authentication on it.

```
@WebService()
@Stateless()
@RolesAllowed("manager")
public class Echo {
Method(operationName = "stringEcho")
    public String stringEcho(@WebParam(name = "val") String val) {
        return "echoing " + val;
    }
}
```

We are using the `@RolesAllowed` annotation to only allow a user with manager role access this EJB and therefore the only users able to invoke the `stringEcho` business method from a Web service client is a user because either their principal is mapped to the role or the group they are a member is mapped to manager role.

Right to this point we applied the access control to our Echo Web service but we are still lacking the authentication process which specifies how the users are going to provide their principals and what is our reference for checking these principals. This requirement is fulfilled using some sub-elements of the `port-component-name` element of the `sun-ejb-jar.xml` file.

Following snippet shows how we specify the authentication method and the security realm for the `Echo` Web Service.

```
<ejb>
    <ejb-name>Echo</ejb-name>
    <webservice-endpoint>
        <port-component-name>Echo</port-component-name>
        <login-config>
            <auth-method>BASIC</auth-method>
            <realm>file_realm</realm>
        </login-config>
    </webservice-endpoint>
</ejb>
```

We are simply using the `login-config` element and its sub-elements to define the authentication method and the security realm.

Sure we still need to define the roles and the mapping either in the `sun-ejb-jar.xml` or in the `sun-application.xml`. The following snippet shows how we can map the manager role to a principal named `jack` and a group named `mgrs`. The snippet can be placed either in the `sun-application.xml` or in the `sun-ejb-jar.xml` file.

```
<security-role-mapping>
    <role-name>manager</role-name>
    <principal-name>jack</principal-name>
    <group-name>mgrs</group-name>
</security-role-mapping>
```

So far we learned how to specify the roles permitted to invoke a Web service method and we specified how to authenticate the identity of any invoker by checking their identity with a security realm. But we are still lacking an important security measure — the transport guarantee.

To enforce transport guarantee we only need to add one more sub-element to the `webservice-endpoint` element. Following snippet shows the Echo service with CONFIDENTIAL transport security guarantee.

```
<enterprise-beans>
    <ejb>
        <ejb-name>Echo</ejb-name>
        <webservice-endpoint>
            <port-component-name>Echo</port-component-name>
            <login-config>
                <auth-method>BASIC</auth-method>
                <realm>file</realm>
            </login-config>
            <transport-guarantee>CONFIDENTIAL</transport-guarantee>
        </webservice-endpoint>
    </ejb>
</enterprise-beans>
```

We can use NONE, INTEGRAL, and CONFIDENTIAL transport security levels as we discussed in *Chapter 1*.

The client code for invoking an EJB-based Web service is the same as client code for a Servlet-based Web service as it should be because of the nature of Web Services.

GlassFish provides Message Security measures which we can use to enforce authentication in the message level (SOAP, HTTPServlet). To learn more about using GlassFish Message Security visit `http://docs.sun.com/app/docs/doc/820-7692/ablrk?a=view`.

In the following sections of this chapter we will review how we can use OpenSSO and OpenSSO Web service security providers to secure our Web Services.

Understanding Web Services security

Security is required whenever we want to only let a small set of users use a service. The small set can be as small as one or it can be as large as thousands of subscribers whom we allowed to use the service. Web Services usually fall into the second category because we do not simply expose functionality when we do not want to let more than one user access it.

So basically, we need all sorts of security measures that we had in a web application present in the Web Services realm. These requirements are as follows:

- Authentication to identify the involved parties, which are **Web Service Producer (WSP)** and **Web service consumer (WSC)**

- Authorization to check the availability of a resource to an identity authenticated in the previous step

- Confidentiality to ensure that no one will be able to tap into the communication

- Integrity to prevent any kind of tampering during the communication between WSP and WSC

- Non-repudiation to provide confidence in the interaction and prevent any party from repudiating its involvement in the interaction

- Credential exchange to send and receive security tokens between different parties involved in the interaction, like token issuer, service provider, and service consumer

We may need to address one or more than one of these items in our system, based on our software design and the business security requirements.

Addressing these needs is a bit different than dealing with them when we are developing classic web applications. This is because Web Services are introduced to cover the interoperability needs of different systems interacting together when none of them were designed specifically to understand how the other systems involved in the process work. So Web security standards are introduced to make sure that all systems meant to expose interoperable secure Web Services follow them in order to let other standard clients interact with them.

The following figure shows a sample scenario that usually happens when a client tries to access a secured Web service. The WSP needs authentication to process the WSC and a mediator is sitting before the WSP to log all incoming requests.

In our scenario, the client should sign the message it is sending in addition to encrypting one of the Web service parameters named `request-ID` to prevent any unauthorized party monitoring the communication from finding the `request-ID` value.

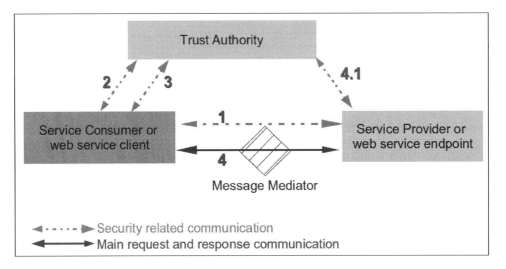

What the above figure shows about clients accessing secured Web Services can be summarized into the following steps:

1. Client requests security metadata from the service provider and the service indicates that the client needs a security token from a particular trust authority (**Secure Token Service (STS)** from now on) along with the STS address. This step is transparent to the application and an application developer does not need to know about it.

2. The client requests security metadata from the STS and the STS responds with the type of security token to be used for further communication. This step is transparent to the application.

3. The client sends its credential as requested by the STS and the STS issues a security token after verifying that credentials are valid and has the required access level.

4. The client invokes the service by sending a signed message, which includes the encrypted request ID and security tokens included in the message header according to the related standards. The service provider verifies the token by consulting the trust authority and verifies the message integrity by checking its signature. If successful, the WSP will send the appropriated response back to the client.

Multiple trust authorities can be chained to ensure that multiple consumer requests can span between different domains and different enterprises.

In the above sample scenario, the WSC can be a developed using .NET framework while the WSP is hosted in a Java EE container and the trust authority is developed using C++ or any other language. To make it possible for such a scenario to take place smoothly several standards were introduced to provide the industry with security implantation guidelines that guarantee the interoperability between different systems. These guidelines and specifications are developed or recommended by different organization such as W3C, WS-I, OASIS, and others. The most important standards and specifications related to Web Services are included in the following table along with use of the standard in the above scenario. Although some of these specifications are not directly introduced for Web Services they are still playing a great role in the overall Web Services security.

Standard	Description
WS-Security	Specifies how integrity and confidentiality should be enforced on a message as well as specifying the standard way to communicate using authentication tokens like username password, X.509 certificates, and others along with the message. Steps 2 and 3 in the previous list involve this standard.
WS-Trust	Specifies how authentication tokens are issued, renewed, and validated in a system of multiple consumers, providers, and token-issuer services. Steps 2, 3, and 4.1 involve this standard.
WS-Policy	Not directly related to Web Services security but a WSP may use it to publish its security requirements and capabilities. For example, which tokens the provider accepts and tokens issued by which issuer are accepted by the provider. Step 1 involves this standard.

Standard	Description
XML Encryption	Introduced by W3C, specifies how we can encrypt content of an XML element and later on decrypt it. Encrypting the request ID involves XML Encryption.
XML Signature	Specifies the structure of a digital signature we can use to sign XML documents to ensure their integrity. Signing the XML message guarantees the integrity involving this standard.
WS-SecureConversation	As the name implies, the standard specifies how we can have a security context in the course of exchanging multiple SOAP messages. The standard specifies something similar to TLS in classic Web.
WS-Federation	Defines mechanisms to allow different security systems with internal security realms to broker information on identities and identity attributes. If we were going to use multiple trust authorities we could have used WS-Federation.
SAML	The Security Assertion Markup Language tries to solve the SSO problem in the Web Services realm. The aim of SAML is specifying a standard to let a WSC communicate its authentication and authorization to a WSP. If we were going to use multiple trust authorities we could have used SAML.
WS-I Basic Security Profile	It specifies how different WS-Security elements should be interpreted and dealt with to achieve the maximum possible interoperability.

As you can see, we have many different standards and recommendations, which we must adhere to achieve a certain level of interoperability. The good news is that most of these standards are under the hood and we as developers are not dealing with them in depth. Instead, we deal with a fine set of APIs provided in different Web Services implementation, like Metro, to develop interoperable Web Services. The following figure shows how these standards are related to each other:

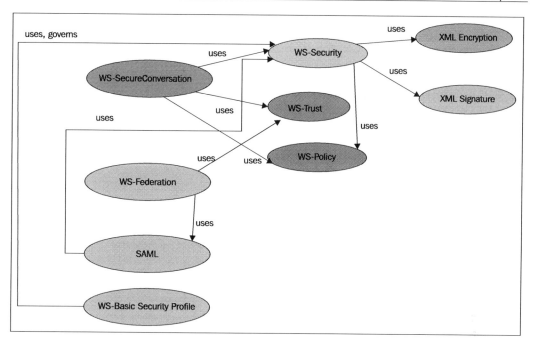

As you can see, the heaviest standard is the WS-SecureConversation, which virtually depends on more than five other standards. There are some other specifications and recommendations for Web Services security that are not widely in use. Some of them are listed below:

- The **eXtensible Access Control Markup Language (XACML)** specifies how to describe and interpret access control policies
- The **XML Key Management Specification (XKMS)** specifies protocols for distributing and registering public keys, suitable for use in conjunction with XML Signature and XML Encryption

Now that you understand the jargons and saw which standards we have in WS-Security, let's take a brief look at the relation between WS-Trust and WS-Security when it comes to authentication and authorization. WS-Security defines required standards that allows us to include an authentication or authorization information into a SOAP message. The included information is tampering- and sniffing-proof. WS-Security defines several types of credentials that can be included into the SOAP message to let the service provider check for authentication or authorization. Important credential tokens are username, X.509 certificate, Kerberos ticket, and SAML assertion. WS-Trust on the other hand defines standards for issuing, renewing, and validating security tokens, which is referred to as STS. These tokens are used by WS-Security to include them in the SAML assertions.

We said that XML Encryption, **XML Digital Signature (XML-DSig)**, and WS-SecureConversation are working together to provide a functionality similar to what we have in TLS. Let's see the differences between TLS and message security-related specifications. The following table shows how TLS and message level security are different.

TLS	Message level security
Uses SSL.	Does not use SSL.
None or all stream protection: Whole data pipe is protected by SSL, no selective protection increases the processing overhead.	Selective protection: Selected XML elements are protected.
Does not work with Intermediaries that may monitor, or audit, or preprocess the SOAP messages.	Any mediator sitting between WSC and WSP can read unsecured parts of the message for logging, audition, preprocessing, load balancing, and so on.
Based on well-established standards.	Based on newer standards.
Well-known key management.	More complex key management.

Understanding SOAP message structure

The **Simple Object Access Protocol (SOAP)** is the base of Web Services communication as it specifies how data should be packed to be understandable to the Web service provider when it receives a request and to the Web service consumer when it receives the response back from the provider.

SOAP messages are XML documents with a defined schema. Each message has an envelope inside which we have a header and a body. The body of the message carries the business-related information, like response to a stock quote request and the header carries metadata, such as information like QoS, security, and others. The following figure shows the structure of a SOAP message:

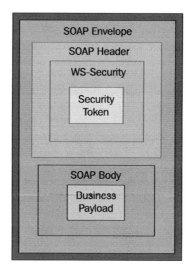

Developing secure Web Services

In this section we will develop a simple Web service, which will echo an incoming string to demonstrate how we can use OpenSSO to enforce a different level of security on the SOAP messages level.

We can develop the sample Web service using any IDE or using the JAX-WS development tools like `wsgen` and `import`. I leave the service development to your capable hands and only focus on the security portion of the story.

 The best IDE that I can suggest is NetBeans IDE 6.8 or a newer version. NetBeans IDE is well integrated with GlassFish and provides us with superb support for Java EE software development.

The source code for the `Echo` class right after developing looks like the following snippet:

```
@WebService()
public class Echo {

    /**
     * Web service operation
     */
    @WebMethod(operationName = "echoString")
    public String echoString(@WebParam(name = "stringToecho")
      String stringToecho) {
        return "Echoing " + stringToecho;
    }
}
```

As you can see, we have nothing but a plain method echoing the string it receives. We will develop the service consumer code later on after we understand more concepts of the OpenSSO Web Services security.

Enforcing security measures on the consumer and provider means that the service container in the WSP side and the execution environment or the container in the WSC side should have a way to communicate with the OpenSSO server. They need this to query the OpenSSO server about the security measures, validate security tokens, place the audition events, and so on. The JAX-WS in general, and the close integration between the OpenSSO and GlassFish in particular, provides us a neat and easy integration of OpenSSO Web Services security agents into GlassFish. Integrating the OpenSSO Web service security agent with other containers like Apache Tomcat, IBM WebSphere, and Oracle WebLogic server is possible with a manual installation process instead of using the Web Services security agent installation application.

The security agent can be used in Java SE environment as well as to enforce security measures on the client communication with the service providers.

A simple scenario using OpenSSO Web Services security will involve a set of OpenSSO components. These components, along with their interactions, are shown in the following figure:

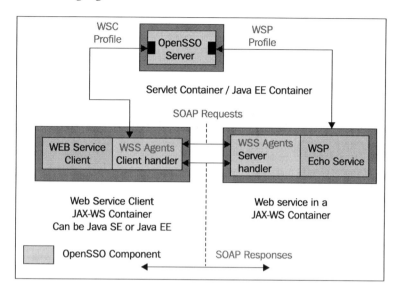

Any client who wants to access service needs to provide the WSP a security token issued by the specified STS and also needs to sign the messages it is sending to the Web service. The previous figure shows how OpenSSO components, WSC, and WSP fits in the scenario.

What happens in the communication between the WSP and WSC is as follows:

1. The WSS agent in the client side will secure the outbound messages by including the security token inside the SOAP header. The token will receive its validity from the OpenSSO server service like the STS.

2. The WSS agent in the server side will validate inbound messages for the security token and check the token status with the OpenSSO server.

3. The WSS agent in the server side will place a security token in the SOAP header of any outbound response.

4. The WSS agent in the client side will validate inbound messages by checking the security token authenticity with the OpenSSO server.

The figure illustrates the case when the client side is a Java SE client using the programmatic method to create the security tokens. If running inside a container with WSS agent installed, the agent can take care of inserting the security tokens automatically.

Downloading and installing Web Services security agents

We used a Java EE security Policy Agent to secure the classic Java EE application and now we are going to use another security Policy Agent that can enforce security over Web Services instead of enforcing it on Java EE applications. Download the latest nightly build of OpenSSO Web Services security providers from `http://www.forgerock.org/downloads/openam/wssagents/nightly/openssowssproviders.zip` and extract it in a directory, which we will call `wss_agent_dir`. Before continuing with these steps make sure that:

- The agent server is stopped and not running.
- The OpenSSO server is up and running.
- Create a password file containing a single line which, is the Agent Authentication Password. For example, the file name is `wsspassword.pwd` and its content is one line as follows:

```
adminadmin
```

I assume the following is our current configuration for the installation process.

Configuration Item	Description
OpenSSO server	We assume that OpenSSO is running on `http://127.0.0.1:8080/opensso`.
Agent server	We assume that agent server ports are as stated above.
Password file	We assume that we have the password file created and it is located at `/opt/wsspassword.pwd`.

After understanding the configuration we can use the following steps to install the Web Services security agent.

1. Now, navigate to `wss_agent_dir/bin` and get ready to install the agent into the agent server. If you are in Linux or UNIX platform you need to give the execution permission to the `wssagentadmin` file. You can do it using the following command:

   ```
   chmod +x wssagentadmin
   ```

   Start the installation with the following command:

   ```
   ./wssagentadmin --install --saveResponse /opt/response.resp
   ```

We used two parameters for the `wssagentadmin` command — the first parameter tells the `wssagentadmin` that we want to install a new agent and the second parameter asks the `wssagentadmin` to save our responses to the `wssagentadmin` configuration questions in file for later use. We will discuss all `wssagentadmin` parameters in the next table.

2. After we execute the command, it will shows a license agreement which we should accept. After accepting the license, `wssagentadmin` will ask a series of questions included in the following table:

Question	Description and our answer
Enter the Application Server Config Directory Path	We should provide a path like: `domains_dir/domain2/config`.
OpenSSO server URL	We should provide a fully-qualified name if we need SSO and its features (discussed in the previous chapter) or a plain URL similar to `http://127.0.0.1:8080/opensso` if we do not need SSO features.
Enter the Agent Profile name	A unique name for this agent, something like `gfbook_wss_agent`.
Enter the path to the password file	Full path to the password file we created in the previous step: `/opt/wsspassword.pwd`.

When the agent installation successfully finishes, we can see a new directory created inside the `wss_agent_dir` named `WSSAgent_001`. If it is not the first agent instance installation we can expect the `001` to be something else, showing how many agent instances we've installed using the `wss_agent_dir` as an installation base. The `WSSAgent_001` directory contains the following directories:

  ○ A `logs` directory containing logfile and debug messages if debug mode is enabled

  ○ A `config` directory that includes the `AMConfig.properties` file, containing the agent instance bootstrap attributes

3. Now we should continue our work in the OpenSSO administration console. Navigate to `http://127.0.0.1:8080/opensso` and log in using `amadmin` and your specified password.

4. Go to **Access Control | Default realm | Agents,** you should see a window similar to the following figure. Most of our work will be with the **Web Service Client** and **Web Service Provider** sections.

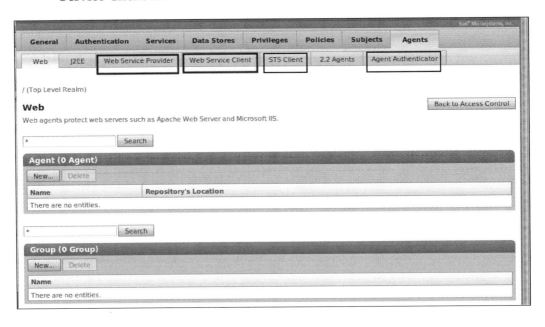

Now we need to create two security profiles—one for our WSP and one for our WSC to let them use the OpenSSO Web service security agent.

Creating a Web Service Client profile

The Web Service Client agent profile specifies the configuration that is used to secure the outbound Web service requests from a Web service client. The profile name should be unique across all agents. To create the profile:

1. Go to the **Web Service Client** tab and click on the **New** button under the **Agent** panel.

2. Specify the required attribute for creating the profile as follows and then click on the **Create** button to create the profile.

    ○ **Name:** EchoService_Client or anything else meaningful to you

    ○ **Password:** adminadmin

3. Click on the **EchoService_Client** profile to open the configuration page.

4. Here we can specify which security mechanism is accessible to our client. We will select **STSSecurity** to use the STS of OpenSSO for issuing the security tokens. When we select **STSSecurity** the option for **STS Configuration** will get enabled and we can select one of the available **STS Client** profiles, for example the default profile which is named **SecurityTokenService**.

5. Make sure that **Preserve Security Headers in Message** is selected.

6. Go down to the **Signing and Encryption** section. Make sure that all of the following items are selected because we want to sign the outgoing requests messages and later on verify the received responses to ensure that the message is not tampered with during transmission. We will discuss the signing and signature verification in more detail at the end of this section.

   ° **Is Request Signed Enabled**

   ° **Is Response Signature Verified**

7. Now we should specify the Web service endpoint we want to enforce these measures for. In our example the endpoint URL is `http://localhost:38080/EchoService/EchoService`.

8. Save the changes by clicking on the **Save** button.

The WSC profile is created. Now we are going to create the provider profile.

Creating a Web Service Provider profile

The **Web Service Provider** profile specifies the configuration that is used to perform the following tasks:

- Validating inbound Web service requests from Web service clients
- Securing outbound responses according to the configuration

To create the provider follow these steps:

1. Navigate to the **Web Service Provider** tab under the **Agents** tab and click **New**.

2. Specify a name and a password for the profile and click on the **Create** button. For example:

   ° **Name: EchoService_Provider** or anything else meaningful to you

   ° **Password**: `adminadmin`

3. Click on the **EchoService_Provider** to edit its configuration.

4. Select all **Security Mechanisms**. And make sure that **Preserve Security Headers in Message** is selected.

5. Now we should specify **Signing and Encryption** configurations. Make sure that all of the following items are selected. We are enforcing a signature verification of any request and signing our response so that WSC can verify the responses it receives before delivering them to the actual client code. We will discuss the signing and signature verification in more detail at the end of this section. The items to be kept selected are:

    ○ **Is Request Signature Verified**

    ○ **Is Response Signed Enabled**

6. In the **End Points** section specify the Web service end point we want to enforce these measures for it. In our example the endpoint is `http://localhost:38080/EchoService/EchoService`.

7. Save the changes by clicking on the **Save** button.

We are done creating a Web Service Provider profile. The next step, and last one in OpenSSO administration console, is updating the Agent Authenticator Profile. Updating this profile will let the agent authenticator access the read-only attributes of allowed agent. To do so:

1. In the **Agents** tab click on the **Agent Authenticator** and then click on **agentAuth** to open its editor page.

2. Add the **EchoService_Provider** and **EchoService_Client** from the list of available agent profiles to the list of selected profiles and click on the **Save** button. The following figure shows the **agentAuth** edit page:

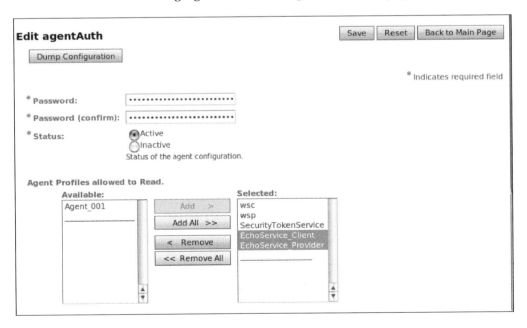

After finishing step 2 we are done with configuring the security provider profiles.

Securing the Echo Web Service

We do not need to do anything special to secure the Echo Web service. The policies we specified in the WSP profile will be enforced automatically. So this section of the book is complete.

Now let's turn to developing a WSC and see what we need to do in order to get the client-side WSS integrated into our application.

Developing an Echo Service Consumer

We will develop the client application on top of JAX-WS 2.0 and assuming that you know how to use your IDE to develop a Java SE application I will only include the source code for the main parts of the WSC.

The WSS client agent will integrate with our Java SE application, so we need to include some libraries in the application classpath. The following list shows all that we need to include in the classpath. Remember that these libraries are in addition to JAX-WS (Metro 2.0 in our case) required libraries.

- `wss_agent_dir/lib/openssoclientsdk.jar`
- `wss_agent_dir/lib/opensso-sharedlib.jar`
- `wss_agent_dir/lib/openssowssproviders.jar`

These libraries contain all the necessary classes that the WSC agent requires to interact with the OpenSSO server and to enforce the required securities.

The WSS client agent needs to interact with the OpenSSO server, so we should have a bootstrap file to boot the agent with required information like OpenSSO address, shared secret, and other attributes. This file is named `AMConfig.properties` and is located inside the agent instance `config` directory. In case you forgot, the directory is located at `wss_agent_dir/WSSAgent_001/config`. We should place this file in the application classpath, for example in the source code default package.

Now, let's see how we can use the WSS Provider to enforce the security we defined in the OpenSSO administration console for the `EchoService_Client` profile.

The complete source code for the sample application is included in the code bundle. Here we will only evaluate the portion related to WSS agents and Web Services security.

The overall procedure of invoking a Web service using a WSS provider involves the following steps:

1. Creating the SOAP message as we usually do when we are invoking unsecured Web Services.
2. Initializing an OpenSSO WSS handler for the profile we created to enforce the security on the SOAP message.
3. Securing the message using the handler.
4. Sending the message to the service provider.

Now let's take a look at the mentioned steps in source codes that actually performs the job. Starting with the step 1 snippet which is as follows:

```
String providerName = "EchoService_Client";
StringBuffer soapMessage = prepareRequestSOAPMessage("Sample
    String");
MimeHeaders mimeHeader = new MimeHeaders();
mimeHeader.addHeader("Content-Type", "text/xml");
MessageFactory msgFactory = MessageFactory.newInstance();
SOAPMessage message = msgFactory.createMessage(mimeHeader,
    new ByteArrayInputStream(soapMessage.toString().getBytes()));
```

Here is the detailed explanation of what is happening in the source code.

1. In the above snippet we only defined a variable containing the name of the WSC profile we want to use and we previously created in OpenSSO. The snippet also invokes a method, which creates a SOAP request for our `EchoService`. Now it's time to move on to step 2.

   ```
   SOAPRequestHandler handler = new SOAPRequestHandler();
   HashMap params = new HashMap();
   params.put("providername", providerName);
   handler.init(params);
   ProviderConfig pc = ProviderConfig.getProvider(providerName,
       ProviderConfig.WSC);
   ```

2. As you can see in the snippet, we initialized the `SOAPRequestHandler` using the information we stored in the `EchoService_Client` profile on the OpenSSO server.

   ```
   SOAPMessage encMessage = handler.secureRequest(
       message, new Subject(), params);
   ```

3. We enforce the security requirements on the message using the created `handler`. We are passing an empty `subject` to the method because we did not configure our WSP to enforce authentication. In the next section we will discuss how we can enable authentication on the WSP for inbound requests.

   ```
   String response = invokeEchoService(pc.getWSPEndpoint(), request);
   ```

4. Finally in the last step, as shown in the above snippet, we are sending the message to the and receive the response back from the Echo Web service.

As you just saw we only enforced signing and encryption of SOAP messages in the WSP and WSC profiles configuration. If you look more closely at the WSC and WSP configuration pages you can find a section named **Key Store** as shown in the following figure:

In this configuration section we can specify which keystore we want to use and which key in the specified keystore should be used to sign the messages using the XML Signature standard that we discussed previously.

By default, as you can see in the figure, OpenSSO uses its generated keystore with a key pair identified with `test` alias. We can specify our own keystore file and then use the alias of the private and public keys which we want to use to sign, encrypt, verify, and decrypt the SOAP messages.

Authenticating a service call using WSP

In the previous section we learned how we can use WSC and WSP to sign and verify the signature of the message prior to consuming it. Now we want to discuss how to protect a Web service by placing an authentication layer in front of the service to ensure that only the users with valid credentials can invoke our service.

So far we saw that we can enforce signing and verification by changing some configuration elements. To add authentication, we only need to adjust few settings in the WSP configuration to enforce authentication and specify which security service we want it to authenticate the users against. In the WSP part we need to specify the security mechanism we want to use and configure the mechanism to comply with our environment and requirements.

Configuring WSP for enforcing authentication

Open the **EchoService_Provider** configuration page by going to **Authentication | Agents | Web Service Provider**, and then the **EchoService_Provider** link in the list of agents. Now under the **Security Mechanism** subsection of the **Security** section we can see a list of security mechanisms that we can select to specify types of credentials we accept during the request authentication. For example, if we select only the **UserNameToken** the provider will not accept SAML or any other type of token. The following table describes important security mechanisms supported in OpenSSO WSP.

Security Mechanism	Description
X509Token	Uses the Public Key Infrastructure (PKI) to authenticate the client. In this method, both client and server trust the CA issued to the other party's certificate or they trust each other's public keys. This mechanism is similar to CLIENT-CERT authentication method we discussed in *Chapter 1*. For more information take a look at http://docs.oasis-open.org/wss/2004/01/oasis-200401-wss-x509-token-profile-1.0.pdf.
SAML-HolderOfKey	A WSC should supply a SAML assertion with the holder-of-key confirmation method to identify the requester and to authenticate itself to the WSP. SAML-HolderOfKey is derived of the WS-I Basic Security Profile. For more information take a look at http://www.oasis-open.org/committees/download.php/16768/wss-v1.1-spec-os-SAMLTokenProfile.pdf.
LibertyX509Token	Secures the Web service with the X.509 Certificate Token Profile. Although it is similar to X509Token it complies with the processing rules defined by the Liberty Alliance Project. For more information take a look at http://www.projectliberty.org/liberty/content/download/1300/8265/file/liberty-idwsf-security-mechanisms-v1.2.pdf.

Security Mechanism	Description
SAML-SenderVouches	Secures the Web service with SAML and a different confirmation method. The difference is the way that the assertion which confirms that WSC is acting on behalf of the SAML token's owner. For more information take a look at `http://www.oasis-open.org/committees/download.php/16768/wss-v1.1-spec-os-SAMLTokenProfile.pdf`.
KerberosToken	Carries basic information (username and optionally, a password or shared secret) in a Kerberos token, for purposes of authenticating the user identity to the WSP. For more information take a look at `http://www.oasis-open.org/committees/download.php/16788/wss-v1.1-spec-os-KerberosTokenProfile.pdf`.
UserNameToken	Secures the Web service with a username and password and optionally, a signature of the requester. In this method WSC identifies the requester by username and, optionally, a password (or a shared secret or password equivalent) to authenticate its identity to the WSP. For more information take a look at `http://docs.oasis-open.org/wss/2004/01/oasis-200401-wss-username-token-profile-1.0.pdf`.
LibertySAMLToken	Secures the Web service with the Liberty SAML Token Profile. Although it is similar to SAML-SenderVouches, it complies with the processing rules defined by the Liberty Alliance Project. For more information take a look at `http://www.oasis-open.org/committees/download.php/16768/wss-v1.1-spec-os-SAMLTokenProfile.pdf`.

Now that we understand what type of tokens we can configure the WSP to accept, let's enforce authentication using a username and a password for any invocation of our Web service method. To do so:

1. Under the **Select Mechanism** section, tick the **UserNameToken**.

2. For the **Authentication Chain**, select the **ldapService** in the drop-down box.

3. Leave all other options as they are and click on the **Save** button to save the configuration.

We are finished with configuring the WSP, now we need to configure the WSC to use the `UserNameToken` mechanism to carry the client credentials to the server for authentication.

Configuring WSC to support authentication

Configuring the WSC is just few clicks away. The following instructions shows how to configure the WSC to use the `UserNameToken` mechanism:

1. Open the **EchoService_Client** configuration page by clicking on **Authentication | Agents | Web Service Client** and then **EchoService_ Client** link in the list of agents.

2. Under the **Security Mechanism** select the **UserNameToken**.

3. Click on **Save** button.

We are done with configuring both WSC and WSP to use the `UserNameToken` mechanism. The last step in running our sample application with `UserNameToken` mechanism support is changing the client source code to provide the WSC with the credentials we want to use for authenticating the request.

> You should remember from *Chapter 7* that we added few users to our OpenSSO user store to test our sample web application. You should have noticed that we use the same authentication chain that uses the same module instance where we stored our test users. So we can use the same users and passwords to test the Web service sample.

To change the sample code we only need to change the invocation of `handler. secureRequest` (to include a properly initialized `Subject` instance) as follows:

```
List userCredentials = new ArrayList();
PasswordCredential credential = new  PasswordCredential("james",
    "james");
userCredentials.add(credential);
final Subject subj = new Subject();
subj.getPrivateCredentials().add(userCredentials);
SOAPMessage encMessage = handler.secureRequest(message,
    subj, params);
```

As you can see we are simply creating a `PasswordCredential` object using a valid username and password, then we are adding this credential to the `Subject` instance, and finally passing the properly initialized `Subject` instance to the `handler. secureRequest` method.

Now if we run the sample application an authentication goes through prior to invoking the Web service, and if the provided username and password are valid, the invocation will go through.

Web Services security is a vast and major topic of which we only scratched the surface in this chapter. There are tons of different standards and specifications in play to integrate and secure complex Web Services deployments. You can read more about OpenSSO and Web Services security in the OpenSSO reference manuals available at `http://docs.sun.com/app/docs/coll/1767.1`.

Summary

In this chapter we looked at Web Services security with OpenSSO capabilities in mind. We discussed what the major standards are in Web Services security and what the capabilities of OpenSSO are for enforcing security on Web Services. Finally, we installed OpenSSO Web Services Security Provider Agent and developed a simple, secure pair of WSP and WSC.

Index

Thank you for buying
GlassFish Security

About Packt Publishing

Packt, pronounced 'packed', published its first book "*Mastering phpMyAdmin for Effective MySQL Management*" in April 2004 and subsequently continued to specialize in publishing highly focused books on specific technologies and solutions.

Our books and publications share the experiences of your fellow IT professionals in adapting and customizing today's systems, applications, and frameworks. Our solution based books give you the knowledge and power to customize the software and technologies you're using to get the job done. Packt books are more specific and less general than the IT books you have seen in the past. Our unique business model allows us to bring you more focused information, giving you more of what you need to know, and less of what you don't.

Packt is a modern, yet unique publishing company, which focuses on producing quality, cutting-edge books for communities of developers, administrators, and newbies alike. For more information, please visit our website: www.packtpub.com.

About Packt Open Source

In 2010, Packt launched two new brands, Packt Open Source and Packt Enterprise, in order to continue its focus on specialization. This book is part of the Packt Open Source brand, home to books published on software built around Open Source licences, and offering information to anybody from advanced developers to budding web designers. The Open Source brand also runs Packt's Open Source Royalty Scheme, by which Packt gives a royalty to each Open Source project about whose software a book is sold.

Writing for Packt

We welcome all inquiries from people who are interested in authoring. Book proposals should be sent to author@packtpub.com. If your book idea is still at an early stage and you would like to discuss it first before writing a formal book proposal, contact us; one of our commissioning editors will get in touch with you.

We're not just looking for published authors; if you have strong technical skills but no writing experience, our experienced editors can help you develop a writing career, or simply get some additional reward for your expertise.

Java EE 5 Development with NetBeans 6

ISBN: 978-1-847195-46-3   Paperback: 400 pages

Develop professional enterprise Java EE applications quickly and easily with this popular IDE

1. Use features of the popular NetBeans IDE to improve Java EE development

2. Careful instructions and screenshots lead you through the options available

3. Covers the major Java EE APIs such as JSF, EJB 3 and JPA, and how to work with them in NetBeans

4. Covers the NetBeans Visual Web designer in detail

EJB 3 Developer Guide

ISBN: 978-1-847195-60-9   Paperback: 276 pages

A Practical Guide for developers and architects to the Enterprise Java Beans Standard

1. Gain a rapid introduction to the EJB 3 essentials while learning about the underlying principles

2. Create Entities, Message-Driven Beans, Session Beans and their clients

3. Look at running an EJB client from an application client container

4. Learn how to package and deploy an EJB

5. Use JQPL (Java Persistence Query Language)

6. Explore the entity manager interface

Please check **www.PacktPub.com** for information on our titles

Made in the USA
Lexington, KY
17 March 2011